California Politics

CQ Press, an imprint of SAGE, is the leading publisher of books, periodicals, and electronic products on American government and international affairs. CQ Press consistently ranks among the top commercial publishers in terms of quality, as evidenced by the numerous awards its products have won over the years. CQ Press owes its existence to Nelson Poynter, former publisher of the *St. Petersburg Times,* and his wife Henrietta, with whom he founded Congressional Quarterly in 1945. Poynter established CQ with the mission of promoting democracy through education and in 1975 founded the Modern Media Institute, renamed The Poynter Institute for Media Studies after his death. The Poynter Institute (*www.poynter.org*) is a nonprofit organization dedicated to training journalists and media leaders.

In 2008, CQ Press was acquired by SAGE, a leading international publisher of journals, books, and electronic media for academic, educational, and professional markets. Since 1965, SAGE has helped inform and educate a global community of scholars, practitioners, researchers, and students spanning a wide range of subject areas, including business, humanities, social sciences, and science, technology, and medicine. A privately owned corporation, SAGE has offices in Los Angeles, London, New Delhi, and Singapore, in addition to the Washington DC office of CQ Press.

California Politics

A Primer

Third Edition

Renée B. Van Vechten
University of Redlands

Los Angeles | London | New Delhi
Singapore | Washington DC

Los Angeles | London | New Delhi
Singapore | Washington DC

FOR INFORMATION:

CQ Press

An Imprint of SAGE Publications, Inc.

2455 Teller Road

Thousand Oaks, California 91320

E-mail: order@sagepub.com

SAGE Publications Ltd.

1 Oliver's Yard

55 City Road

London EC1Y 1SP

United Kingdom

SAGE Publications India Pvt. Ltd.

B 1/I 1 Mohan Cooperative Industrial Area

Mathura Road, New Delhi 110 044

India

SAGE Publications Asia-Pacific Pte. Ltd.

3 Church Street

#10–04 Samsung Hub

Singapore 049483

Publisher: Charisse Kiino

Development Editor: Nancy Matuszak

Editorial Assistant: Davia Grant

Production Editor: Libby Larson

Copy Editor: Judy Selhorst

Typesetter: C&M Digitals (P) Ltd.

Proofreader: Sally Jaskold

Indexer: Michael Ferreira

Cover Designer: Candice Harmon

Marketing Manager: Amy Whitaker

Printed in the United States of America

Library of Congress Cataloging-in-Publication Data

Van Vechten, Renee.
California politics: a primer / Renée B. Van Vechten, University of Redlands. — Third edition.

pages cm

ISBN 978-1-4833-4013-5 (pbk.) —
ISBN 978-1-4833-4012-8 (web pdf)

1. California—Politics and government. I. Title.

JK8716.V36 2014
320.4794—dc23

This book is printed on acid-free paper.

Certified Chain of Custody
SUSTAINABLE FORESTRY INITIATIVE
Promoting Sustainable Forestry
www.sfiprogram.org
SFI-01268
SFI label applies to text stock

14 15 16 17 18 10 9 8 7 6 5 4 3 2 1

Contents

Preface

Seismic political events have rumbled through California since the last edition of this book was published, shaking up the status quo, causing a few great upheavals, and illustrating enduring political lessons of politics. A new sheriff is in town: the inimitable Jerry Brown retook the governor's office (but no sleeping on a bare mattress in a spare apartment this time around), and with steely jaw set, took an ax to the budget and whacked off large pieces, creating horror and angst that eventually gave way to begrudging acceptance of this cold fiscal prudence. Elections became trendy again: after the new citizen-led redistricting commission redrew district lines that forced many incumbents into uncomfortable races, voters test-drove a brand-new primary election system that bypasses political party affiliation and creates "top-two" races that yield plenty of close calls and surprises. The Democrats took over: with every executive seat held by a Democrat and supermajorities in both legislative houses (intermittently, it turns out), Republicans have been scrambling to avoid irrelevance. The state economy is in recovery mode: the budget has been passed on time three years in a row, eye-popping structural budget deficits have finally been erased, a budget surplus appeared in 2013, and voters actually approved a (small and temporary) sales tax hike.

Yes, things have changed. Two years ago California was verging on economic collapse and seemed utterly broken, not just broke. *Ungovernable* was the buzzword on a lot of lips. Trust in government seemed to have vanished irretrievably. Yet has all that much changed? Is Jerry Brown right when he insists that yes, the state "*is* governable"?

It's still an open question. The economy has been slow to recover, and some people are faring much better than others; stubbornly, unemployment remains high, and foreclosures on properties continue, although rates have slowed considerably. Citizens' trust in government remains dismally low. Perhaps most dangerously, public employee pensions that the state has promised to pay in the coming years threatens to suffocate the state's budget just a few years down the road.

What will it take to solve these problems and to fashion a high-functioning governing system for a state that is effectively one of the largest countries in the world? What would it take for Californians to trust in their government or to regain their faith in representative democracy? This short text, *California Politics: A Primer,* attempts to outline the puzzle that is California politics, providing readers with analytical tools to piece together an answer to these overarching questions. By emphasizing how history, political culture, rules, and institutions influence choices that lie at the heart of governing, the text moves beyond mere recitation of facts, pressing the reader to think about how these forces conspire to shape politics today and how they will determine the state of affairs tomorrow.

Because this book is intended to provide the essentials of California politics, brevity conquers detail, and scope outshines depth. Yet what is included presents an effective snapshot for understanding how the state is governed and how its politics works. Timely examples succinctly clarify trends and concepts, and instructors may read these as cues for further elaboration in class. Heavy emphasis on visuals in the form of figures, charts, graphs, maps, and photos also allows readers to discern the basics quickly, but readers should also take time to uncover the clues to understanding politics and tease out the rich patterns contained in these illustrations and in the accompanying captions.

What's New to the Third Edition

This third edition of *California Politics: A Primer* contains thoroughly updated chapters that have been embellished with examples and tightened organizationally. Particular attention has been paid to recent developments in electoral politics, the "rules of engagement" for legislators (voting thresholds and retooled term limits), the role of special interest groups in influencing policymaking, and the criminal justice system (prison realignment).

Graphics have been fully updated for this edition, incorporating major data releases by the U.S. Census Bureau, state agencies, and public affairs research organizations. Some of these graphics, such as the cartogram (Map 7.1) in chapter 7, suggest to the reader novel ways of perceiving current trends. Many of the updated graphics are incorporated into PowerPoint lecture slides that are designed to provide instructors with helpful guidance and guideposts for classroom instruction. The updated test bank of questions contains both conceptual and factual questions that are presented in a variety of formats, including multiple-choice, fill-in-the-blank, true/false, and short-answer response formats as well as longer essay questions. Adopters should go to http://cqpress.college.com/sites/californiair/ to register and download materials.

Acknowledgments

The clean and vigorous style in which this book is written is meant to engage the reader in an unending discussion of California politics that makes plenty of room for other participants. Those who have been essential to enlarging the debate by making this book possible are the expert crew at CQ Press, namely: Charisse Kiino, publisher extraordinaire; Nancy Matuszak, perpetually insightful, optimistic, and adept development editor, the epitome of grace under pressure; and an adroit and exceptionally talented production and marketing team that includes Libby Larson, Judy Selhorst, and Erica DeLuca. The book's continued success is testament to their professional prowess, and my gratitude and admiration for their wordsmithing talents are limitless. I also extend sincere thanks to those colleagues who have taken the time to provide essential feedback on previous editions, especially Shaun Bowler, whose first review was invaluable, and Mark Petracca, an adviser for the ages, as well as numerous anonymous reviewers whose insights and advice provided the thrust for improvements: Lucille Acquaye-Baddo, Los Angeles Harbor College; Chris Den Hartog, California Polytechnic Institute–San Luis Obispo; Diana Dwyer, California State University–Chico; Richard Groper, California State University–Los Angeles; Lisa Henkle, California Baptist University; Nathan Monroe, California State University–Merced; Maria Sampanis, California State University–Sacramento; Diane Schmidt, California State University–Chico; Michelle Rodriguez, San Diego Mesa College; and Cindy Tucey, University of California, Santa Cruz. I also extend my thanks to the many extraordinary public employees of California who helped provide critical source material for the book, from the staff of the Legislative Analyst's Office to the secretary of the Senate, and many in between. Brian Ebbert of the Assembly Clerk's Office deserves special mention for his considerate responses to my sporadic requests for information, as does Rick Battson (a senate chief of staff in his previous life), who provided a thoughtful assessment of the second edition. Most important, I have limitless appreciation and love for my family, to whom this effort is dedicated: my parents, Ann and Joe, whose careful guidance shaped my life's path; my forgiving husband, Charlie, who gallantly competes with the computer for my attention (and who is a far more brilliant and loving companion); and Ava and Zachary, whose growth and progress are a source of joy. May they inherit a political system that they can meaningfully shape and in which they can take pride.

Introduction

Reconsider California as one of the ten largest countries in the world. With a gross domestic product of approximately $2 trillion, its economy rivals those of Italy, France, and Brazil.[1] Its territory includes breathtaking coastal stretches, fertile farmland, deserts, the highest and lowest points in the continental United States, dense urban zones, twenty-one mountain ranges, and ancient redwood forests. Consider further how the state's almost thirty-eight million inhabitants govern themselves: they generally distrust representative institutions and assume that bickering politicians will squander taxpayers' money. Many eligible citizens never vote, and more than 20 percent of registered voters spurn the two major parties by declaring "no party preference." Wealthy corporations, citizens, and interest groups routinely use the initiative process to force policy changes that will affect the entire citizenry. Virtually everyone relies on such public goods as roads, emergency services, and schools, and yet California's backlog of critical infrastructure projects continues to swell as the population—along with citizens' loathing of taxes and impatience with politicians—grows.

Global economic tides, immigration, climate change, federal mandates, terrorist threats, chronic money shortages, and a host of other factors place conflicting pressures on those who make policy decisions for one of the world's most diverse political communities. The decision-making process is further complicated by a hybrid political system (a combination of direct and representative democracy) that tends to produce conflict without compromise. If **politics** is a process through which people with differing goals and ideals try to manage their conflicts by working together to allocate values for society—which implies that government institutions should enable officials to craft long-term solutions to major problems—then California's system is prone to repeated failures. Given all of this, California is widely regarded as "ungovernable."

This wasn't always so: a newly "modernized" constitution implemented in the late 1960s transformed the legislature into a highly paid, well-staffed institution that quickly gained a reputation as a policy and political reform leader among the states. In 1971 the legislature was described as possessing "all the characteristics that a legislature should have," having "proved itself capable of leading the nation in the development of legislation to deal with some of our most critical problems."[2]

It didn't take long for popular perceptions to change, however. In 1978 the people revolted against "spendthrift politicians" by passing Proposition 13, a measure that addressed ballooning property tax rates.[3] In the 1980s, as immigration was blamed for bigger government and rising costs, voters helped redefine the state's responsibilities toward immigrants by approving initiatives that either gave "guidance to the legislature" on such matters or evaded the legislature altogether.[4] Legislators were also targeted for being "arrogant and unresponsive" and for spending money on themselves while neglecting "schools, transportation, and basic needs."[5] By the time term limitations were passed in 1990 (capping the number of terms any state elected official could serve in a lifetime), it seemed the legislature's reputation could sink no lower. Many observers regarded California's legislators as simply incapable of governing.

FIGURE 1.1 Gross Domestic Product, 2012 (in millions)

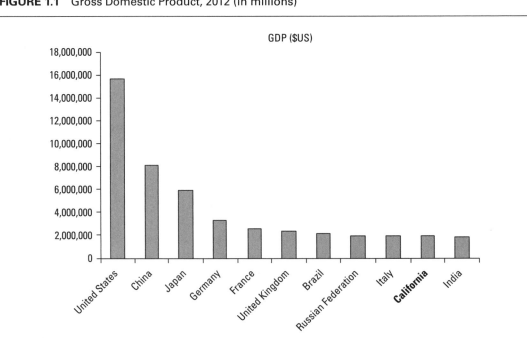

Sources: World Bank, "Gross Domestic Product 2012," World Development Indicators database, http://databank.worldbank.org/data/download/ GDP.pdf; U.S. Department of Commerce, Bureau of Economic Analysis, "Interactive Data" (state GDP, TOTAL industries number), http://www.bea .gov. See also Center for Continuing Study of the California Economy, "California Poised to Move Up in World Economic Rankings in 2013," press release, July 2013, http://www.ccsce.com/PDF/Numbers-July-2013-CA-Economy-Rankings-2012.pdf.

Today, California's issues exist on a massive scale. For example, more than one of every eight U.S. residents lives in California, and one of every four Californians is foreign-born. Multibillion-dollar budget gaps have been commonplace, patched year to year through gargantuan loans, the placement of state workers on unpaid leaves (furloughs), and the slashing of state services. Prisons have remained overcrowded by tens of thousands of inmates, and state unemployment rates have remained higher than the national average (8.7

percent in California in July 2013).[6] It is little wonder that in February 2013 only 35 percent of adult Californians approved of the job the legislature was doing.[7]

In spite of their approval ratings, state elected officials work hard year-round to represent hundreds of thousands of people—a job that requires them to balance the needs of their own districts against those of the entire state. That balancing act is but one reason California politics often appears irrational, but, like the U.S. government, the system was designed that way, mostly through deliberate choice but also through the unintended consequences of prior decisions. California's crazy quilt of governing institutions reflects repeated attempts to manage conflicts that result from millions of people putting demands on a system that creates both winners and losers—not all of whom give up quietly when they lose. As happens at the federal level, state officials tend to respond to the most persistent, organized, and well-funded members of society; on the other hand, losers in California can reverse their fortunes by skillfully employing the tools of direct democracy to sidestep elected officials altogether.

Principles for Understanding California Politics

It may seem counterintuitive given the depth of its problems, but California politics can be explained and understood logically—although the results of the process are just as often frustrating and irresponsible as they are praiseworthy and necessary. In short, the fundamental concepts of **choice, political culture, institutions, collective action, rules,** and **history** can be used to understand state politics just as they are used to understand national or even local democratic politics. These concepts are used throughout this book to explain how governing decisions are made by Californians or on their behalf and to provide a starting point for evaluating how governable California is.

We begin with the premise that **choices** are at the heart of politics. Citizens make explicit political choices when they decide not to participate in an election or when they cast a vote, but they also make implicit political choices when they throw aluminum cans in a recycling bin or send their children to private schools. Legislators' jobs consist of a series of choices that involve choosing what to say, which issues to ignore, whose recommendations to take, which phone calls to return, how to word a law, and what votes to cast.

In large and diverse societies that are crammed with people who are motivated by different goals, interests, and values, a successful political system provides a process for narrowing choices to a manageable number and allows many participants to reconcile their differences as they make choices together. The decisions that emerge from this process express the customs, values, and beliefs about government that a society holds and give that political system a distinct culture—a **political culture** that varies from state to state. One of the features that defines California's political culture is a historical fondness for reforming the political system and an aversion to politicians—themes that will resurface throughout this book.

Political systems also facilitate compromises, trade-offs, and bargains that lead to acceptable solutions or alternatives. **Institutions** help organize this kind of action. Political institutions are organizations built to manage conflict by defining particular roles and rules for those who participate in them. In short, they bring people together to solve problems on behalf of society. Democratic elections are a good example: there are rules about who can vote and who can run for office, how the process will be administered, and how disputes resulting from them will be resolved. Through institutions like elections, **collective action** (working together for mutual benefit) can take place. The same can be said of other institutions—such as traffic courts and political parties—for in each, people work together to solve their problems and allocate goods for a society.

Rules also matter. **Rules** define who has power and how they may legitimately use it, and rules create incentives for action or inaction. For instance, legislators who do not face term limits may extend their political careers by choosing to run for reelection in perpetuity, but term-limited legislators who want to remain in public service have an incentive to run for other offices when opportunities arise. Rules are also the results of choices made throughout **history,** and over time a body of rules will change and grow in response to cultural shifts, natural disasters, scandals, economic trends, and other forces, creating further opportunities and incentives for political action.

Recognizing that both choices and the rules that condition them are made within a given historical context goes a long way toward explaining each state's distinctive political system. A state's political culture also contributes to that distinctiveness. These are the elements that make New York's state government so different from the governments of Nevada, California, and every other state, and we should keep them in mind as we consider how California's governing institutions developed. In essence, a unique set of rules, its culture, and its history are key to understanding California politics and help explain why elected officials have such a difficult time governing the state.

Is California ungovernable? From online blogs to *New York Times* editorials, the consensus for years has been a resounding yes, but Governor Jerry Brown snubs that conclusion as he points to budgets that were balanced on his watch and an improving economy—facts that affirm his leadership and have contributed to his generally high approval ratings (57 percent in early 2013, although closer to 50 percent later in 2013).[8] It remains to be seen whether Brown is merely holding a tidal wave of problems at bay, for the current arrangement of political institutions severely handicaps government's capacity to solve the state's pressing problems and hinders representatives' ability to

BOX 1.1   **Comparative FAST FACTS on California**

	California	New York	United States
Capital:	Sacramento	Albany	Washington, D.C.
Statehood:	September 9, 1850 (31st state)	July 26, 1788 (11th state)	Declared independence from Great Britain July 4, 1776
Number of U.S. House members, 2014: *	53	27 (−2 from 2000)	435
Number of counties:	58 (since 1879)	62	50 states
Largest city by population:	Los Angeles, 3,863,839**	New York City, 8,175,133	New York
Total population:	37,966,000**	19,465,197***	316,110,352***
Percentage of persons with a bachelor's degree or higher:	30.3	32.5	28.2
Percentage of foreign-born persons: ***	26.7	21.7	12.9
Median annual household income: ***	$61,632	$56,951	$50,502
Percentage of persons living below poverty level: ***	14.4	14.5	15.9

*Based on 2010 reapportionment.

**California Department of Finance, "California Grew by 0.8 Percent in 2012; Total State Population Nears 38 Million," press release, May 1, 2013, http://www.dof.ca.gov/research/demographic/reports/estimates/e-1/documents/E-1_2013_Press_Release.pdf.

***Current U.S. and New York population figures based on U.S. 2010 census, monthly population estimates as of May 1, 2013. U.S. Census Bureau, American FactFinder, "Monthly Population Estimates for the United States: April 1, 2010 to December 1, 2013," http://factfinder2.census.gov/faces/tableservices/jsf/pages/productview.xhtml?pid=PEP_2012_PEPMONTHN&prodType=table. Income, national origin, and poverty rates based on U.S. Census Bureau, American Community Survey, 2007–2011, five-year estimates, accessed May 2013.

Ethnic Makeup of California:

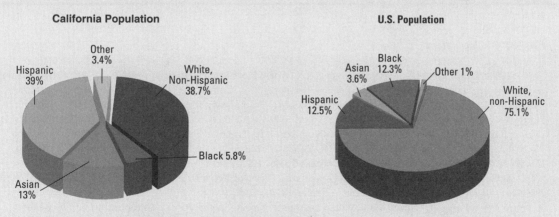

California Population

Other 3.4%
Hispanic 39%
White, Non-Hispanic 38.7%
Black 5.8%
Asian 13%

U.S. Population

Black 12.3%
Asian 3.6%
Other 1%
Hispanic 12.5%
White, non-Hispanic 75.1%

Sources: California Department of Finance, "Report P-3: Population Projections by Race/Ethnicity, Detailed Age, and Gender, 2010–2060," January 2013, http://www.dof.ca.gov/research/demographic/reports/projections/P-3; U.S. Census Bureau, American FactFinder.

The steps of the state capitol in Sacramento serve as the location where California governors are sworn into office at least every four years and provide a daily stage for public rallies and demonstrations.

plan sufficiently for the future. Still, Brown has demonstrated that political leadership is possible. This book explores the reasons for this state of affairs and pushes the reader to ask what it will take to enable California's government to serve the public's interests effectively, comprehensively, and sensibly over the long term.

Notes

1. World Bank, "Gross Domestic Product 2012," World Development Indicators database, http://databank .worldbank.org/data/download/GDP.pdf; U.S. Department of Commerce, Bureau of Economic Analysis, "Interactive Data" (state GDP, TOTAL industries number), http://www.bea.gov. See also Center for Continuing Study of the California Economy, "California Poised to Move Up in World Economic Rankings in 2013," press release, July 2013, http://www.ccsce.com/PDF/Numbers-July-2013-CA-Economy-Rankings-2012.pdf.

2. John Burns, *The Sometime Governments: A Critical Study of the 50 American Legislatures, by the Citizens Conference on State Legislatures* (New York: Bantam Books, 1971), 8.

3. Howard Jarvis and Paul Gann, "Arguments in Favor of Proposition 13," in *Primary Election Ballot Pamphlet* (Sacramento: California Secretary of State, 1978).

4. S. I. Hayakawa, J. Orozco, and Stanley Diamond, "Arguments in Favor of Proposition 63," in *General Election Ballot Pamphlet* (Sacramento: California Secretary of State, 1986).

5. Paul Gann, "Argument in Favor of Proposition 24," in *General Election Ballot Pamphlet* (Sacramento: California Secretary of State, 1984).

6. U.S. Department of Labor, Bureau of Labor Statistics, "Unemployment Rates for States: Monthly Rankings Seasonally Adjusted, July 2013," last modified August 19, 2013, http://www.bls.gov/web/laus/laumstrk.htm.

7. Mark DiCamillo and Mervin Field, "Release #2438," The Field Poll, February 21, 2013, http://www.field.com/fieldpollonline/subscribers/Rls2438.pdf. The respondents were 834 California registered voters, and the interviews took place February 5–17, 2013. The poll's margin of error was ±3.5 percent.

8. See James Fallows, "Jerry Brown's Political Reboot." *The Atlantic,* May 22, 2013, http://www.theatlantic.com/magazine/archive/2013/06/the-fixer/309324. The 57 percent approval rating figure is from DiCamillo and Field, "Release #2438."

CHAPTER 2

Critical Junctures

California's Political History in Brief

Early California

The contours of California's contemporary political landscape began to take shape in 1542, when Spanish explorer Juan Cabrillo claimed the Native American lands now known as San Diego for a distant monarchy, thereby paving the way for European settlements along the West Coast. Aided by Spanish troops, colonization accompanied the founding of Catholic missions throughout Baja (lower) and then Alta (northern) California. These missions, as well as military presidios (army posts), were constructed along what became known as El Camino Real, or the King's Highway, a path that roughly followed a line of major tribal establishments. Over the next two hundred years, native peoples were either subordinated or decimated by foreign diseases, soldiers, and ways of life, and the huge mission complexes and ranches, or rancheros, that replaced these groups and their settlements became the focal points for social activity and economic industry in the region.

The western lands containing California became part of Mexico when that country gained independence from Spain in 1821, and for more than two decades Mexicans governed the region, constructing presidios and installing military leaders to protect the cities taking shape up and down the coast. Following the Mexican-American War of 1848 that ended with the Treaty of Guadalupe Hidalgo, California became the new U.S. frontier astride a new international border. The simultaneous discovery of gold near Sacramento provoked an onslaught of settlers in what would be the first of several significant population waves to flood the West Coast during the next 125 years. The rush to the Golden State was on.

MAP 2.1 California's Missions

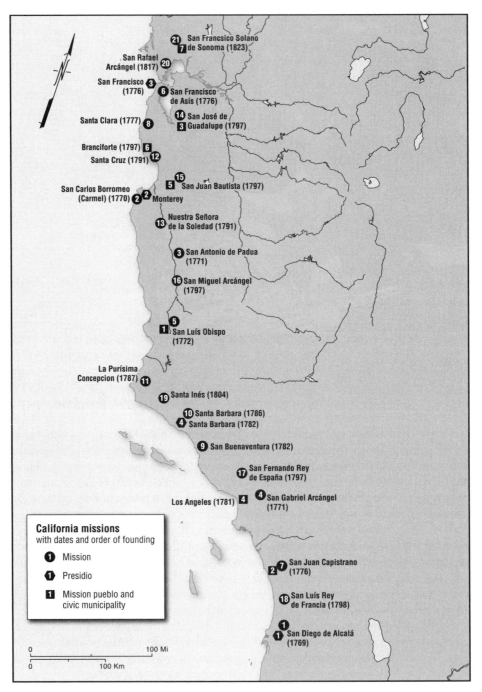

San Francsico Solano
de Sonoma (1823)

San Rafael
Arcángel (1817)

San Francisco
(1776)

San Francisco
de Asís (1776)

Santa Clara (1777)

San José de
Guadalupe (1797)

Branciforte (1797)

Santa Cruz (1791)

San Juan Bautista (1797)

San Carlos Borromeo
(Carmel) (1770)

Monterey

Nuestra Señora
de la Soledad (1791)

San Antonio de Padua
(1771)

San Miguel Arcángel
(1797)

San Luís Obispo
(1772)

La Purísima
Concepcion (1787)

Santa Inés (1804)

Santa Barbara (1786)

Santa Barbara (1782)

San Buenaventura (1782)

San Fernando Rey
de España (1797)

Los Angeles (1781)

San Gabriel Arcángel
(1771)

San Juan Capistrano
(1776)

San Luís Rey
de Francia (1798)

San Diego de Alcalá
(1769)

California missions
with dates and order of founding

- Mission
- Presidio
- Mission pueblo and
  civic municipality

0   100 Mi

0   100 Km

The Rise of the Southern Pacific Railroad

Spurning slavery and embracing self-governance, a group of pre–gold rush settlers and mayors convened to write a state constitution in 1849; a year later the U.S. Congress granted the territory statehood, and shortly thereafter Sacramento became the state's permanent capital. Although gold had already lured nearly one hundred thousand adventurers to the state in less than two years, the region remained a mostly untamed and distant outpost, separated from the East Coast by treacherous terrain and thousands of miles of ocean travel. Growing demand for more reliable linkages to the rest of the United States led to the building of the transcontinental railroad in 1869, an undertaking that resulted in the importation of thousands of Chinese laborers and millions of acres of federal land grants to a few railroad companies. Eleven million acres in California were granted to the Southern Pacific Railroad alone.[1]

The wildly successful enterprise not only opened the West to rapid development but also consolidated railroad power in the Central Pacific Railroad, later renamed the Southern Pacific Railroad. Owned by barons Collis Huntington, Mark Hopkins, Leland Stanford, and Charles Crocker—the "Big Four"—through the early 1900s the Southern Pacific extended its reach to virtually all forms of shipping and transportation. This had direct impacts on all major economic activity within the

Enduring persistent racial discrimination, punishing conditions, and a lack of labor and safety protections, Chinese immigrants laid thousands of miles of railroad tracks during the 1880s and early 1900s.

THE CURSE OF CALIFORNIA.

state, from wheat prices to land values and from bank lending to the availability of lumber. The railroad barons' landholdings enabled them to control the prosperity or demise of entire towns near rail lines throughout the West. Power didn't come cheap, however, and they fostered "friendships" in the White House, Congress, the state court system, and of course throughout local and state governments by finding every influential person's "price." As famously depicted in Edward Keller's illustration "The Curse of California," which appeared in San Francisco's *The Wasp* on August 19, 1882, the "S.P." (Southern Pacific Railroad) dominated every major sector of the state's economy— and politics—like a determined octopus.

Progressivism

The Southern Pacific's hold over California government during the late 1800s cannot be overestimated. One historian describes the situation in this way:

> For at least a generation after the new constitution went into effect [in 1879] the great majority of Californians believed that the influence of the railroad extended from the governor's mansion in Sacramento to the lowest ward heeler in San Francisco, and that the machine determined who should sit in city councils and on boards of supervisors; who should be sent to the House of Representatives and to the Senate in Washington; what laws should be enacted by the legislature, and what decisions should be rendered from the bench.[2]

The Southern Pacific's grip over California industry and politics was finally smashed, bit by bit, by muckraking journalists whose stories were pivotal in the passing of new federal regulations aimed at breaking monopolies; by the prosecution of San Francisco's corrupt political boss, Abe Ruef; and by the rise of a national political movement known as "Progressivism" that quickly took root in California. Governor Hiram Johnson (1911–1917) personified the idealistic Progressive spirit through his focus on eliminating every private interest from government and restoring power to the people.

To that end, Governor Johnson spearheaded an ambitious reform agenda that addressed a wide range of social, political, and economic issues that were attracting the attention of Progressives in other U.S. states. Not only was his agenda grounded in a fundamental distrust of political parties, which had been hijacked by the Southern Pacific in California, but it was also built on an emerging philosophy that government could be run like a business, with efficiency as a clear objective. Workers' rights, municipal ownership of utility companies, universal education, environmental conservation, morals laws, and the assurance of fair political representation topped the list of items Johnson tackled with the help of the California legislature after he entered office in 1911.

Changes in electoral laws directly targeted the ties political parties had to both the railroads and potential voters. Although secret voting had become state law in 1896, the practice was strengthened and enforced as a means to control elections and ensure fairness. The ability of party bosses to "select and elect" the candidates for political offices was undercut with the establishment of **direct primary elections,** in which any party member could become a candidate for office and gain the nomination of his fellow party members through a regular party election. The legislature also reclassified local elected offices as **"nonpartisan,"** meaning that the party affiliations of candidates did not appear on the ballot if they were running for municipal offices, such as city councils or local school boards, or for judgeships. Efficiency, the Progressives believed, demanded that voters and officials be blind to partisanship, because petty divisions wasted valuable time and resources and the important concern was who was the best person for a position, not his political affiliation.

A more ingenious method of controlling parties was accomplished through a new law that allowed **cross-filing,** which meant that any candidate's name could appear on any party's primary election ballot without the candidate's party affiliation being indicated. In effect, Republicans could seek the Democrats' nomination and vice versa, thereby allowing candidates to be nominated by more than one party. This rule, which remained on the books until 1959, initially helped Progressives but later allowed Republicans to dominate state politics despite state party registration that favored the Democrats after 1934.

Civil service exams were also instituted, which changed the hiring of local and state government employees from a system based on patronage (*who* one knew) to one based on merit (*what* one knew about a position and *how well* one knew it). But perhaps the most important political reform the Progressives instituted was a transformation of the relationship citizens had to California government. They accomplished this first by guaranteeing **women the right to vote** and then by adopting the tools of **direct democracy**: the recall, the referendum, and the initiative process (discussed in chapter 3). By vesting the people with the power to make laws directly—even new laws that could override those already in place—Progressives redistributed political power and essentially redesigned the basic structure of government. No longer was California a purely representative democracy; it now had a **hybrid government** that combined direct and representative forms of democracy. Elected officials would now compete with the people and special interests for power through the initiative process. The Progressives had triggered the state's first giant political earthquake.

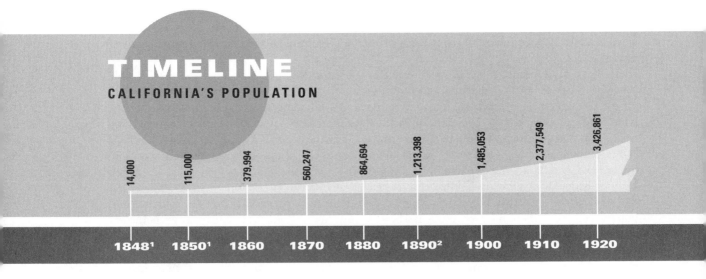

TIMELINE
CALIFORNIA'S POPULATION

1848[1]	1850[1]	1860	1870	1880	1890[2]	1900	1910	1920
14,000	115,000	379,994	560,247	864,694	1,213,398	1,485,053	2,377,549	3,426,861

[1] Source for population estimates 1848–1850: Andrew Rolle, *California: A History* (Wheeling, IL: Harlan Davidson, 2003).
[2] Population estimates from 1848–1880 are for nonnative populations. Native populations were not included in the U.S. census prior to 1890.

It should be noted that the Progressives' efforts to widen access to political power did not extend to every group in California, and some of the laws they passed were specifically designed to exclude certain people from decision making and restrict their political power. The most egregious examples reflected the white majority's racial hostility toward Chinese-born and other Asian-born residents, which took the form of "Alien Land Laws" that denied landownership, full property rights, and other civil rights to anyone of Asian descent—laws that would not be removed from the state's books for another half century.

The Power of Organized Interests

Ironically, the Progressives' attacks on political parties and the Southern Pacific created new opportunities for other kinds of special interests to influence state government. Cross-filing produced legislators with minimal party allegiances, and by the 1940s these individuals had come to depend heavily on lobbyists for information and other "diversions" to supplement their meager $3,000 annual salary. The legendary Artie Samish, head of the liquor and racetrack lobbies from the 1920s to the 1950s, personified the power of the "third house" (organized interests represented in the lobbying corps) in his

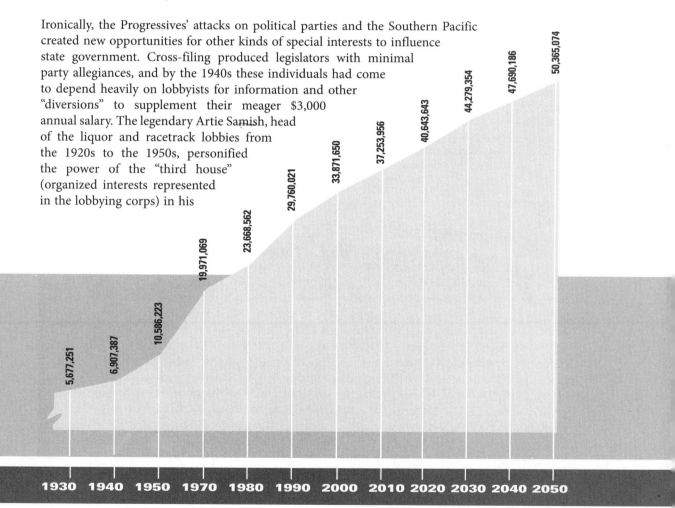

Source for population estimates 1860–2015: U.S. Census Bureau.

Source for population estimates 2020–2050: California Department of Finance, Demographic Research Unit.

ability to control election outcomes and tax rates for industries he represented. "I am the governor of the legislature," he brazenly boasted in the 1940s, "To hell with the governor of California."[3] He was convicted and jailed for corruption not long after making this statement, but his personal downfall hardly disturbed the cozy relationships between lobbyists and legislators that continued to flourish in—and taint—California state politics.

Growth and Industrialization in the Golden State

To outsiders the image of California as a land of mythical possibility and wealth persisted even as the Great Depression took hold in the 1930s. As depicted in John Steinbeck's *The Grapes of Wrath,* hundreds of thousands of unskilled American migrants from the mid- and southwestern Dust Bowl ("Okies" as they were pejoratively called by Californians) flooded the state, provoking a stinging social backlash that lasted at least until war production created new labor demands. The Depression also helped breathe life into what was neither the first nor the last unconventional political movement: in 1934 outspoken writer and socialist Upton Sinclair easily won the Democratic nomination for governor by waging an "End Poverty in California" (EPIC) campaign, which promised relief for lower- and middle-class Californians through a radical tax plan. His near-win mobilized conservatives, inspired left-wing Democrats to pursue greater funding of social programs, and propelled the first modern attack ads—the media-driven smear campaign—into being.

Rapid urban and industrial development during the first decades of the twentieth century accompanied the invention of the automobile and the step-up in oil production preceding World War II. Ribbons of roads and highways wrapped new towns and tied them to bulging cities, and people kept arriving in California at spectacular rates. Industrialization during World War II restored the state's golden image, bringing defense-related jobs, federal funds, manufacturing, construction, and a prosperity that only accelerated postwar. The building sector boomed while orange trees blossomed. To address labor shortages, the federal "Bracero" program created a new agricultural labor force by facilitating the entry of Mexican laborers into the United States, beckoning millions of men and their families to the country. Their efforts laid the foundations for California's thriving modern agribusiness sector.

Tract-housing developments materialized at an unprecedented rate and so did demands for roads, water, schools, and other critical infrastructure. In 1947 the state fanned the spread of "car culture" with an ambitious ten-year highway plan that cost $1 million per working day. Flood control and colossal irrigation projects begun in the 1860s had transformed the San Francisco Bay and the Sacramento–San Joaquin River Delta region from wetlands filled with wildlife into a labyrinth of levees, tunnels, canals, and dams that allowed midcentury farmers to feed bulging populations. Los Angeles continued to invent itself by sprawling across floodplains with manufacturing plants and neighborhoods that depended on water imported from the north, triggering "water wars" that continue to this day. Infrastructure spending centered on moving water to the thirsty south, building schools, establishing a first-class university system, and keeping freeways flowing—priorities that governors Earl Warren and Edmund "Pat" Brown advanced through the early 1960s.

The Initiative Process Takes Hold

The political landscape was also changing. Cross-filing, which had severely disadvantaged the Democrats for forty years, was effectively eliminated through a 1952 initiative that required candidates' party affiliations to be printed on primary election ballots. With this important change, Democrats finally realized majority status in 1958 with Pat Brown in the governor's office and control of both legislative houses.

Several U.S. Supreme Court cases also necessitated fundamental changes in the way that Californians were represented in both the state and national legislatures. Between 1928 and 1965, the state employed the "federal plan," modeling its legislature on the U.S. Congress, with an upper house based on geographic areas (counties rather than states) and a lower house based on population. Although many attempts had been made to dismantle the plan because it produced gross over-representation of northern and inland rural interests and severe underrepresentation of southern metropolitan residents in the state senate (three-fourths of sitting senators represented low-density rural areas), it remained in place until a federal court struck it down; per the U.S. Supreme Court ruling in *Reynolds v. Sims* (1964), the California system was found to violate the "one person–one vote" principle.[4] After 1965 political influence passed from legislators representing the north to those representing the south and also from rural to urban interests. Moreover, putting legislators in charge of redrawing their own districts reopened the possibility for gerrymandering, the practice of manipulating district boundaries to virtually ensure the reelection of incumbents and the continuation of the majority party in power.

The revival of parties in the legislature during the 1960s was greatly assisted by the Democratic Speaker of the California state assembly, "Big Daddy" Jesse Unruh, who understood how to influence the reelection of loyal partisans by controlling the flow of campaign donations. Unruh also helped orchestrate an overhaul of the legislature through Proposition 1A, a measure designed to "Update the State!" via constitutional cleanup in 1966. Prop 1A professionalized the lawmaking body by endowing it with the "three S's": salary, staff, and session length. The hope was to create a legislative body that could separate itself from the enticements of lobbyists by giving it the necessary resources to compete on more equal footing with the executive branch, and 73.5 percent of California voters welcomed the political shake-up. Lawmakers' annual pay doubled to $16,000 to reflect their new full-time status, and ample staff were hired to write and analyze bills.

Professionalization helped refresh the legislature's image, but the shine soon faded. It quickly became apparent that these changes still did not adequately equip legislators to deal effectively with all of the major issues facing Californians. Voters took matters into their own hands, and in 1978 the power of the initiative process was fully realized in Proposition 13. This citizen-generated anti-tax measure forever changed the rules regarding taxation and state budgeting, effectively altering the balance of power in the state by transferring that authority from cities and counties to state government.

Propelled by anger over the legislature's inability to reconcile skyrocketing property taxes and a multibillion-dollar state budget surplus, voters overwhelmingly approved Prop 13, which limited annual property tax to 1 percent of a property's assessed value.[5] Moreover, a two-thirds vote of the legislature became required to raise any tax, a rule that empowers a minority determined to forestall any tax increases. This has had significant impact on the legislature's ability to pass balanced budgets on time. Finally, Prop 13 sparked the dramatic use of the initiative process that continues today.

The faith in self-governance and mistrust of politicians that spurred Progressives into action and citizens to approve Prop 13 continued to cause political tremors in California politics. The view that citizens were more trustworthy than their representatives only intensified during the 1980s after three legislators were convicted of bribery in an FBI sting labeled "Shrimpscam" (a fictitious shrimp company "paid" legislators to introduce bills favoring the company), reinforcing the perception that Sacramento was full of corrupt, self-indulgent politicians. Similar political reforms have since targeted *governing institutions* such as the legislature; Proposition 140 is the most notable of these (discussed in chapter 4), which in 1990 imposed term limits on lawmakers and all elected state constitutional officers.

Parties and elections also have been targets: allowing all persons to vote in any political party's primary election regardless of party membership was attempted in 1996 (Proposition 198's blanket primary was overturned by the U.S. Supreme Court) and later succeeded as an "open primary" law in 2010 (Prop 14). Also in 2010, voters transferred the authority to draw electoral district lines (boundaries defining the geographic areas that legislators represent) from lawmakers

The passage of Proposition 13 in June 1978 opened a new chapter in California history, demonstrating the power of the initiative and the strength of antitax forces. The initiative's authors, Howard Jarvis and Paul Gann (not pictured here), led the anti-taxation effort. Prop 13's strict limits on property taxes sparked similar "taxpayer revolts" across the United States.

to a citizen commission (Prop 11). *Policymaking* has been altered through changes in the rules. Proposition 98, approved in 1988, significantly constrains the legislature by mandating that public schools (grades K–12) and community colleges receive an amount equal to roughly 40 percent of the state's general fund budget each year. And Proposition 39, approved in 2000, affects the voters' ability to approve school bonds by lowering the supermajority requirement to 55 percent (from two-thirds).

Hyperdiversity in a Modern State

Probably no condition defines politics in California more than the state's great human diversity, which is as much a source of rich heritage and culture as it is the root of competing and sometimes divisive political pressures. Differences stemming from ethnicity, race, religion, age, sexuality, ideology, socioeconomic class, and geography (to name but a few sources) do not inevitably breed conflict; however, these differences often are the source of intense political clashes in the state. The political realm is where these differences are expressed as divergent goals and ideals in the search for group recognition, power, or public goods, and the vital challenge for California's political representatives and institutions is to aggregate interests rather than aggravate them.

A post–World War II baby boom swelled the state's population even as waves of immigration and migration throughout the mid- to late twentieth century produced minor political tremors. A marked national population shift from the Rust Belt to the Sun Belt boosted California's economy, as well as its population, over the latter half of the twentieth century. Another wave of people from Southeast Asia arrived during the late 1960s to the mid-1970s, following the Vietnam War, and the most recent influx of immigrants occurred during the 1980s and 1990s, when the state's economic prosperity encouraged large-scale migration from Mexico and other Latin and Central American countries.

Immigration, legal and illegal, as well as natural population growth, has therefore produced a hyperdiverse state in which many groups vie for political legitimacy and attention, for public services and goods, and for power and influence. Same-sex couples demand the right to be wed in the same manner as heterosexual couples; immigrants and their undocumented children desire to pay in-state (rather than out of state) tuition rates at state colleges and universities; women seek workplace promotions at the same frequency and pay rates as men. In California, "special interest" groups that possess voting strength, money, or political power have had an easier time using the instruments of state power (including the initiative process) to achieve their goals, which may or may not represent the public interest. Groups that do not possess these assets may try to make statements in other ways. For example, racial tensions have occasionally erupted into large-scale riots, as happened in southeastern Los Angeles in 1992 (and in 1965 in what came to be known as the Watts Riots).

Continuing racial and ethnic diversification will dominate California society in the coming years, and this social change will have important political ramifications. Constituting 40 percent of the state's population and already the state's largest ethnic group, Latinos are projected to become the absolute majority segment by 2040. Historically underrepresented at the polls, at what point will they become fully active in California politics? How will they achieve this change? Will they do so with or without the help of the state? What kinds of political earthquakes, if any, will the shift produce?

Changing demographic patterns such as these help drive public policy debates, as they often raise questions about what it means to be a citizen. Impassioned campaigns have been waged over whether to make English the state's official language (approved by 73.2 percent of voters in 1986), whether to teach children only in English (passed by 60.9 percent of voters in 1998 as Proposition 227), whether to deny citizenship to children born in the state to undocumented workers (a federal constitutional issue), and whether to allow undocumented immigrants the ability to obtain in-state tuition rates or Cal Grants (the California Development, Relief, and Education for Alien Minors Act, known as the DREAM Act, became law in 2011). AB 60, a law passed in 2013, will allow undocumented immigrants to become eligible to obtain driver's licenses, something many Californians have opposed for symbolic and practical reasons, a right that has already been enabled in Colorado, Illinois, and New Mexico, among other states.[6]

Settlement patterns also raise questions about cultural assimilation versus cultural preservation. Some subpopulations tend to concentrate into geographic areas identified by dominant ethnic communities, such as "Little Saigons," "Chinatowns," or barrios. "Communities of interest" such as these have performed the historical role of absorbing foreign laborers and refugees, including the approximately fifty thousand Vietnamese who arrived after the Vietnam War and the approximately three million Latinos who joined family members in the United States as part of a 1986 federal

A foreign culture transplanted or an American culture transformed? Ethnic subgroups in California have established communities of character, as this barrio in East Los Angeles shows.

amnesty program. Chinatown in San Francisco remains the largest enclave of its kind, with the largest concentration of ethnic Chinese outside China. The dual trends of "balkanization" (communities separated by race or ethnicity) and "white flight" (the movement of Caucasians out of urban zones and to the inland counties) have become more pronounced during recent decades and have political implications, particularly for voting (see chapter 9).

The sheer volume of basic and special needs created by this hyperdiversity has tended to outstrip government capacity in the areas of public education, legal and correctional services, environmental protection, public welfare, and health services. Constant and growing population needs will continue to animate budget and policy debates, providing plenty of fissures that will test the foundations of state government.

Recalling a Governor

The most significant political earthquake of the new millennium in California hit in 2003 with the recall of Governor Gray Davis, a dizzying, circus-like event that solidified the state's image as a national outlier. Although the petition drive gained momentum slowly at first, it built on growing discontent over skyrocketing electricity costs, a weakening economy, and an overdue budget that contained unpopular fixes such as raising the car tax. The mild-mannered, uncharismatic Governor Davis was also perceived as a "pay-to-play" politician who rewarded friendly, generous public employee unions with larded contracts. After Republican U.S. representative Darrell Issa infused the recall effort with more than $1 million, enough signatures were gathered to trigger a special recall election.

For the first time in the state's history, Californians would be asked if they wanted to keep their sitting governor in office or replace him, and if enough voters wanted to replace him, they would have the opportunity to choose a successor. Hundreds of potential candidates jostled for attention (135 names were eventually listed on the ballot), including actor Arnold Schwarzenegger, who surprised Jay Leno and the audience of *The Tonight Show* by announcing his candidacy during an appearance on the show.

The spectacular election season lasted only seventy-six days (a normal cycle is about twice as long), during which time the candidates spent $80 million, captivated the mainstream media, and participated in televised debates. On October 7, 2003, 55.4 percent of voters selected "yes" on the recall question, and 48.7 percent chose Schwarzenegger to replace Davis. With 61.2 percent of registered voters having participated in the election, Californians demonstrated that they'd had enough "politics as usual" by exploiting the tools of direct democracy to shake up their government once again.

Pushing Ahead with More Reforms

Arnold Schwarzenegger's approach to governing involved broad, centrist appeals to Californians on common themes such as the environment and reforming government. A self-proclaimed environmentalist, he signed the nation's first law to regulate greenhouse gas emissions, AB 32, a law now being enacted through the development of a cap-and-trade system of carbon emissions credits and other mandates. In true populist fashion, Governor Schwarzenegger called special elections in

2005 and 2009 to gather support for measures to address a jaw-dropping $27 billion budget deficit, although with only one exception the public resoundingly rejected all the initiatives he endorsed. The measure that succeeded in 2009 reflected the prevailing antigovernment, antipolitician sentiment, as it prevented legislators from receiving pay raises during a year when there is a budget deficit—a precursor to a harsher measure that passed a year later, one prohibiting lawmakers from receiving their paychecks should they fail to pass a budget on time.

Elections remained at the epicenter of political change throughout Schwarzenegger's two terms, and also after his successor, Jerry Brown, retook the office of governor in 2010. The election in 2008, a presidential election year, drew the highest voter turnout in almost thirty years, sending strong shocks through the state's political system with voters' approval of the Voters FIRST Act (Proposition 11), an initiative that stripped lawmakers of their responsibility for redrawing state legislative districts and mandated that a new nonpartisan citizens' commission assume the job; a later initiative added congressional redistricting to the commission's duties. Although proponents hoped to extract politics from the sensitive process of remapping district boundaries, the supercharged election of 2012 proved the process is inherently political: some incumbents were pitted against each other and others dropped out altogether to avoid terrible fights, and the state Republican Party lost its challenge to the maps that eventually resulted in Democrats' gaining a supermajority in the legislature.

The "top-two primary," approved by voters in 2010 (Prop 14), also rattled the representational system by permitting all registered voters, including independents, to choose among all candidates for an office, not just their own parties' candidates, in primary elections. The new rules force the top two vote-getters into a runoff in the November general election. Thus, in November 2012 a total of nineteen state assembly, state senate, and congressional races pitted Democrats against fellow Democrats, and eight races set Republicans against fellow Republicans, provoking aggressive contests in some districts. Advocates of Prop 14 hoped that more moderates would replace those strident ideologues whose tendency to resist compromise can disable the legislative process, but so far there is little evidence that the new system will ultimately reduce polarization (or the tendency for members of both parties to cluster at either end of the ideological spectrum).[7] However, observers point to specific cases in which the more moderate candidates were selected over their competitors in the general election.[8] Additionally, the new system allows independents, or "no party preference" voters, to participate fully in primary elections. Over time researchers will be able to verify or invalidate these preliminary conclusions and measure how deep lawmakers' ideological fault lines run under the new system.

The Return of Jerry Brown

Edmund G. "Jerry" Brown was one of the youngest governors in California history when he assumed office in 1975 at age thirty-six, and he became the oldest governor when he retook the oath of office in 2011 at age seventy-two. Tested through several high-profile experiences in elective office, including Oakland mayor and state attorney general, Brown spent the first years of his new governorship wrangling the state's deficit-plagued budget into balance by slicing spending and seeking a voter-approved tax measure to fund public education (Prop 30). By sharply reducing funding for items considered sacred to fellow Democrats, including health care programs and education, and by using the initiative process to help enact his agenda, he showed that he would govern with calculated moderation. He also promised to "hold the line" against expansions in government programs that Democratic lawmakers might propose (Democrats won supermajorities in both the assembly and the senate in 2012), even as he has tried to plan for long-range population growth by supporting controversial projects such as high-speed rail that would eventually connect Sacramento to San Diego, currently estimated to cost between $70 and $100 billion.[9]

Brown has rebuilt himself into a trustworthy, practical "doer" who spurns the trappings of power. He has left behind the radically austere lifestyle of his "Governor Moonbeam" years, when he slept on a mattress in a rented Sacramento apartment, yet he still aims for efficiency. For example, he has trimmed the governor's staff to half the number that Governor Schwarzenegger had employed, and moves about the capital without a large security detail. Brown is expected to run for reelection without serious opposition in 2014, and his tenure ultimately may be the strongest challenge to the idea that California is ungovernable.

Conclusion: Political Earthquakes and Evolving Institutions

Like real seismic events, political earthquakes are difficult to predict. The tensions that produce them are ever present and recognizable in the fault lines that ripple the ground on which government is built. Periodic ruptures release some of that tension. Although political earthquakes may be triggered by conditions or events that are difficult to control—such as a weakening global economy, Supreme Court decisions, or wars—the shock waves that these events produce have the potential to effect transformations both large and small.

Throughout California's history, political earthquakes have reconfigured relationships between the elected and the governed, between citizens and their governing institutions, and among citizens. Each of these upheavals involved choices about who may use power and how they may do so legitimately. Rules have also mattered: in some cases the shake-ups were about whether to change the rules themselves, whereas in other cases the rules shaped the alternatives available and determined who could choose among them. Many political events become supercharged emotionally because they raise questions about shared values and about the kind of social and political culture in which people will live. Finally, history also plays a role in creating opportunities for action or in creating conditions that shape alternatives. As this historical review demonstrates, California's past pulses in the political institutions, culture, rules, and choices of today.

Notes

1. Andrew Rolle, *California: A History*, 6th ed. (Wheeling, IL: Harlan Davidson, 2003), 174.
2. Quote is attributed to Robert G. Cleland in Evelyn Hazen, *Cross-Filing in Primary Elections* (Berkeley: University of California, Bureau of Public Administration, 1951), 9.
3. Arthur Samish and Robert Thomas, *The Secret Boss of California* (New York: Crown Books, 1971), 10.
4. *Silver v. Jordan*, 241 Fed. S. 576 (1965) and *Reynolds v. Sims*, 377 U.S. 533 (1964), following *Baker v. Carr*, 369 U.S. 186 (1962).
5. Proposition 13 limited property tax rates to 1 percent of a property's assessed value in 1975; for properties sold after 1975, the rate would be 1 percent of the property's sale price. These rates would not be allowed to increase more than 2 percent per year.

6.   Ivan Moreno, "Undocumented Immigrant Driver's Licenses Bill Signed into Law in Colorado," Huffington Post, June 5, 2013, http://www.huffingtonpost.com/2013/06/05/immigrant-drivers-license_n_3391941.html.

7.   John Sides, "Can California's New Primary Reduce Polarization? Maybe Not," The Monkey Cage, March 27, 2013, http://themonkeycage.org/2013/03/27/can-californias-new-primary-reduce-polarization-maybe-not. See also Lucas Eaves, "Recent Study Misses Big Picture in Evaluation of Top-Two Primary," Independent Voter Network, May 22, 2013, http://ivn.us/2013/05/22/how-to-define-success-the-impact-of-the-top-two-primary -in-california.

8.   Eaves points to the election of Democratic candidates who were not supported by Democratic leadership as evidence that the system is inducing intended change and, if only by implication, more moderation. He cites Eric Swalwell's victory over incumbent Pete Stark. Eaves, "Recent Study Misses Big Picture."

9.   In 2008, voters approved Proposition 1A, which provides $9.95 billion in funding for high-speed rail. After a report in 2011 that revised the costs upward to nearly $98 billion, Governor Brown ordered redesigns that would bring costs down. In 2012, high-speed rail authorities reported new cost estimates to be closer to $68 billion, a figure that the state's General Accounting Office found to be "reasonable." "GAO: Calif. High-Speed Rail Estimates Reasonable," CBS Sacramento Local, March 28, 2013, http://sacramento .cbslocal.com/2013/03/28/gao-calif-high-speed-rail-estimates-reasonable. See also Ralph Vartabedian, Dan Weikel, and Richard Simon, "Bullet Train's $98-Billion Cost Could Be Its Biggest Obstacle," *Los Angeles Times,* November 2, 2011, http://articles.latimes.com/2011/nov/02/local/la-me-1102-bullet -train-20111102; and Mike Rosenberg, "High Speed Rail Chief: Bullet Train Won't Cost $100 Billion," *San Jose Mercury News,* March 14, 2012, http://www.mercurynews.com/california-high-speed-rail/ci_20168582/ high-speed-rail-chief-bullet-train-wont-cost.

CHAPTER 3

Direct Democracy

Medical use of marijuana. No horsemeat to be sold for human consumption. Term limits for all state elected officials. Funding for stem cell research. Each of these measures became state law because citizens signed petitions to get them on the ballot and majorities of voters approved them. Neither the governor nor the legislature was involved in their creation or passage. For more than one hundred years California has had a "hybrid" government that is part representative, part direct democracy, a design that the nation's founders carefully avoided.[1]

Until 1911 California's government reflected the U.S. founders' belief that elected representatives working in separate departments—namely, the executive and legislative branches—would check each other with overlapping powers, filter the passions of their constituents through a deliberative process, find compromises, and create good public policy. Lawmakers and presidents would compete for power, and these arrangements would safely allow ambition to counteract ambition, as James Madison noted in the *Federalist Papers*. Spurning this logic, California Progressive reformers at the beginning of the twentieth century removed those checks by establishing the initiative, referendum, and recall, thereby creating a hybrid government in which the people can make laws without the help of representatives. What we might call the first branch of California government is the people's power to govern themselves through the instruments of direct democracy. Article II of the state constitution affirms this view: "All political power is inherent in the people . . . and they have the right to alter or reform it when the public good may require."

The Statewide Initiative Process

At the state level, the *direct initiative* gives Californians the power to propose constitutional amendments and laws that fellow citizens will vote on without the legislature's involvement. Twenty-three other states also have initiative processes, although each has different requirements for bringing measures to the voters; the indirect method allows legislatures to consider and sometimes amend citizen-initiated measures before they are presented to the public for a vote. The California legislature is barred from making changes of any kind to ballot propositions, either before or after an election (see Box 3.1).

Prior to the "Prop 13 revolution" that emboldened Californians to use the initiative process, Oregon led the states with the most initiatives. Since then, propositions have appeared more often on California's ballots: from 1979 to 2012, Californians considered 195 different initiatives put forward by citizens, compared to 148 in Oregon and 103 in Colorado.[2] Considering all types of measures, including bonds, referenda, and legislatively referred initiatives (the most typical kind in Oregon), California still leads the states with more than 400 measures having been put to voters between 1979 and 2012.[3] More propositions have also been approved by Californians (120 as of 2012) than by voters in other states. Proposed measures typically fail before they make it to the ballot because their sponsors fail to gather enough signatures in time, or too many submitted signatures are invalidated by the secretary of state.

Initiatives cover all manner of subjects at the state level. Issues that surface frequently include taxation, welfare, public morality, immigration, education, criminal justice, and civil rights. Most prevalent are measures that focus on government and the political process—reforms intended to change the rules for political participation or control the behavior of elected officials—and it is no coincidence that term limits for statewide officials exist almost exclusively in states with the initiative process (Louisiana is the only exception). Requiring that two-thirds of all lawmakers agree to raise a tax or fee is another example of how Californians have played a vital role in setting the context for political decision making by imposing significant institutional controls on the legislative process. Without a doubt, initiatives have fundamentally altered California government and politics (see Table 3.1 and Figure 3.1).

Unfortunately, such piecemeal reforms are forced on government incoherently, resulting in political rules that overlap unnecessarily and encourage stalemate and inflexibility. Few citizen-imposed laws ease the rules for legislators, but Prop 25 (passed in 2010) is a rare example of this. It lowered the legislative vote requirement to pass the budget from a two-thirds supermajority to a simple majority, a change that has resulted in budgets being passed on time and without the need to satisfy a few minority-party members who might trade their votes for budgetary benefits. The law did, however, oblige legislators to forfeit their pay permanently if the budget is late.[4] The bottom line is that the initiative process both directly and indirectly conditions the actions of all California elected officials, who work in fragmented institutions that are not systematically organized to encourage collective action. As a result, representative and direct democracy coexist uneasily.

Citizens can propose laws at the city, county, and state levels in California. Any registered voter may propose a law (an *initiative statute*) or a change to the state constitution (a *constitutional amendment*). However, because most citizens cannot overcome the financial and time barriers associated with the initiative process, which hinges on gathering hundreds of thousands of valid voter signatures for statewide propositions, well-funded interest groups now dominate a system that was intended to *reduce* their influence. In practice, nearly anyone who can spend about $3 million to hire a signature-gathering firm can qualify a measure for the ballot. Special interest groups, corporations, wealthy individuals, political parties, and even elected officials with such resources use the state's initiative process to circumvent regular lawmaking channels because it "is the only way for [them] to get the policy they want."[5] Although the process remains primarily a check against government corruption

TABLE 3.1   Selected Landmark Initiatives in California, 1966–2012

Number	Description	Year
Proposition 1A	Constitutional reform, legislative professionalization	1966
Proposition 9	"Political Reform Act" (campaign finance reform)	1974
Proposition 13	Property tax limitation	1978
Proposition 98	Minimum annual funding levels for education	1988
Propositions 140, 28	State officeholder term limits; may spend twelve years total in either house	1990, 2012
Proposition 184	Three-strikes law	1994
Proposition 187	Ineligibility of illegal aliens for public services	1994
Proposition 209	Ending affirmative action in state institutions	1996
Proposition 215	Medical use of marijuana	1996
Proposition 5	Tribal state gaming compacts, tribal casinos	1998
Proposition 227	Elimination of bilingual education	1998
Propositions 11, 20	Citizens' redistricting commission to redraw state and congressional districts	2008, 2010
Proposition 8	Definition of marriage	2009
Proposition 14	Open primary elections ("top-two primary")	2010
Proposition 30	Temporary taxes to fund education	2012

and unresponsiveness, the Progressives of the early twentieth century would probably be surprised at how the process works today.

Preparation Stage: Drafting and Titling

The first step in bringing an idea to the ballot is drafting, or writing, the text of the proposed law. Measures are worded carefully to fit the needs and goals of their sponsors, and it is the authors' responsibility to correct errors or ambiguities that may later provide opponents with a convenient excuse to challenge them in court. A proposed initiative must be submitted with $200 to the attorney general's office, where it is assigned a title and a summary, one hundred words or fewer in length, that captures the measure's purpose. From that point on the wording of the proposed law cannot be changed. The state also prepares a fiscal analysis of the proposed law if the attorney general requests one.

Qualification Stage: Gathering and Verifying Signatures

During the qualification stage, the initiative's proponents must circulate strictly formatted petitions and gather enough valid voter signatures to qualify the measure for the ballot. There are no geographic requirements such as those in other states (no minimum or maximum numbers that

MAP 3.1 States with the Initiative Process, 2013

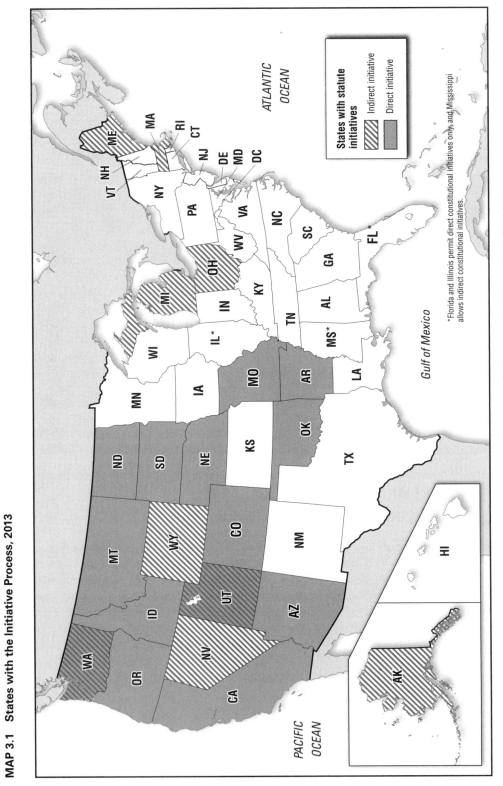

States with statute initiatives

- Indirect initiative
- Direct initiative

*Florida and Illinois permit direct constitutional initiatives only, and Mississippi allows indirect constitutional initiatives.

Source: National Conference of State Legislatures, "Initiative and Referendum States," http://www.ncsl.org/legislatures-elections/elections/chart-of-the-initiative-states.aspx.

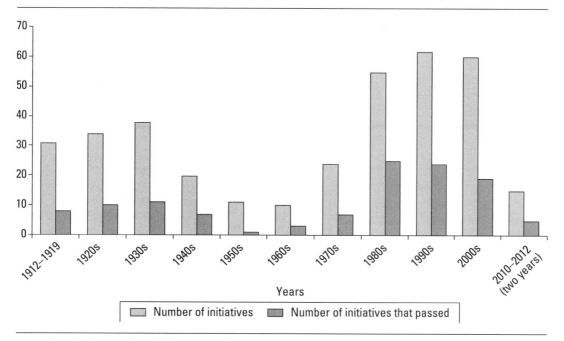

Source: California Secretary of State, "Initiative Totals by Summary Year, 1912–January 2013," http://www.sos.ca.gov/elections/ballot-measures/pdf/initiative-totals-summary-year.pdf.

Note: Excludes measures referred by legislature. Two initiatives in the 1980s and one initiative in 1999 qualified for the ballot but were removed from the ballot by court order.

must be gathered in each county, for instance), meaning that signatures can come from anywhere in California. Signature requirements are based on a percentage of all votes cast for governor during the previous election: the requirement is 5 percent for an initiative (504,760 signatures, based on the 2010 gubernatorial election) and 8 percent for a constitutional amendment (807,615 signatures). Proponents have 150 days to circulate and collect signatures on their formal petitions. Usually a signature collection company is hired to coordinate and execute the statewide effort, and the rule of thumb is to gather twice as many signatures as required because up to 40 percent or so will likely be invalidated later.[6] In practice this means collecting more than a million signatures at an average cost of $2 to $3 per valid signature, and a last-minute scramble to meet a deadline can push the price up to more than $10 per signature.[7] Means of collecting signatures include in person in public places, such as in front of grocery stores or at churches using the "clipboard method" (by one person) or "table method" (one person sits at a table while a companion approaches passersby); direct mail (generally not cost-effective); and door-to-door (rare). Electronic signature gathering is not yet allowed.

To complicate matters a bit, each person who signs an initiative petition must be a registered voter in the county where the petition is signed, and completed petitions must be submitted to the appropriate elections official (typically the county clerk or registrar of voters) in the county where each petition was filled out. County elections officials must receive and verify the signatures at least 131 days before the next general or special election, and they use a random sampling technique to determine how many signatures are valid. If the secretary of state concludes that enough registered voters signed the filed petitions, the measure is certified, given a number, and becomes known as "Proposition [number]."

FIGURE 3.2 Sample Ballot with Initiatives

OFFICIAL BALLOT
SAN DIEGO COUNTY, CALIFORNIA
PRESIDENTIAL GENERAL ELECTION - November 4, 2008

MEASURES SUBMITTED TO THE VOTERS

STATE

PROP 8 ELIMINATES RIGHT OF SAME-SEX COUPLES TO MARRY. INITIATIVE CONSTITUTIONAL AMENDMENT. Changes California Constitution to eliminate the right of same-sex couples to marry. Provides that only marriage between a man and a women is valid or recognized in California. Fiscal Impact: Over next few years, potential revenue loss, mainly sales taxes, totaling in the several tens of millions of dollars, to state and local goverments. In the long run, likely little fiscal impact on state and local governments.

YES ◯

NO ◯

PROP 9 CRIMINAL JUSTICE SYSTEM. VICTIMS' RIGHTS. PAROLE INITIATIVE CONSTITUTIONAL AMENDMENT AND STATUTE. Requires notification to victim and opportunity for input during phases of criminal justice process, including bail, pleas, sentencing and parole. Establishes victim safety as consideration for bail or parole. Fiscal Impact: Potential loss of state savings on prison operations and increased county jail costs amounting to hundreds of millions of dollars annually. Potential net savings in the low tens of millions of dollars annually on parole procedures.

YES ◯

NO ◯

STATE

PROP 10 ALTERNATIVE FUEL VEHICLES AND RENEWABLE ENERGY BONDS. INITIATIVE STATUTE. Authorizes $5 billion in bonds paid from state's General Fund, to help consumers and others purchase certain vehicles, and to fund research in renewable energy and alternative fuel vehicles. Fiscal Impact: State cost of about $10 billion over 30 years to repay bonds. Increased state and local revenues, potentially totaling several tens of millions of dollars through 2019. Potential state administrative costs up to about $10 million annually.

YES ◯

NO ◯

PROP 11 REDISTRICTING. INITIATIVE CONSTITUTIONAL AMENDMENT AND STATUTE. Changes authority for establishing state office boundaries from elected representatives to commission. Establishes multilevel process to select commissioners from registered voter pool. Commission comprised of Democrats, Republicans, and representatives of neither party. Fiscal Impact: Potential increase in state redistricting costs once every ten years due to two entities performing redistricting. Any increase in costs probably would not be significant.

YES ◯

NO ◯

Emotions ran high on both sides as the vote on Proposition 8, a measure banning same-sex marriage, neared. Voters narrowly approved it in November 2008, 52.3 percent to 47.7 percent. The state supreme court upheld the measure, but a federal court later invalidated it. The U.S. Supreme Court ultimately dismissed a challenge to the lower court's ruling, and same-sex marriages resumed in California in summer 2013.

Campaigning Stage: Persuading Potential Voters

Most initiative attempts fail during the qualification stage, but for successful proponents, the campaigning stage begins the moment the secretary of state certifies their measure, and in the coming months they will usually raise and spend millions of dollars to mobilize or sway voters. A thriving initiative industry has grown around the need to manage fund-raising, television and radio advertising, social media messages, and mass mailings. The price of initiative campaigns has skyrocketed in recent decades, and the most expensive in U.S. history have taken place in California (see Table 3.2). It is not uncommon for supporters and opponents combined to spend $100 million on highly controversial measures. Records were set in 2012 with Props 32 and 30. Prop 32 would have required that union members give permission annually for their dues to be deducted from their paychecks, the automatic deduction being an "injustice" fought by business interests and a "right" staunchly defended by unions. About $105.6 million was spent on that single ballot campaign. In the same election were dueling propositions concerning taxes for education, Governor Jerry Brown's Prop 30 and political activist Molly Munger's Prop 38, which topped the charts at $150.5 million spent either to promote or to defeat them. Not surprisingly, more money tends to be spent when industries are directly affected in some way, whereas uncontroversial measures tend to attract little or no spending.

TABLE 3.2   Five Most Expensive Ballot Measure Campaigns (adjusted figures)

Proposition	Election year	Subject	Total spent	Spent by proponents	Spent by opponents	Pass/fail (% margin)
87	2006	Alternative energy	$174,931,000	$69,486,000	$105,445,000	F (45/55)
30, 38	2012	Taxes for education	$150,500,000	For 30: $58,400,000 For 38: $47,600,000	Against 30: $44,500,000 Against 38: < 0.1	30: P (55/45) 38: F (29/71)
5	1998	Indian gaming	$129,341,000	$92,249,000	$37,092,000	P (62/38)
32	2012	Union dues	$105,600,000	$35,300,000	$70,300,000	F (43/57)
8	2008	Same-sex marriage ban	$94,352,000	$44,296,000	$50,056,000	P (52/48)

Sources: Figures for 2012 are from John Matsusaka, *Book of the States* (Lexington, KY: Council of State Governments, 2013). Proposition 8 figures are from "Proposition 8: Tracking the Money: Final Numbers," *Los Angeles Times*, http://theenvelope.latimes.com/la-moneymap,0,4156785.html story. Figures for Props 87 and 5 from Center for Governmental Studies, *Democracy by Initiative: Shaping California's Fourth Branch of Government*, 2nd ed. (Los Angeles: Center for Governmental Studies, 2008), http://policyarchive.org/handle/10207/bitstreams/5800.pdf.

Note: All figures have been adjusted to 2012 dollars and rounded.

Postelection Stage: Court Challenges and Implementation

Only a simple majority is needed to pass an initiative or recall an elected official, but a supermajority (two-thirds vote) is required for any general obligation bond and most school bonds (55 percent). Initiative laws generally take effect the day after they are approved, unlike bills, which normally go into effect on January 1 the following year. Election results don't always settle issues, however. Opponents often file lawsuits as soon as the votes are counted, triggering expensive court battles over a measure's constitutionality, meaning, or validity. These battles can last years and may result in partial or total invalidation of the measure. A court challenge to Proposition 8, the constitutional amendment defining marriage as between a man and a woman, was initiated shortly after the proposition's passage in 2008. The case twisted through the state courts, where it was eventually upheld by the California Supreme Court, and then was pushed through the federal courts, where it was struck down at the district court level as unconstitutional. The U.S. Supreme Court declined to hear the case in 2013, effectively allowing the lower court's ruling to stand, and same-sex marriages became legal in summer 2013.

Public officials may also search for ways to get around laws they find objectionable, and there is always the likelihood that a contentious issue will be revisited in a future proposition, because new laws often have unintended consequences and because losers always have another chance to prevail. This is another reason that governing decisions seem prone to second-guessing in California, which feeds the perception that the state is ungovernable.

The Power of the Initiative Process

Initiative use is robust for other reasons. Aspiring politicians and lawmakers build their reputations by sponsoring propositions that can't get traction in the legislature. Corporations and special interest groups find initiatives appealing because they know that successful measures can translate into financial gain or friendlier regulation. Competition also plays a role: at times adversaries take their fights to the ballot with dueling measures that propose very different solutions to a problem, as seen in the rival "taxation for education" measures proposed in 2012 (Props 30 and 38). That rule will remain in effect for all future elections.[8] (On a side note, if two similar "rival measures" both receive enough votes to pass, the one attracting more votes goes into effect. On a second side note, in a move only the savviest of politicians might attempt, Brown signed a bill requiring that constitutional amendments be listed on the ballot first, thus ensuring that his measure would appear at the top of the ballot.) Only rarely do genuine grassroots movements mushroom into initiative movements, and even those tend to be elite- or activist-driven efforts. Still, such movements can have enormous consequences for governing.

Today, the power of the average voter has been eclipsed by industry initiative activity and special interest group imperatives. There are no limits on contributions to ballot campaigns, and two-thirds of all donations are in amounts of $1 million or more.[9] The result: voters endure fanatical campaigns waged by organizations and corporations with deep pockets, their strategies packaged in media barrages containing oversimplified messages. Usually armed only with these biased accounts, voters must decide on complex policies frequently crafted without the benefit of compromise, and these policies may set rules that are difficult to amend later. Not surprisingly, confused voters tend to vote no, especially when the ramifications of voting yes are not clear. Most citizens believe there are too many propositions, that the ballot wording is too complicated, and that the system is controlled by special interests. A recent survey revealed that less than 20 percent of adults think that the system is fine the way it is; three out of four people (76 percent) feel that minor or major changes are needed.[10] Given California's history, it is only a matter of time before citizens further reform the process (see Box 3.1). Representatives may also introduce reforms through regular lawmaking channels, as they did recently with SB 202, a law that ended the practice of voting on initiatives in primary elections. Now voters will encounter ballot propositions only in general elections or special elections called by the governor.

Referendum

Citizens may also reject or approve recently signed laws or parts of laws, or redistricting maps, which are now drawn by the independent California Citizens Redistricting Commission. To prompt a referendum, petitioners must collect the same number of signatures required for an initiative (504,760) within three months. If the referendum qualifies for the ballot, voters will decide whether a particular legislative act should be rejected. **Petition referenda** are rare: only forty-seven measures have qualified for the ballot since 1912, and voters have historically been more likely to repeal a law than to approve it (59.6 percent of laws were rejected through referenda; 40.4 percent were approved). In 2012, one of the citizens commission-drawn maps, the state senate map, was challenged through

referendum (Prop 40) after opponents charged that it was biased in favor of Democrats. The effort failed after the sponsors of Prop 40 realized they were likely to lose and announced they would not campaign for it.

A far more common type of referendum is a **bond measure,** first approved by the legislature and then passed along to voters for approval. The constitution requires that voters approve state borrowing above $300,000. Bond measures authorize the state treasurer to sell bonds on the open market, which essentially are promises to pay back with interest any amounts loaned to the state. Bonds are typically used to finance multimillion- or billion-dollar infrastructure projects ranging from water restoration to library renovation, and since 2000 the average bond has cost more than $5 billion (see chapter 8). During recent budget crises the state borrowed approximately $15 billion through the sale of bonds in order to close budget gaps. Most bond measures generate little controversy, and around 60 percent pass, although some projects continue to generate conflict as they're implemented, such as a proposed $10 billion high-speed rail project that voters approved in 2008 (Prop 1A), now continually under fire as projected costs mount, plans are continually modified, and economic forecasting models change. Notably, financing state government projects with billion-dollar bonds involves substantial penalties and hidden costs: a sizable share of the state's annual budget each year is dedicated to paying interest, or "servicing the debt," and taxpayers end up paying twice the face amount of what is borrowed after the interest and capital are repaid. Few voters are aware that a $10 billion bond will actually cost around $20 billion to pay off.

Recall

California is one of nineteen states allowing voters to remove and replace state elected officials between regular elections, and it is one of at least twenty-nine permitting the recall of local officials.[11] In a California recall election, voters are asked whether the representative in question should be removed from office; they may then choose a replacement from a certified list of candidates, regardless of whether they cast an initial yes or no vote. This method of removing a politician before his or her term ends differs categorically from impeachment, whereby charges of misconduct in office are leveled, a trial is held by the state senate and two-thirds vote to convict, and the assembly votes to impeach. Nationwide, the majority of recall attempts are aimed at local officials such as judges, city council members, or school board members; state officials are also frequently targeted, usually unsuccessfully—although two state legislators in Colorado who had voted for stricter gun control legislation were singled out by the National Rifle Association and were successfully recalled by voters in September 2013.

Low recall success rates are partly ensured through fairly high signature requirements and relatively short deadlines. For lawmakers and appeals court judges in California, for instance, petitioners have 160 days to meet the signature threshold, which is equal to 20 percent of the votes cast in the last election for the official being recalled. For statewide officials, signatures must be obtained from voters in at least five different counties, with minimums in each jurisdiction tied to the prior election results. The requirements tend to be higher for recalling governors; in some states the signature threshold to bring about a recall is as high as 40 percent of eligible voters. Citizens wishing to recall a governor in California have a little more than five months to submit valid signatures equal to 12 percent of the votes cast during the previous gubernatorial election (more than 1.2 million signatures based on the 2010 election).

No specific grounds for removal are needed to launch a recall in California, but proponents must state their reasons on the petitions they circulate. Since 1913, 157 recalls have been launched against state elected officials in California, but only 9 of these qualified for the ballot and only 5 ultimately succeeded. The most recent target was Republican state senator Jeff Denham, who survived a recall election in 2008, but by far the most dramatic was the 2003 recall of Governor Gray Davis, discussed in chapter 2. Ironically, it takes a majority vote to remove an incumbent, but the replacement wins by plurality vote (the most votes of all cast), so Arnold Schwarzenegger could have won with far less than the 48.7 percent he received in an election that featured 135 candidates.

Direct Democracy at the Local Level

Direct democracy also exists in all California counties and municipalities, and while it is more frequently used at this level and local initiatives are adopted more often than state propositions, the process seldom sparks intense interest. Controversial decisions on school boards lead to the most

BOX 3.1 Reforming the Initiative Process

Is the initiative process ripe for reform? Californians overwhelmingly support their right to make laws alongside the state legislature, but many acknowledge the process isn't perfect. Its built-in biases have long been recognized, and resource-rich special interests have advantages over average citizens at every stage, a situation that contradicts the original intent of empowering the many at the expense of the few. Fixing these problems and others will require balancing individual power and free-speech rights. Opinion is sharply divided over whether and how to address these complex issues and how effective any solutions would be.

Problems and Suggested Remedies

Problem: It is far easier for paid circulators to collect enough valid signatures than it is for volunteer-based groups; virtually anyone can qualify an initiative by paying a professional signature-gathering firm $2–$3 million or more.
Remedy: Extend the signature-gathering period well past the current 150 days so that smaller groups have more time to spread their messages and volunteers throughout the state, or ban paid signature gathering.

Problem: Big money dominates the initiative process.
Remedy: Limit campaign donations from groups and individuals. Disclose donor information as close as possible to the date a draft is titled and prominently display that information on initiative petitions and advertising throughout the campaign.

Problem: It is difficult to trace donors to ballot campaigns.
Remedy: Require in-ad disclosure of top donors to campaign committees; make online resources such as Cal-Access easier to navigate.

Problem: Ballot measures are confusing and complex.
Remedy: Hold legislative hearings to generate more substantive discussion about a measure's probable impacts and broadcast them online and through traditional news media. If two conflicting measures are being considered in the same election, place them together in the ballot pamphlet and explain which will prevail if both pass. In addition, direct voters to online resources to help them in their search for more comprehensive information.

Problem: There are too many initiatives.
Remedy: Require the legislature to vote on proposed laws first. After a public hearing on a measure, the legislature could vote on passing it, with or without any changes that the initiative's authors may approve or reject. Courts could be given a role in verifying that the legislature's version respects the authors' intent.

Problem: It is too difficult to revise initiatives once they become law. They cannot be changed except through future ballot measures, even if flaws are discovered.
Remedy: Allow the legislature to amend measures after a certain amount of time, holding lawmakers to strict guidelines or further review.

Problem: The state constitution is cluttered with redundant and contradictory amendments.
Remedy: Enable more frequent, comprehensive reviews of the state constitution to weed out obsolete, unnecessary, or contradictory language. Alternatively, require a constitutional revision commission to meet periodically and make recommendations that voters or lawmakers may act upon.

Problem: Too many initiatives are declared unconstitutional.
Remedy: Require that a measure be reviewed at a legislative hearing or by a panel of active or retired judges to determine whether the proposed law is consistent with the California state constitution. Inform voters of any conflicts, and give authors the option to withdraw their measures.

For further reading, see Center for Governmental Studies, *Democracy by Initiative: Shaping California's Fourth Branch of Government,* 2nd ed. (Los Angeles: Center for Governmental Studies, 2008), http://policyarchive.org/handle/10207/bitstreams/5800.pdf.

recalls (about 75 percent of all recalls are against elected school board members), yet they remain relatively rare events, and the same is true of referenda on local decisions or ordinances. On the other hand, citizens have the power to generate laws and use the process to address all manner of issues with a local flair, and they do so with varying success. In 2011–2012, about half of the 135 different petitions that were circulated in 537 city and county jurisdictions later qualified for the ballot, and more than half of them passed.[12] Most local initiatives relate to matters of growth and development, taxation, and political reform.[13] Recent initiatives have dealt with rezoning public property for private use, imposed term limits on city council members or county supervisors (a more common reform in the past ten years), changed the manner and conduct of elections (for instance, San Francisco now allows Saturday voting), affected utility rates, altered the compensation packages for public employees (cutting or eliminating pensions, for example), and touched on every manner of civil rights, liberties, and public morals, such as regulating marijuana dispensaries, marriage, immigration, gambling, and alcohol.

County measures rarely make it to the ballot, and local measures, be they in cities or counties, rarely generate much attention or press unless the issues are controversial or deep-pocketed interests are at stake. For example, pornographic film actors in Los Angeles County must wear condoms during filming thanks to Measure B, which passed in November 2012, a local law that an adult film company has sued to overturn because the owners believe it violates freedom of expression.[14] Another example is found in the city of Redlands, where voters in 2010 considered banning big-box retailers such as Wal-Mart from establishing new megastores within city limits. Local activists, who raised and spent about $9,000, lost to the large retailer, which bankrolled $450,000 to defeat the measure.

The procedures for circulating a petition for a city or county initiative are similar to those at the state level and are spelled out in the state's election codes: signature requirements, strict circulation guidelines, signature verification carried out by the county registrar of voters, and certification either by the registrar or the city clerk. Signature requirements vary among cities because they are based on prior turnout (for ordinances or local laws) or voter registration (for charter amendments); thus, it takes about 7,200 signatures to qualify an initiative ordinance in San Francisco, but only 4,500 in Murietta, for instance. In the city of Los Angeles the threshold is 61,486 qualifying signatures based on turnout for the prior mayoral race, yet the *county* of Los Angeles requires 232,155 valid signatures based on voter registration. Unlike the state process, citizens must first file a notice of intent to circulate a petition, and, depending on the number of valid signatures gathered, the local governing board (city council or county supervisors) may first consider and adopt a proposed measure without alteration before it is submitted to voters. This process is known as the *indirect initiative,* and if the local governing body approves a measure, then it becomes law without being put to a vote of the people. Local initiatives are placed on ballots as "Measure [letter]," such as "Measure U," as distinct from state propositions, which are assigned numbers. In 2011–2012, approximately seventy-five cities considered one or more local ballot measures.

Conclusion: The Perils and Promises of Hybrid Democracy

The tools of direct democracy—the initiative, referendum, and recall—render California a hybrid government in which citizens possess the power to make or reject laws and elect or eject representatives. California's unique blend of representative and direct democracy gives the people tremendous power to govern themselves, but, ironically, citizens generally do not feel as if they are in control. In an outsized state with a sprawling population, money is a megaphone, and the initiative

FIGURE 3.3 Subject Matter of Municipal and County Citizen-Proposed Initiatives, 2007–2010

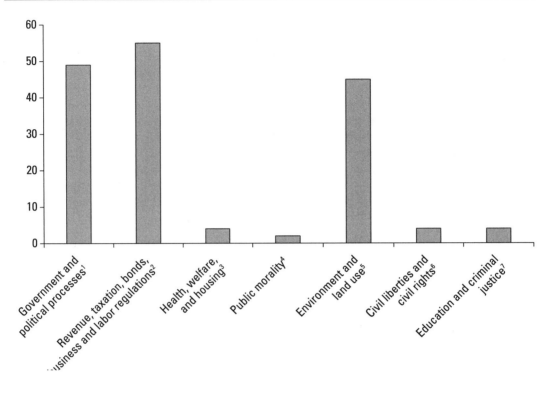

Sources: California Secretary of State, "Report on County Initiative Measures during 2009–2010," http://www.sos.ca.gov/elections/ballot-measures/pdf/county-initiative-09-10.pdf; and California Secretary of State, "Report on Municipal Initiative Measures during 2009–2010," http://www.sos.ca.gov/elections/ballot-measures/pdf/municipal-initiative-09-10.pdf.

Note: Measures were reported to the secretary of state on a biannual basis, although a few cities failed to submit reports each year. This count includes only measures that were brought by citizens and excludes recalls and local bond measures placed on the ballots by city councils. Of ninety-four citizen-initiated measures brought to local California ballots in 2007–2008, the passage rate was 54.3 percent. Of sixty-nine citizen-initiated measures on local ballots in 2009–2010, only forty passed, yielding a 58 percent passage rate.

[1]Includes changes to elections, powers of elected officials, appointed versus elected positions, compensation and benefits for public officials and civil service, term limits, districting, and vital city services and administration.

[2]Includes tax rates, utility rates, school bonds, labor contracting, appropriations, and business and labor regulations.

[3]Includes rent control.

[4]Includes medical marijuana dispensaries.

[5]Includes zoning changes, land-use planning, and big-box retail-related measures.

[6]Includes eminent domain and right to buy/sell fireworks.

[7]Includes prohibitions on military recruitment of children.

process favors the well funded. Whether it's because of the money they can spend to spread their message across major media markets, the blocs of voters they can mobilize, or the time they can dedicate to campaigning, resource-rich special interests overshadow a process that was established to give voice to the powerless.

The initiative process creates winners who use public authority to establish their version of reform and their vision of "better" policy that reflects their values and interests. It also produces losers who have the right to overcome their opponents by imposing their vision of good government through future ballots, should enough voters agree with them. This give-and-take over time is the essence of political struggle, but in a purely representative democracy, conflicts are harnessed by elected officials and saddled to a lawmaking institution where they are tamed through deliberation and compromise. The initiative process in California unleashes political conflicts to a diverse population where debate takes place, but bargaining and compromise are precluded. After all, initiatives offer one-size-fits-all solutions and are not open to amendment before passage. Unlike bills, which pass through many hands and many points where they can be challenged, tweaked, reconsidered, or adjusted to accommodate concerns, the referendum, recall, and initiative take one unchanging form that demands merely a yes or no response from voters at one point in time. Simple messages and emotional appeals are easier to broadcast across the expanse of California than the nuances and complexities normally associated with policy crafting.

Furthermore, neither the initiative nor the referendum lends itself to an integrated set of laws or institutional rules. Thus, new reforms are layered upon prior reforms in California, and newer laws are imperfectly fitted to existing statutes, an incremental process that tends to breed a disordered system of governing. This is a key reason the Golden State's government appears illogical. In fact, state building through the ballot box has proceeded incoherently for decades, often in response to scandals and crises, but often with hopeful desire for better government.

Even though voters make far fewer decisions at the ballot box than legislators make in a typical morning at the capitol, the political, fiscal, and social impacts of initiatives and referenda can profoundly upset the status quo—frequently with unintended consequences. Yet direct democracy is sacred in California. Despite the systemic flaws that people see in the initiative process, at least six in ten citizens believe they make better public policy decisions than elected officials do,[15] and voters continually reshape their government with the goal of "making things work." California's hybrid democracy doesn't ensure that things will get better or that government will work more efficiently, but direct democracy feeds citizens' hopes that it will. For better or worse, Californians will continue to use direct democracy to restructure their relationships with their government and with each other.

Notes

1. The term *hybrid democracy* is attributed to Elizabeth Garrett, "Hybrid Democracy," *George Washington Law Review* 73 (2005): 1096–1130.

2. California Legislative Analyst's Office, "1974 to Present: Ballot Measures by Type," accessed August 28, 2013, http://lao.ca.gov/laoapp/ballot_source/ballot_measures_by_type.aspx; Oregon Blue Book, "Initiative, Referendum, and Recall," accessed August 28, 2013, http://bluebook.state.or.us/state/elections/elections06 .htm; Initiative and Referendum Institute, accessed August 28, 2013, http://iandrinstitute.org; Colorado State Legislature, "Ballot History by Year," accessed August 28, 2013, http://www.leg.state.co.us/lcs/ballothistory.nsf.

3. According to the California Legislative Analyst's Office, 406 measures were on ballots between 1979 and 2010; an additional 13 were considered by California voters in 2012 (one was a referendum). During the same period in Oregon, voters considered 283 measures (including five votes intended to advise the legislature, and excluding one that was not counted by court order), and Colorado ballots included 168. These states represent the top three most active users of the initiative process.

4. In practice the "pay suspension" rule does not work as intended. In 2011 the Democratic-controlled legislature sent Governor Brown a budget just ahead of the June 15 deadline, but Brown and minority-party Republicans accused Democrats of submitting a budget filled with gimmicks and "questionable legal maneuvers." Brown promptly vetoed it (the first time a governor had done so since 1901), making the budget effectively late. In response, Controller John Chiang suspended the legislators' salary and per diem for twelve days (averaging about $4,800 per legislator), and Democrats sued to recover lost pay. On April 24, 2012 (in a tentative ruling affirmed the following day), superior court judge David Brown ruled that Chiang had violated the separation of powers clause of the state constitution, because only the legislature may determine whether a budget is balanced. As of this writing, the case, *Steinberg Perez v. Chiang* (2012), is on appeal. See Judy Lin, "Ruling Undermines Measure Blocking Lawmakers' Pay," *San Jose Mercury News,* April 25, 2012, http://www.mercurynews.com/news/ci_20478590/ruling-undermines-measure-blocking-lawmakers-pay; and Steven Harmon, "Brown Vetoes Budget, Criticizes 'Gimmicks,'" *Contra Costa Times,* June 16, 2011, http://www.mercurynews.com/california-budget/ci_18289420.

5. Elisabeth R. Gerber, Arthur Lupia, Mathew D. McCubbins, and D. Roderick Kiewiet, *Stealing the Initiative: How State Government Responds to Direct Democracy* (Upper Saddle River, NJ: Prentice Hall, 2001), 12.

6. Signature invalidation rates vary by county. The San Diego County registrar of voters reported that of the nine statewide petitions received in 2012, and of the 3 percent of the total signatures submitted (18,856 of 628,525), 17.5 percent were found to be invalid. One study published by the Center for Governmental Studies (CGS) reports that Los Angeles and Oakland have much higher invalidation rates (around 30 to 35 percent) due to duplicate signatures, signatures of unregistered voters, or names submitted in counties where they are not registered to vote. CGS estimates the average invalidation rate to be as high as 40 percent. See Center for Governmental Studies, *Democracy by Initiative: Shaping California's Fourth Branch of Government,* 2nd ed. (Los Angeles: Center for Governmental Studies, 2008), http://policyarchive.org/handle/10207/bitstreams/5800.pdf.

7. Ballotpedia calculates the average cost per required signature (CPRS) based on the amounts paid to the signature collection firms (publicly reported information) and the actual numbers of signatures needed. Based on figures for the 2012 election ballot measures, the highest amounts paid per signature were $10.86 (Prop 30) and $9.81 (Prop 38). The lowest was $1.18 for Prop 40, a redistricting referendum for which the proponents eventually ceased campaigning. Among the remaining measures, the average cost per signature was $2.78. "California Ballot Initiative Petition Signature Costs," Ballotpedia, last modified June 28, 2013, http://ballotpedia.org/wiki/index.php/California_ballot_initiative_petition_signature_costs.

8. The "roll-off," or reduction in number of votes for down-ticket measures, in this case was about 1 percent, meaning that 12,667,751 people cast their votes for Brown's "top of the ticket" Prop 30, whereas 12,331,091 voted for Prop 38, a difference of 336,660 votes (or 0.97 percent). Ultimately, however, Brown's measure won by such a large margin that the roll-off did not matter to the election outcome.

9. Center for Governmental Studies, *Democracy by Initiative,* 14.

10. Mark Baldassare, Dean Bonner, Sonja Petek, and Jui Shrestha, "California's Initiative Process: 100 Years Old," Public Policy Institute of California, September 2011, http://www.ppic.org/main/publication_show.asp?i=265. The polls were conducted in May 2011 (2,005 adults) and September 2011 (2,002 adults). Of those surveyed, 54 percent said that the initiative process in California today is controlled by special interests "a lot," 34 percent said "some," 6 percent said "not at all," and 6 percent responded that they didn't know. See also Mark Baldassare, Dean Bonner, Sonja Petek, and Jui Shrestha, "Californians and the Initiative Process," Public Policy Institute of California, November 2008, http://www.ppic.org/content/pubs/jtf/JTF_InitiativeJTF.pdf. In these

earlier polls, conducted September 2008 (2,002 adults) and October 2008 (2,004 adults), 59 percent agreed with the statement "There are too many propositions on the state ballot," and 78 percent agreed that "ballot wording for citizens' initiatives is often too complicated and confusing for voters to understand what happens if the initiative passes." In 2008 a combined 64 percent believed that minor or major change is needed in the initiative process, compared to 76 percent in 2011.

11. According to the National Conference of State Legislatures, "at least 29 states" permit recall elections to be held in local jurisdictions, but it notes that "some sources place this number at 36." See NCSL, "Recall of State Officials," last modified June 6, 2012, http://www.ncsl.org/legislatures-elections/elections/recall-of-state -officials.aspx.

12. California Secretary of State, "Report on County Initiative Measures during 2011–2012," http://www.sos .ca.gov/elections/ballot-measures/pdf/county-initiative-2011-2012.pdf. By law, figures on local initiatives are reported to the California secretary of state; however, some cities fail to report by the deadline.

13. For a more comprehensive report, see Tracy M. Gordon, *The Local Initiative in California* (San Francisco: Public Policy Institute of California, 2004), http://www.ppic.org/content/pubs/report/R_904TGR.pdf.

14. Vivid Entertainment filed a lawsuit against the county of Los Angeles in January 2013. As of September 2013, the case had not yet been heard in district court.

15. Baldassare et al., "California's Initiative Process."

CHAPTER 4

The State Legislature

Should parents be granted unrestricted administrative access to their thirteen-year-old's Facebook and other social media accounts? Should the importation and sale of shark fins be banned? Should affordable health and dental care be available to all Californians, regardless of citizenship status? Legislators answer just such questions. Throughout the lawmaking process, they are obligated to express the will of the citizens they represent, and they make decisions that touch almost every aspect of people's lives.

Design, Purpose, and Function of the Legislature

In California's system of separated powers, the legislature makes law or policy, the executive branch enforces or implements it, and the judicial branch interprets the other branches' actions and the laws they make. Chapters 2 and 3 discussed how the people also dabble in lawmaking through the initiative process, but primarily legislators are responsible for solving the state's problems. California's full-time lawmakers are far better suited to the task than are average citizens. They grapple with complex issues year-round and are assisted by professional staff members who help assess anticipated outcomes, research the history of similar attempts, evaluate alternatives, and analyze the costs of proposed laws.

California's legislature resembles the U.S. Congress in both structure and function. Like its federal counterpart, it is bicameral; that is, it is divided into two houses that check each other. Legislators in both the state's eighty-member lower house, called the **assembly**, and the forty-member upper house, the **senate**, represent districts that are among the most populous in the nation: based on the 2010 census, assembly

BOX 4.1 FAST FACTS on the California Legislature

Lower house:	Assembly, 80 members
Upper house:	Senate, 40 members
Term length:	Assembly, 2 years; senate, 4 years
Term limits:	12 years (combined) in the assembly and/or senate
Majority party in assembly and senate:	Democratic
Leaders:	Speaker of the assembly, president pro tem of the senate, minority leaders of the assembly and senate
Leaders' salaries:	$109,584* annually plus a per diem of $160/day**
Legislators' salaries:	$95,291* annually plus a per diem of $160/day**

Source: California Citizens Compensation Commission, "Salaries of Elected Officials," effective December 2, 2013, http://www.calhr.ca.gov/cccc/pages/cccc-salaries.aspx. On June 19, 2013, commissioners voted to restore a 5 percent pay reduction that had been implemented on December 3, 2012.

*Legislators also receive a car allowance of $300 per month, which replaced the state-paid vehicle and gas card in 2011. Legislative salaries hit an all-time high in 2008 when regular members were paid $116,208 plus per diem.

**Per the senate and assembly rules committees, per diem amounts are set by the Victim Compensation and Government Claims Board and are intended to cover daily expenses associated with working away from home. Total amounts vary annually with the number of days in session and by chamber. On average in 2012, assembly members collected a total of $28,656 in per diems, and senators collected $28,514.

districts average 465,600 people, and senate districts are larger than U.S. House districts, averaging 931,350 residents.[1]

Unlike members of the U.S. Congress, however, California legislators are term limited. In 1990 voters adopted Proposition 140, an initiative that restricted the number of terms that assembly members and senators could hold. In 2012 voters changed the rules through Prop 28, effectively reducing the total number of years that lawmakers can serve to twelve (from fourteen), but allowing them to serve those years in one house alone or to split their time between the two chambers. A lifetime ban means that lawmakers are prohibited from serving in those offices once they've reached that limit. Prop 28 proponents argued that the change would stabilize a legislature that has been wracked by rapid membership turnover every two years, because lawmakers would be allowed to accumulate more experience in one place and would not be itching to jump into the next office whenever it became available. They expect that turnover rates approaching 50 percent will be a thing of the past.[2] Overall, term limits have profoundly influenced individual representatives' perspectives and the way the legislature operates, a point revisited later in this chapter.

Legislators are elected from districts that are redrawn once per decade based on the U.S. Census. The task of redrawing district boundaries has traditionally rested with senate and assembly committees, but Proposition 11 (passed in 2008) handed the mapmaking power over to an independent citizens' commission. Republicans immediately perceived the commission's maps as throwing an electoral advantage to the Democrats, although the fourteen-member commission contained an equal number of Democrats and Republicans as well as independents, who were charged with drawing districts based on "strict, nonpartisan rules designed to ensure fair representation."[3] In addition, "every aspect" of the process was open to scrutiny by the public and the press. None of the challenges to the new boundaries survived judicial scrutiny or a referendum challenge, although the Democrats did gain a supermajority in the legislature in 2012, chiefly due to party registration that favors the Democrats statewide. Proponents primarily hoped that Prop 28 would increase the election of moderates, but so far the results have underwhelmed observers, as briefly described in chapter 2.

Although a few high-profile criminal cases have been brought against California lawmakers over the past century, hundreds of public-spirited men and women have served and are serving resolutely and honorably as California state legislators. Yet a fervent antipolitician, antigovernment sentiment prevails among Californians, and the individuals who work hard to sustain representative democracy are scorned rather than appreciated for the challenging work they do. As this chapter shows, lawmakers work hard to fulfill the expectations of their constituents and to meet the relentless demands of a state with a population of thirty-eight million.

California Representatives at Work

California's legislature has come a long way from the days when allegiances to the Southern Pacific Railroad earned it the nicknames "the legislature of a thousand steals" and "the legislature of a thousand drinks." Today its full-time, professional members are the highest paid in the nation, earning more than $100,000 per year, including per diem payments intended to cover living costs. Special interests and their lobbyists still permeate Sacramento politics with their presence, money, and messages, but legislators' loyalties these days are splintered by district needs, statewide demands, and partisanship. Their crammed schedules are split between their home districts and Sacramento.

Nowadays, term limits create large classes of freshman legislators every two years, pushing others into campaigns for the next office and year-round fund-raising. Prop 28 (which lays out the new term limits rules) may slow that trend, but legislators' desire for job security will continue to keep turnover high. Nearly everyone in the legislature is on a learning curve, anticipating the next election and aware that the clock is ticking. In past years, supermajority rules and rigid ideological positioning drove Democrats and Republicans to gridlock over raising taxes and cutting social programs, key components of balancing the budget on time. Now that only a simple majority is needed to pass the budget, and Democrats have won enough seats in both houses to raise taxes without minority-party Republican votes, Republican representatives have fallen to new levels of irrelevance in most policy debates.

In many ways the legislature is a microcosm of California. More than ever before, the demographics of the assembly and senate resemble the state's population (see Figure 4.1). There are more women and ethnic minority members representing a wider range of ages and backgrounds, and more than 40 percent of senate and assembly members identify as ethnic minorities.[4] The extent to which a legislature is, as U.S. founder John Adams put it, "an exact portrait, in miniature, of the people at large"[5] is a measure of **descriptive representation**. The extent to which members translate those outward features, as well as their values, into meaningful policies is **substantive representation**.

FIGURE 4.1 Profile of California's Population versus California State Legislature, 2013

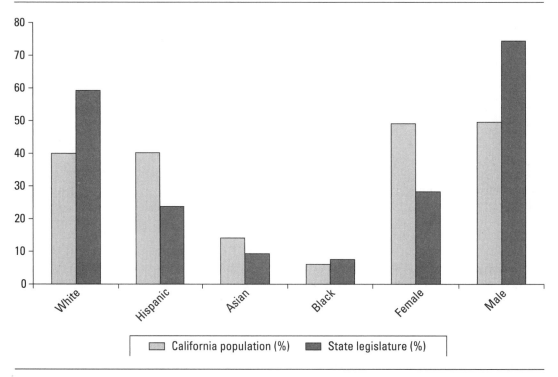

Sources: California Department of Finance, "Report P-3: Population Projections by Race/Ethnicity, Detailed Age, and Gender, 2010–2060," January 2013, http://www.dof.ca.gov/research/demographic/reports/projections/P-3; author's data, snapshot of legislature in June 2013.

Policymaking and Lawmaking

Assembly members and senators fulfill their representative functions chiefly through performing various aspects of lawmaking. To deal with approximately 5,000 bills and measures introduced in a two-year session, they gather information through research generated by their staffs, pay attention to the cues given by their colleagues, hear arguments from hundreds of people—mostly lobbyists—about proposed laws, and visit sites such as schools and interact with community leaders and citizens to get a better sense of their districts. They introduce bills addressing problems that lobbyists or constituents bring to their attention. As members of committees (where the bulk of policymaking occurs), they help shape or amend legislation after fielding complaints, statements, and predictions from witnesses who will potentially be affected by proposed changes. They deliberate and vote both in committee and later on the assembly or senate floor, where every member has a chance to vote on every bill. As all bills must be passed in identical form by both houses before they can be presented to the governor for signature or veto, members also continue building support for, or opposition to, measures that are moving through the other house.

BOX 4.2   Term Limits: Political Earthquake

Have term limits for legislators been good or bad? Both supporters and detractors can find ammunition in the findings. One thing neither side can deny, however, is that the reform has dramatically changed the rules of representation and the environment in which legislators work. Legislators elected in 2012 or after will help alter current understandings of the law's effects, because voters changed term limits (with Prop 28) to allow twelve years "in the assembly, senate, or both, in any combination of terms."

Prior to the passage of Prop 140 in 1990, state legislators were condemned for being out-of-touch careerists who had developed cozy relationships with lobbyists. Observers blamed stagnant rates of member turnover on uncompetitive elections, and the legislature was still reeking from a Federal Bureau of Investigation (FBI) sting two years earlier in which fourteen state officials were charged with bribery, including three legislators who went to jail.

The electorate was ready for change when an initiative modeled on one passed shortly before in Oklahoma qualified for the ballot. It restricted senators to two terms (a total of eight years) and assembly members to three terms (six years) during their lifetimes. Echoes of the early California Progressives were heard in proponents' sweeping promises to restore a "government of citizens representing their fellow citizens."* The measure quickly gained momentum and passed with just over 52 percent of the vote. Since then, support for term limits among Californians has solidified and increased, and twenty other states subsequently adopted similar measures, although these were invalidated or repealed in six states, bringing the current total number of states with term limits to fifteen. In 2012, modifications to the term limits law were approved by 61 percent of the voters, who accepted arguments that politicians were "more focused on campaigning for their next office than doing their jobs."** Ever hopeful that tweaking the law might help restore more accountability, voters will now allow lawmakers to stay up to twelve years in one chamber so they might "develop the expertise to get things done."

Term limits had immediate impacts in 1990. Long-term legislators were forced to campaign for other elected offices, and staff members were driven into private lobbying firms when Prop 140 slashed legislative budgets. Within a few years, long-standing Speaker Willie Brown was mayor of San Francisco, assembly careers were ending for good, and sitting senators were anticipating their next career moves. Overall, the wide-ranging effects of term limits have touched virtually every aspect of legislative life, and they have ranged from positive to negative.

Willie Brown, Speaker of the California state assembly from 1980 to 1995, was an easy target of term limits supporters for his perceived abuses of power and flashy style.

Electoral Changes

- Competition has increased for political offices at all levels, from county boards of supervisors to seats in the U.S. Congress, as more termed-out legislators run for them.
- Intraparty competition has risen as legislative members of the same party vie for the same seats—usually in the state senate, but also in Congress, on county boards of supervisors and city councils, and as executive constitutional officers. This effect is exacerbated by the recently instituted "top-two primary," which sometimes produces general election races in which each candidate squares off against other members of his or her own party.

(Continued)

BOX 4.2 **(Continued)**

- Open-seat primary elections created through term limits are ferociously competitive; open-seat general elections in a handful of districts are highly competitive as well.
- Incumbents still have huge advantages—about 96 percent are reelected. Many cruise to victory without serious challengers, and some face no challengers at all. Because individuals may be reelected five times to the assembly, those incumbent-dominated contests reduce electoral competitiveness overall.
- For legislators elected under Prop 140 rules (those elected before 2012), the senate is a logical step up for assembly members, and nearly all senators have been former members of the state assembly. A few have or will return to the assembly to finish serving out a final term before reaching *their* lifetime limit (fourteen years; their last term would be in 2024). This pattern will change as new legislators seek reelection to spend up to twelve years under Prop 28 rules, rather than risk losing their seats to run for the other chamber. It's likely that the senate will contain more new legislators who have never had assembly experience.

Membership Changes

- Far higher numbers of open seats have encouraged the candidacies and election of ethnic minority members—higher than would be expected through redistricting alone. As of mid-2013, 40 percent of legislators were Latino, African American, or Asian American.
- Higher turnover has led to record numbers of female candidates for office since 1990, although the total percentage of women in the legislature follows a longer historical upward trend unconnected to term limits.
- Women are occupying more leadership roles in both houses than ever before; these trends are more apparent among Democrats, in part because Democratic women have served as lawmakers in greater numbers than have Republican women.

Institutional Changes

- Newer legislators have recently experienced the effects of current laws in their districts and have fresh ideas about how to address problems arising from them.
- "Institutional memory" has drained away as career legislators and their staffs have left at regular intervals; members are less expert across a range of policy areas than in the past, and their knowledge of how state systems interrelate is poorer. As legislators stay in one chamber and accumulate more years in one office under Prop 28, their longevity is expected to breed expertise and longer-term perspectives.
- Under Prop 140, the average senator has had about two and a half times as much legislative experience as the average assembly member. Under Prop 28, senators' and assembly members' experience is expected to equalize.
- Senate staff members tend to be more experienced than assembly staff members and consider the upper house the "watchdog" of the more turnover-prone assembly. This "attitudinal" difference, shared by staff and senators alike, will probably persist because the senate has half as many members as the assembly, and senators enjoy four years between elections rather than two.
- Lobbyists who represent powerful groups, have experience, and are well connected can quickly establish relationships and exert undue influence over legislators. Lobbyists must work harder to get to know new legislators, however, as new members are likely to regard lobbyists with skepticism.
- Executive branch departments command informational resources and benefit from less frequent institutional turnover, rendering oversight by the legislature even more difficult than in the past.

Behavioral Changes

- "Lame duck" legislators (those in their last terms) lack electoral accountability to their current districts. Many look to their next possible constituency when considering how to vote; some feel less obligated to lobbyists in their last terms and more frequently feel free to "vote their conscience."
- Long-term, comprehensive lawmaking suffers as term-limited legislators lack the time and incentive to tackle many big projects or issues that will outlast their tenures. Smaller, district-level projects are more attractive to term-limited legislators. Longer tenures under Prop 28 may mitigate these effects.
- Changes to the law were implemented because of a pervasive sense that "everyone is running for the next office." Term-limited legislators will still run for other offices (about two-thirds of legislators will do so within two years of their term limits), and most will find work in the public sector, but institutional turnover is expected to decrease as more legislators "play it safe" by staying in the same office until their twelve-year clocks run out.

Sources: Author's data. See also Thad Kousser, Bruce Cain, and Karl Kurtz, "The Legislature: Life under Term Limits," in *Governing California: Politics, Government, and Public Policy in the Golden State*, 3rd ed., ed. Ethan Rarick (Berkeley: Public Policy Press, Institute of Governmental Studies, 2013); and Ava Alexandar, *Citizen Legislators or Political Musical Chairs? Term Limits in California* (Los Angeles: Center for Governmental Studies, 2011).

*California Secretary of State, "Argument in Favor of Proposition 140," November 1990 ballot pamphlet.

**Jennifer A. Waggoner, Kathay Feng, and Hank Lacayo, "Argument in Favor of Proposition 28," in *Presidential Primary Election Ballot Pamphlet* (Sacramento: California Secretary of State: 2012), http://voterguide.sos.ca.gov/past/2012/primary/propositions/28/arguments-rebuttals.htm.

As in Congress, much of a legislator's workload is derived from membership on committees, the institution's powerhouses. The assembly boasts a total of about seventy-five standing committees, budget subcommittees, and "select" committees on issues ranging from agriculture to public safety—enough for each member of the majority party to become a chair if desired. The senate has about three-quarters the number of assembly committees. In both chambers, committees are staffed by policy specialists whose intimate knowledge of past and present policy solutions accord them key roles in analyzing the bills referred to the committees.

In bygone eras the committee chairmen would rule over their fiefdoms for decades, dispensing with legislation at a whim and blessing the bills voted out of their committees and sent to the assembly or senate floor for final consideration by all members. Power is more difficult to centralize in an era of term limits, because turnover leads to relatively less expert members and more competition for choice chairpersonships. Given that most senators are former assembly members, they have at least four years of legislative experience (and often more) when they are appointed as committee chairs. By contrast, many freshmen with no legislative experience have chaired committees in the assembly for the past two decades, but this will change as assembly members gather more experience under the new term limits law.

Each bill bears the imprint of a unique set of players, is shaped by the rules, and is affected by timing. More often than not, the concerns of important groups are gathered throughout the bill passage process and accommodated to some degree. Observers are often surprised at the overt influence that special interests wield in the process. When they raise objections to provisions in bills, legislators listen and respond. Lawmakers tend to be sensitive to the fears and threats expressed by well-financed, vocal, influential, and large organizations that support their parties or are active in their districts—as some say, "The squeaky wheels get the oil." For instance, if a bill to raise the minimum wage is being considered, then lobbyists for big retailers and restaurant chains will likely be arguing that it is a "job killer" bill in face-to-face meetings with lawmakers or their staff and will be forcefully presenting their cases in committee hearings, just as labor union lobbyists will be vigorously arguing opposite points. This scenario recently occurred when Brown signed AB 10, a law that will raise the minimum wage to $9.00 per hour in July 2014 and will increase it to $10 per hour in 2016.

Relationships also matter. Partisans tend to support fellow partisans, but legislators who get to know others "across the aisle" tend to be more willing to support them legislatively. Over time, representatives tend to develop what is commonly referred to as "social capital": a shared sense of norms, interpersonal networks, and trust among colleagues. Because in the final analysis compromise is key, relationships among the players—from legislative staff to legislators to lobbyists to the governor's staff—help facilitate the necessary give-and-take to co-construct workable policy solutions.

Bills vary in scope, cost, urgency, and significance and cover every imaginable topic. Most go no further than being referred to a committee, and not bringing up a bill in committee after it has been referred is the easiest way for a chair to kill it. Of lowest significance are simple **resolutions** passed to express the legislature's position on particular issues. For example, in April 2013, when the International Olympic Committee initially ruled to eliminate wrestling as an official Olympic sport, the state senate passed a resolution urging the committee to reverse its decision. On a more substantive issue, in March 2009 the assembly passed a resolution "memorializing its opposition to Proposition 8" on the grounds that the proposition improperly revised the state constitution. No Republicans supported the resolution, but it was adopted by a majority vote of Democrats.

Inexpensive **local bills**, which deal with such concerns as specific land uses, may matter a lot to the people directly affected by the legislation but usually have only minor impacts on state government. Many bills relate to the administration of government and make technical changes or amendments to existing state law. These proposed **statutes** might impose mandates, or obligations, on local governments or agencies, such as requiring the governing boards of state colleges and universities to provide for live audio transmission of all public meetings. New laws (statutes) are also needed to authorize public agencies to take on new responsibilities or to collect fees, such as charging consumers for the disposal of old tires. Other bills create new categories of crime, authorize commissions or studies, or set up programs. For example, it takes a law to set up a recovery program for unused paint or compact fluorescent lightbulbs that might otherwise be illegally dumped, or to require that tattoo artists get annual permits from the state health department to operate legally.

Legislators also introduce bills that at first glance may appear to make small changes, but that, if enacted into law, would have tangible effects on Californians and their local governments. For instance, hydraulic fracturing, commonly known as "fracking," involves drilling horizontal wells deep into underground shale deposits and injecting chemical-laced water at high pressure to release trapped oil or natural gas. To grapple with the growing practice, lawmakers have introduced bills to temporarily halt fracking altogether, require pre- and postfracture groundwater testing, force companies to disclose the chemicals used, require regulation of hydraulic fluids as hazardous waste, commission studies of the environmental impacts, and demand that companies give thirty

The Senate Rules Committee holds a hearing to consider the appointment of Mary Nichols to chair the California Air Resources Board (CARB). A former state Department of Resources secretary and chair of CARB under Jerry Brown from 1978 to 1983, she reassumed the post in 2007 and continues to serve in this position in the Brown administration.

days' notice before commencing fracking activity. Some of these controversial bills will be defeated and then reintroduced in future legislative sessions, and at least one (SB 4) became law on January 1, 2014. Each new law will impose novel procedures that local and/or state officials must figure out how to implement, and each type of regulation could also have serious implications for property owners, oil and gas companies, and, ultimately, the prices consumers pay for energy.

Of major import are multimillion- or billion-dollar, long-range, intricate bills that affect many different groups and usually require years of study and compromise. Examples include revising workers' compensation benefits, and regulating ecosystems such as the Sacramento–San Joaquin River Delta and its related maze of waterways. Reshaping the state health care system to comply with federal regulations is another "big-ticket" item that lawmakers have already spent years working on in anticipation of "Obamacare," the Affordable Care Act, which becomes operational in 2014. Unfortunately, term-limited members lack incentive to unwind knotty problems that take years to understand and for which they will receive little credit, although this does not stop all legislators from trying to "make a difference." Longer time in one house may counteract this tendency, and with the help of veteran committee staff and lobbyists, especially those who have greater longevity and knowledge than the legislators themselves, many members can work to craft solutions to problems that take time to understand well.

FIGURE 4.2   How a Bill Becomes a Law

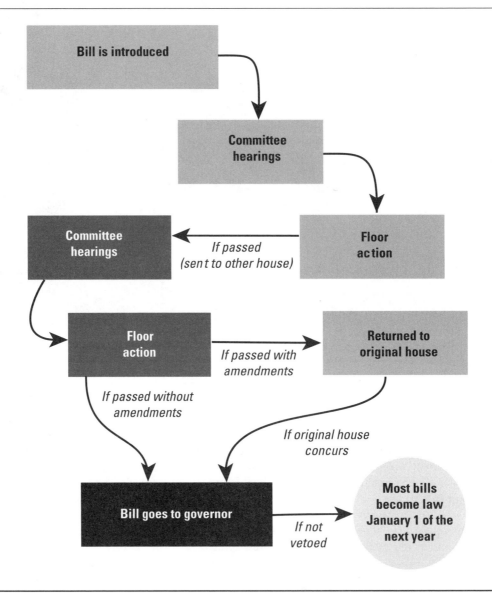

Given the scope and complexity of the state's ongoing issues, legislators need help. Thousands of staff members work directly for legislators in the capitol and in district offices (**personal** staff) or for committees in both chambers (**committee** staff). Inside each legislator's office are individuals hired to prepare bills their boss will introduce, analyze the thousands of other bills that cross a legislator's desk during a two-year term, assist with scheduling, and perform constituent relations. Committee staff manage all aspects of shepherding bills through a committee, from scheduling witnesses to writing analyses for each bill. The smaller senate retained more veteran professional committee staff and more experienced legislators under the original term limits law and has tended to view itself collectively as having a stronger filter for "bad ideas." This may change as members accumulate a dozen years of experience in a single chamber and they encourage personal and committee staffs to stay as well.

Legislators also heavily depend on institutional housekeepers like the assembly chief clerk's staff or the senate's secretary to ensure that legislators follow standing rules and parliamentary procedures. The nonpartisan **Legislative Analyst's Office (LAO)** has been the so-called conscience and eyes and ears of the legislature since 1941, providing professional analysis of the annual budget as well as fiscal and policy advice based on continuing, in-depth research of statewide programs. With analysts divided into nine subject areas, including education, housing, social service, health, and finance, the LAO remains one of the premier sources of information about state programs and the budget (http://www.lao.ca.gov). Similarly, since 1913 the nonpartisan **Legislative Counsel** has acted as an in-house law firm, crafting legislators' proposals into formal bills, rendering legal opinions, and making bill information available electronically (http://www.leginfo.ca.gov). Finally, staff work for both political parties' leadership and steadily provide their own bill analyses and vote recommendations to their party members.

It should also be noted that the majority party controls the fate of nearly all bills because a simple majority vote (41 in the assembly, 21 in the senate) is all that's needed to pass most bills, although a good number of bills are noncontroversial and pass unanimously. With a simple majority also needed to pass the annual budget, the majority party can enact its agenda without being held hostage by a minority party trying to extract concessions in exchange for votes. The bottom line: today, minority-party Republicans are at the mercy of majority-party Democrats when it comes to lawmaking, and their bills rarely move out of committee—unless they are deemed "harmless" by the Democrats. Usually the majority party can safely ignore the minority unless votes are needed to pass urgency bills or fiscal measures such as new tax or fee hikes that require a two-thirds supermajority (54 in the assembly, 27 in the senate), a discouraging position for those in the minority. The 2012 elections laid a new milestone when, for the first time since 1883, Democrats secured a supermajority in both houses.[6] With fifty-five Democrats in the lower house and twenty-eight in the upper house (a threshold that was crossed and lost with several special elections in 2013), they enjoyed a "veto-proof" majority for several months, meaning that they could raise taxes or override a gubernatorial veto without relying on Republican votes. As Governor Brown opined in a 2013 interview, "The Republicans appear to have no power . . . they aren't needed for any votes."[7]

Annual Budgeting

It takes the legislature more than half the year to work out an annual budget for the fiscal year (FY) that starts July 1. The process formally begins on January 10 when the governor submits his version to the legislature, and it should end by June 15, when the budget is officially due—but long-overdue budgets have been the norm for decades. The almost regular delays stopped after voters passed Prop 25 in 2010, an initiative that lowered the vote threshold needed to enact the budget to a simple majority, and also eliminated legislators' salaries and benefits for each day the budget is not passed after the June 15 deadline.

During the winter and spring of a normal fiscal year, the committees in both houses divvy up the work of determining how much money is needed to keep government programs running. They use the governor's budget as a benchmark for estimating costs and potential state revenues. Big-ticket items such as education are automatically funded, leaving a relatively small chunk of the budget pie for discretionary purposes; therefore, each legislator fights hard for the crumbs. The inherently partisan process becomes incendiary during tight budget years and is tempered when there is "unified government," meaning that both houses of the legislature and the governor's office are controlled by one party, as has been the case since Jerry Brown's election in 2010.

TABLE 4.1   A Day in the Life of Senator Norma J. Torres

June 18, 2013 Tuesday	
9:30 a.m.–10:00 a.m.	ON CONSENT: Senate Public Safety AB 423 + EG (Room 4203)
9:30 a.m.–10:00 a.m. (note overlaps)	Staff meeting (CO)*
10:30 a.m.–11:00 a.m.	Meeting with Metrolink re: AB 8 & SB 11 (CO)
11:00 a.m.–11:15 a.m.	Meeting with Speaker Pérez (Room 219)
11:30 a.m.–12:00 p.m.	Meeting with California Federation of Teachers legislative director re: AB 950 (CO)
12:00 p.m.–1:30 p.m.	Democratic Caucus (Maddy Lounge)
1:30 p.m.–2:00 p.m.	ON CONSENT: Senate Committee on Judiciary AB 491 + EG (Room 112)
1:30 p.m.–2:30 p.m. (note overlaps)	Senate Transportation & Housing AB 1024 + LE (Room 4203)
1:30 p.m.–3:00 p.m. (note overlaps)	Senate Elections & Constitutional Amendments Committee
3:00 p.m.–4:00 p.m.	Enterprise Zone Working Group Part 2
4:30 p.m.–4:45 p.m.	Meeting with California Bankers Association re: AB 279 (Dickinson) & AB 385 (Dickinson) (CO)
5:00 p.m.–5:30 p.m.	Senate Education Committee briefing with staff (CO)
5:30 p.m.–6:00 p.m.	Senate Banking & Financial Institutions Committee briefing with staff (CO)
6:00 p.m.–8:00 p.m.	Receptions (three member fund-raising receptions in various locations)

*CO = capitol office.

Constituency Service and Outreach

Constituency service entails "helping constituents navigate through the government system,"[8] particularly when their troubles stem from bureaucratic "red tape." Legislators hire caseworkers to help them respond quickly to requests, and these personal staff members, who typically work in district offices, spend their days tracking down answers from workers in state agencies like Caltrans and scheduling appointments at other state agencies for frustrated constituents, among other things. Legislators take constituency service seriously, although this part of the job is not mentioned in the state constitution. Many consider it "paramount to return every phone call, letter, and e-mail" and make government seem friendlier through personal contact.[9]

Most legislators try to communicate frequently with the residents of their districts through e-mail, Facebook, Twitter, official websites, or bulk-mail newsletters. Other activities include addressing select groups, such as Rotary and other clubs, or attending special public events (store openings, groundbreakings for public facilities, parades, and so forth). This kind of constituent outreach, or **public relations**, as some members call it, helps educate constituents, helps the representatives get to know their constituents and the issues they care about, and provides incumbents with necessary ammunition for reelection by enhancing their name recognition and reputation.

Executive Branch Oversight

Who monitors programs to ensure that a law is being carried out according to the legislature's intent? Ideally, assembly members, senators, and their staff members should be systematically reviewing programs and questioning administrators by having them appear as witnesses in committee hearings, but term-limited legislators often don't have the time or staff resources to determine if the laws they have created are being faithfully executed. In practice, they rely on investigative reports in the media, lobbyists, citizens, and administrators to sound the alarm about needed fixes. Once a problem is identified, the assembly and senate can rescue legislative intent in a number of ways. For example, they might address the offending administrators personally or write a bill to clear up confusion. On the rare occasion when an issue grabs the media's attention, lawmakers might respond more dramatically, by interrogating uncooperative administrators in a public forum and then threatening to eliminate their positions, yank authority away from them, or reduce their program funding (a governor can also fire irresponsible administrators). In addition, senators influence programs through their power to confirm hundreds of gubernatorial appointees to influential state boards and commissions, such as the major executive departments and the seventeen-member California Community Colleges Board of Governors. Leaders in both houses are also charged with directly appointing members of a few select boards, such as the twelve-member California Coastal Commission, which is made up of individuals chosen (four apiece) by the Senate Rules Committee, the assembly Speaker, and the governor.

Leaders

Aside from the governor, the Speaker of the assembly and the president pro tem of the senate are among the most powerful figures in Sacramento. Along with the governor and the minority leaders of

The assembly floor is normally a beehive of activity when the house is in session. A view from the rear of the chamber shows Republican members' desks on the left-hand side and Democratic members' desks on the right (from the Speaker's view the Democrats are seated to the left and Republicans to the right, reflecting their traditional ideological placement). Members cast votes by pressing buttons on their desks, and votes are registered on digital display boards at the front of the chamber.

each house, these individuals form the "Big Five" of California government: the leaders who speak for all their fellow party members in their respective houses and are ultimately responsible for cobbling together last-minute political bargains that clinch the budget or guarantee the signing of big bills.

A party leader's job is to keep his or her majority in power or to regain majority status. Nonstop fund-raising, policymaking, rule making, and deal making all serve that overarching objective. Leaders oversee their *party caucus* (all the members of a party in one house) and help shape the electorate's understanding of what it means to support a "Democratic" or "Republican" agenda. Still, institutional agendas are fluid, and more often than not they emerge from commonalities among legislators' individual designs more than they are imposed by elites at the top. However, the general rule is: what leadership wants, leadership gets. Leaders' ability to obtain desired results rests on many factors, including their having credible weapons such as the power to remove members from choice committees or kill their bills. Leaders may also endorse opponents, cut off campaign funds, reduce office budgets midyear, or move members out of offices or parking spaces to new and undesirable locations. For instance, Assemblyman Anthony Portantino's office budget was slashed in summer 2011 after he cast the only Democratic vote against the state budget bill.

The Speaker is the most visible member of the assembly and its spokesperson at-large. He or she negotiates budgets, bills, and policies on behalf of the entire membership; curries a high profile with the press; and cultivates a distinct culture of discipline and institutional independence through a unique and personal leadership style. The Speaker actively uses the campaign funds he or she raises to reward faithful party members and punish traitors. The senate's president pro tem plays these same roles, and in a term-limited era when legislative experience is concentrated in the upper house, the senate leader's visibility has increased relative to that of the Speaker. Under Prop 28, it is likely that the two leaders will maintain rough parity as the years pass.

The Speaker appoints chairs and members to all assembly committees, as does the president pro tem in the senate through his or her chairing of the all-powerful, five-member Rules Committee. The president pro tem also can use the Rules Committee's power over the governor's key administrative appointments as a bargaining chip in budget and bill negotiations—a tool the Speaker lacks.

These days neither the Speaker nor the senate president pro tem regularly leads floor sessions. Visitors catch glimpses of these leaders as they crisscross the floor to speak privately with members in an effort to find support for bills and negotiate deals while normal business proceeds. More often than not, a colleague acting as an assistant "pro tem" guides floor proceedings.

Leaders never forget that they are chosen by colleagues and stay only as long as they can maintain high levels of trust and confidence by meeting their colleagues' political needs. This was as true

Senate President Pro Tem Darrell Steinberg (D-Sacramento; left) listens as Minority Leader Bob Huff (R-Diamond Bar) explains his opposition to a bill being debated on the senate floor.

for flashy former Speaker Willie Brown (1980–1995) as it is for Speaker John Pérez (2010–2014) today. No tyrants can survive, if only because so many potential replacements impatiently wait in the wings—and under term limits, they needn't wait long before the next opportunity arises. Brown presided over the assembly for almost fifteen years. In the span of fifteen years following his departure there were *ten* Speakers.

Conclusion: Of the People, for the People

Although the legislature's basic framework has changed little since the constitutional revision of 1879, major changes in electoral law, campaign finance rules, ethics law, redistricting rules, compensation levels, and terms of office have molded and remolded California's legislative environment. Initiatives continue to complicate the already difficult task of condensing a multitude of competing interests, opinions, backgrounds, values, expectations, and ideas into an effective decision-making body. Californians have been quick to alter the political rules in attempts to make their representatives resistant to what is generally regarded as the poisonous influence of partisanship, money, and power, yet they have done so with limited success.

The battle to replace Assembly Speaker Karen Bass (center) was resolved when top contender Kevin de León conceded to John Pérez, who became the first openly gay Speaker in California history in 2010. Bass was later elected to Congress, and de León became a state senator.

Lawmaking is *supposed* to be hard, and an institution that features overlapping powers and shared responsibilities among many elected officials inevitably makes it difficult. In California the policymaking process is further complicated by direct democracy and hyperdiversity. Bills bear the imprints of competing interest groups, parties, leaders, funding sources, personal ambitions, rules, history, and a host of other factors that influence choice and impede the easy resolution of issues. The lawmaking process is messy. Short of creating a tyranny, no reform will change that.

The California legislature comes closer to the U.S. Congress in form than any other state legislature in the nation. Perhaps that is one reason for its dismal approval ratings, but it also remains the best hope for each citizen to achieve a degree of representation that would be unimaginable under an unelected bureaucracy, a dictatorial governor, or even a part-time legislature responsible for helping to govern one of the largest "countries" on the globe. The lawmaking body is closer to the people than the other two branches could ever be: neither the elected executives nor judges can understand the needs and interests of California's communities as thoroughly as firmly anchored representatives can.

Notes

1. The U.S. Census 2010 apportionment population in congressional districts is 710,767; California contains fifty-three U.S. House districts. National Atlas of the United States, "Congressional Apportionment," http://www.nationalatlas.gov/articles/boundaries/a_conApport.html#one.

2. It should be noted that although high turnover in 2012 was also prompted by redistricting, term limits have provided the impetus for high turnover in non-redistricting years since 1990. In 2012, turnover reached 47.5 percent.

3. Proposition 11, Section 2(d).

4. Of the 118 legislators in office in June 2013 (with 2 vacancies), 32 were women. Among the 118 legislators, 69 were white, 9 were African American, 27 were Hispanic/Latino, 11 were Asian American, and 2 were of Middle Eastern descent (Jordanian and Armenian). In all, 50 of 118 (42.4 percent, the highest proportion in history) were "nonwhite."

5. Quoted in Hannah Pitkin, *The Concept of Representation* (Berkeley: University of California Press, 1967), 60.

6. The Republican Party achieved supermajority status in both chambers at least a dozen times between 1891 and 1933.

7. James Fallows, "Jerry Brown's Political Reboot," *The Atlantic,* May 22, 2013, http://www.theatlantic.com/magazine/archive/2013/06/the-fixer/309324/?single_page=true.

8. Donald Lathbury, "Two-Thirds Majority Battle Still on Radar," California Majority Report, September 22, 2008, http://www.camajorityreport.com/index.php?module=articles&func=display&ptid=9&aid=3581.

9. Author's interview with freshman assembly member in Sacramento, California, in March 1999.

CHAPTER 5

The Executive Branch

Question: Who is in charge of California's K–12 education system?

Answer: Although the *governor* guides education policy through budgetary changes and is often held responsible for the overall state of education, it is the elected *state superintendent of public instruction* who heads the system by constitutional mandate, overseeing the *Department of Education,* the agency through which the public school system is regulated and controlled as required by law, taking cues from the administration's powerful *State Board of Education,* also appointed by the governor but technically administered by the superintendent, who in turn implements the educational regulations of the State Board of Education . . . not to mention the *assembly* and *senate education committees* that steer education bills into law.

Confusing? A case of checks and balances gone awry? Somewhere among the governor's need to obtain information and make recommendations, the legislature's regulatory imperative, and the people's desire to elect officers who can be held accountable, the system evolved into a tangled network of authority that even Department of Education employees have difficulty explaining.

California's Plural Executive

The founders of the United States rejected the notion that more than one person could effectively lead an executive branch. They argued that only a single individual, the president, could bring energy to an office that would otherwise be fractured by competing ambitions and differences of opinion. What then are we to make of California's plural executive, which comprises eight constitutional executive officers plus a five-member board, sharing responsibility for administering state government—the longest list among the states? Or the fact that these elected officials may be Republicans and Democrats who are ideologically opposed?

Number of executives:	8, plus the Board of Equalization (12 persons)
Elected executive offices:	Governor
	Lieutenant governor (LG)
	Attorney general (AG)
	Secretary of state
	Controller
	Treasurer
	Superintendent of public instruction
	Insurance commissioner
	Board of Equalization (4 of 5 members are elected)
Balance of political parties:	2 Republicans, 9 Democrats, 1 nonpartisan (2010 elections)
Governor's salary:	$173,987
Salary for AG and superintendent:	$151,127
Salary for controller, treasurer, and insurance commissioner:	$139,189*
Salary for secretary of state, LG, and Board of Equalization members:	$130,490*
Terms of office:	Four years
Term limits:	Two terms (lifetime ban)**

Source: California Citizens Compensation Commission, "Salaries of Elected Officials," effective December 2, 2013, http://www.calhr.ca.gov/cccc/pages/cccc-salaries.aspx.

*A salary decrease of 18 percent went into effect in December 2009; the average decrease was more than $30,000 per official. A further salary reduction of 5 percent was implemented December 3, 2012, and reversed by the commission's vote on June 19, 2013, effective December 2, 2013.

**Once an executive has served two terms in a particular office, he or she may not run for that office again. Term limits took effect with Proposition 140 in 1990. Anyone who served prior to 1990 was not prevented from running again; this includes Governor Jerry Brown, who served two terms as governor from 1975 to 1983.

Term limits on each office—two four-year terms under Proposition 140—also call into question executives' ability or desire to cooperate with one another. As term-limited colleagues, they are potential or actual rivals for each others' seats, driven from one elected position to the next as in a game of musical chairs. Each contender must build his or her own name brand through independent actions that merit attention from the media and the voters. However, despite their responsibilities and industrious efforts to lead the nation's most densely populated state jointly, like most elected officials they remain virtually anonymous to average residents.

The duty of an executive is to carry out laws and policies. Whereas federal administrators direct agencies in their departments to implement a coherent presidential agenda, in California a wide assortment of departments, agencies, and commissions serve different masters: the governor, other California executives, the legislature, the entities they are supposed to regulate, or a combination of any of the above. Years of legislative and administrative turf battles, as well as citizen-driven initiatives, have produced a thicket of offices, boards, agencies, and commissions, some of which

FIGURE 5.1 California Executives and Musical Chairs

Under term limits, an individual may be elected to the same seat only twice. Elected officials are usually looking for their next jobs long before eight years are up, and open statewide offices are attractive options to those who have campaigned statewide and have run other aspects of state government. In a term-limited era, it's all about the "next" office.

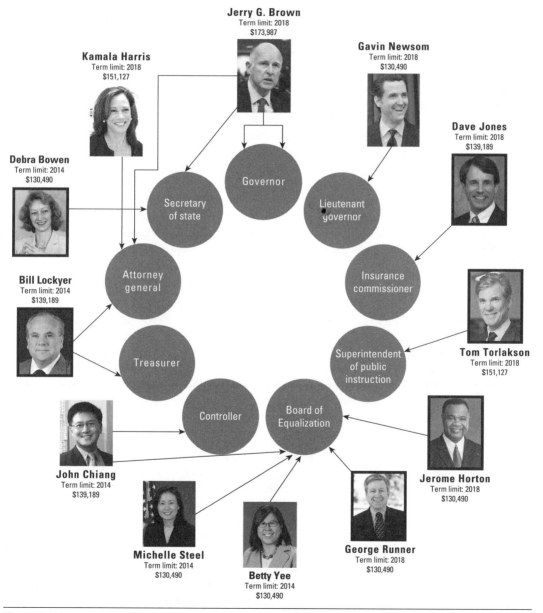

Notes: A **bold frame** indicates that the executive **served as an elected legislator** in the assembly, the senate, or both. Debra Bowen lost a bid for a congressional seat in 2011.

retain independent regulatory power and many more of which follow the governor's lead. In theory, the dispersion of power across several top offices inoculates government against the worst effects of a single, inept leader, but practically speaking, a fragmented power structure works against the production of consistent government policy and counteracts accountability.

California's Governor

According to the state constitution, "The supreme executive power of this State is vested in the Governor," which places him or her first among equals—for none of the elected executive officers answer directly to the governor. The most widely recognized and most powerful figure in California's state government possesses constitutional duties much like those of most other state governors; what distinguishes the office is both the size and hyperdiversity of the constituency (the entire state population) and the resulting volume of conflicts to be addressed.

The usual route to office is through a battering election that commands national headlines. Only former governor Arnold Schwarzenegger initially escaped primary and general election contests, as well as an extended campaign, by winning office through a recall election in 2003, replacing Gray Davis, who was a mere one year into his second term. Strong partisans and prodigious fundraisers tend to survive the regular winnowing process, and those with prior elected experience also tend to be favored—qualities that boosted Jerry Brown to victory in 2010 over his opponent, eBay cofounder Meg Whitman. Brown gained the seat for the second time, having served as governor (1975–1983, prior to the imposition of term limits), secretary of state, mayor of Oakland, and state attorney general.

Head of State

A governor has responsibilities both formal and informal. The role of **head of state** resonates with average citizens: the governor appears at official ceremonies and public events, summarizes California's outlook and his or her agenda in an annual "State of the State" address, receives and entertains foreign dignitaries, and speaks for Californians on both national and international political stages. He or she also functions as the state's official liaison to federal officials in Washington, D.C., and works with other state governors to advance causes nationally.

Chief Executive

The power to execute or carry out the law rests with the governor. Putting the law into practice is not something the governor can do alone, however. Brown employs 120 key "personal" staff to provide advice and assistance with research and communication (Schwarzenegger employed 230), and cabinet secretaries, who oversee major departments containing scores of agencies, assist the governor by implementing mandated programs throughout the state and coordinating the governor's policies. They are among the approximately 850 top-level appointees placed throughout the administration. Collectively, these appointees put into practice the governor's vision of good governance through the daily decisions they make about thousands of issues.

The governor also appoints members to approximately three hundred state boards and commissions with more than 2,250 slots to be filled. Examples include advisory groups, boards that manage county fairs, professional licensing bureaus, and specialized councils that deal with everything from marine fisheries to the arts to sex offenders. Appointments to about one hundred full-time administrative positions and seventy-five boards and commissions require senate approval, and overall only a fraction of appointees serve at the governor's whim. For instance, civil service laws protect virtually all state employees, and roughly 99 percent are hired based on merit rather than nepotism, favoritism, or patronage.[1] Outside of this, on rare occasion the governor may name a replacement to an open U.S. Senate seat. The governor also has the power to fill vacancies throughout the judiciary (superior, appellate, and supreme courts), although his appointees to appellate and supreme courts must first be reviewed and confirmed by two different judicial commissions and are later subject to voter approval at retention elections (see chapter 6). The governor may also issue **executive orders** directing state employees in how to implement the law, but the governor's power falls short of forcing all elected executives—constitutional partners such as the controller or attorney general—to do his or her bidding.

Legislative Powers

Legislatively, the governor plays a significant role by **setting policy priorities** for California not only through proposed laws but also through the budget. The power to **call special legislative**

Edmund Gerald Brown Jr., also known as Jerry Brown, first became governor at age thirty-six and was later reelected at age seventy-two. He has also served as a community college board trustee, California secretary of state, mayor of Oakland, state Democratic Party chair, and state attorney general.

sessions and special elections, combined with long-term, permanent staff members dedicated to research and program oversight, give the governor's office significant institutional advantages over the legislature.

Aides monitor bills at all stages of the legislative process. They propose bills and participate in critical final negotiations over a bill's wording and price tag. They testify before assembly or senate committees about pending measures and help build coalitions of support or opposition among legislators, interest groups, and other stakeholders. They also advise the governor to **veto** or **sign** legislation, as a bill submitted to the governor by the legislature becomes law after twelve days without gubernatorial action. Like governors in four out of five states, the governor of California wields the **line-item veto**, the power to reduce or eliminate dollar amounts in bills or the budget. This is also called "blue pencil" authority, because in the 1960s governors actually used an editor's blue pencil to cross out items in print. Governor Schwarzenegger, for example, used the power to eliminate nearly $1 billion in spending from the 2010 budget; in 2013 Governor Brown worked closely with Democratic lawmakers on the budget but ended up striking about a dozen "small-ticket" items from the final version, such as reducing preschool funding by $5 million. Veto overrides of such spending items or any bill passed by the legislature are rarely attempted or successful. In fact, the last recorded successful override occurred in response to one of "young" Governor Jerry Brown's budget-related line-item vetoes, recorded in early 1980.[2]

Budgeting Power

Budgeting power arguably gives the administration a powerful advantage over the assembly and senate. On January 10 of each year, the governor submits to the legislature a proposed annual state budget for the upcoming fiscal year. The muscular **Department of Finance (DOF)**, a permanent clearinghouse for state financial and demographic information, works in tandem with the governor, executive departments, and agencies to specify the initial budget in January, based on projections, and to revise it in May based on actual tax receipts. The 470 employees of this "superdepartment" work year-round to prepare the following year's budget and enact the previous year's financial plan, and they also analyze any legislation that has a fiscal impact.[3]

Chief of Security

The governor promotes security as **commander in chief** of the state's National Guard, which may be called on at short notice to deliver, for example, emergency services to victims of natural disasters such as earthquakes or fires. The State Military Reserve is the defense force placed under exclusive control of the governor; the land-based California Army National Guard and the Air National Guard, dedicated to cyberspace, space, and air capabilities, provide support. With few restraints the governor also can reduce penalties associated with a crime by offering clemency; that is, he can pardon individuals or commute sentences, even for death row inmates. Pardoning means that the offense stays on the individual's record, but no further penalties or restrictions will be imposed. Such reprieves are not uncommon, and the governor must report all reprieves and the reasons for them to the legislature annually. Throughout his time in office, Governor Schwarzenegger granted a total of sixteen pardons and ten commutations of sentence—one of which was sharply, publicly criticized because it appeared to be done out of favoritism for the convicted son of close associate and former assembly Speaker Fabian Nuñez. In contrast, only two and a half years into his first term, Jerry

Brown had already granted clemency to 214 persons who had demonstrated "exemplary behavior following their conviction."[4]

Sources of Power

The California governor's powers resemble those of U.S. presidents but with important exceptions. The state constitution spells out the governor's duties, but the constitutional blueprint for a plural executive limits a governor's ability to live up to citizens' expectations. For example, as the most visible and recognizable leader in state government, the governor sets policy priorities, yet he or she shares responsibility for day-to-day administration with almost a dozen other elected executive officers who may choose not to follow the governor's agenda. The governor is held to account for actions that condition the overall state of affairs, even if they are outside his or her control. To overcome this structural disadvantage, the governor must draw on other sources of power to be an effective leader.

One source of power is institutional, such as whether the governor's party holds a majority in both the assembly and the senate, as well as the numerical advantage of the majority. Another institutional factor is the cohesiveness of parties in the legislature, because the presence of many moderates may make the governor's job of reaching compromises much easier, whereas rigid partisans who are unwilling to budge from their positions can potentially thwart a governor's plans by obstructing specific bill language or foiling supermajority votes.

Power can also stem from a governor's popularity, personal qualities, and style. The governor's image as a loyal partisan friend or possibly as an untrustworthy party turncoat affects his or her ability to gather votes for preferred bills or provisions in them. For example, Governor Arnold Schwarzenegger alienated fellow Republicans by working with Democrats and championing policies that defied the state party's official platform. Jerry Brown (2010–present), despite having chaired the California Democratic Party at one time, has struck a note of practicality and toughness in his negotiations with Democratic leaders, disappointing them repeatedly with cuts to favored programs but earning him high marks from citizens. Aware of Brown's popularity and generally supportive of his ideological approach, Democratic legislators have had little choice but to back him, even if they cannot count on his unquestioning loyalty. Personal charisma, the power to persuade, the perception of having a mandate, and strategic use of the media can also go a long way in enhancing a governor's power base. Varied, lifelong political experience can also be a source of strength, as it has been for Governor Jerry Brown.

The Constitutional Executive Officers

Should the governor leave the state at any time, the **lieutenant governor** (LG) takes temporary control; should the governor resign, retire early, die, become disabled, or be impeached, the lieutenant governor takes the gubernatorial oath of office. Topping the LG's lackluster list of duties is presiding over the senate, which in practice means exercising a rare tie-breaking vote. The "governor-in-waiting" is also a voting member of the California State University (CSU) Board of Trustees and the University of California Board of Regents and sits on several other regulatory and advisory state boards ex officio, or "automatically" by virtue of his or her position.

Second in power to the governor is actually the **attorney general** (AG), known as the state's chief law enforcement officer. Through the state's Department of Justice, the AG employs deputy attorneys general to help represent the people of California in court cases, provides legal counsel to state officials, coordinates statewide narcotics enforcement efforts, enforces state firearms and gambling laws, fights fraud, assists with criminal investigations, provides forensic science services, and supervises all sheriffs, police chiefs, and state agencies to enforce the law adequately and uniformly. The office is inherently political not only because the state's lead lawyer is elected and may use the position as a stepping-stone to bigger and better offices (AG is also said to be shorthand for "aspiring governor") but also because he or she privileges some causes above others. For example, an AG might step up lawsuits against repeat environmental polluters or sue cities to overturn local ordinances that violate state law.

The **secretary of state** acts as the chief elections officer and oversees all aspects of federal and state elections. This includes registering voters, distributing ballot pamphlets in seven languages, printing ballots, certifying the integrity of voting machines, compiling election results, and certifying and publishing election results on the Web and in print. The Political Reform Division of the secretary of state's office implements rules relating to proper disclosure of lobbying and campaign finance activity and makes that information available electronically (http://www.cal-access.ca.gov). As keeper of official historical records, the secretary of state also charters corporations and nonprofits, maintains business filings, stores complete records of official executive and legislative acts, and safeguards the state archives.

Fragmentation of authority is most evident in the three separate offices that regulate the flow of money through the state government. The prominent **controller** (known as comptroller in other states) is the chief fiscal officer who pays the state's bills and continually monitors the state's financial situation by keeping a tally of the state's accounts. State employees and vendors who sell services or goods to the state might recognize the controller's signature on their payment checks. As the state officer who is ultimately responsible for ensuring that certain moneys due to the state are collected fairly, the controller is the at-large member of the State Board of Equalization and sits on numerous advisory boards, including the Franchise Tax Board (which administers personal income and corporate tax laws) and more than sixty other commissions and organizations relating to state payouts, such as employee pensions and construction projects.

The second money officer is the **treasurer**, the state's banker who manages the state's investments, assets, and bond debt. Every year the state borrows several billion dollars to finance huge infrastructure projects such as the rebuilding of bridges or schools, and this borrowing takes the form of bonds sold to investors. The treasurer manages the state's mountainous debt by selling and repaying bonds on an ongoing basis, trying to secure acceptable credit ratings that lead to lower loan interest rates, and maintaining the state's financial assets. The treasurer also chairs or sits on almost sixty boards that are authorized to raise and spend money on huge infrastructure concerns such as rail and road transportation, building and repairing schools, ensuring clean and available water, and housing.

The **Board of Equalization** represents the third money office and consists of the state controller and four other regional officials elected from districts containing more than nine million Californians apiece. The board's job is to standardize the tax systems in the state, which bring in more than $50 billion per year. The fee-based programs the board administers generate 34 percent of the state's annual revenues and essential funding for counties, cities, and special districts.[5] The board helps collect local sales taxes and fees that provide more than $9 billion to local governments. Aided by fifty-eight elected county tax assessors, the board ensures that residents pay fair rates on properties, and it also collects state sales and use fees, as well as liquor, tobacco, and fuel excise taxes that fund essential state services. The board is the only one of its type elected in the fifty states, and was evenly split between two Republicans and two Democrats after the 2010 elections.

In the same antitax spirit that led to the passage of Proposition 13, voters rebelled against spiraling auto insurance rates and elevated the **Office of Insurance Commissioner** from a governor-appointed subagency to a full-scale executive office in 1988. To protect consumers, the elected commissioner oversees the $123 billion-a-year insurance industry by reviewing and preapproving rates for car and home owners' (property and casualty) insurance. The commissioner also makes sure that insurance companies are solvent, licenses agents and companies operating in California, investigates fraudulent practices, and enforces rulings against violators. In recent years the department has taken a stronger role in reviewing health insurance rate increases as well.

As noted in this chapter's opener, the **superintendent of public instruction** leads the Department of Education as well as the State Board of Education, advocating for student achievement as the state's only nonpartisan executive officer. The superintendent is the point person for statewide student

Next to the governor, the most powerful executive officer in California is the attorney general. Here Attorney General Kamala Harris views firearms seized from persons possessing them illegally. In one six-week sweep, Department of Justice officers seized twelve hundred guns. Some of these were taken from persons who had been determined to be mentally unstable or who had active restraining orders against them.

testing and reporting, including implementation of the state's high school exit exams; data collection on a range of education-related issues such as dropout rates, yearly funding levels for K–12 and community college education, and student achievement levels; and implementation of education-related federal court opinions, the No Child Left Behind Act, and related U.S. education policy initiatives. Like other state constitutional officers tasked with coordinating policy among a snarl of governing bodies, the superintendent sits as an ex officio member on more than one hundred education-related boards and commissions.

Although these executive officers are free to consult each other and frequently find themselves in each other's company, at no point do they meet as a governing board, and no central mechanism exists to coordinate their work. Sometimes this arrangement makes for strange bedfellows, as Governor Schwarzenegger found in 2009 when he wrote an executive order closing state offices two Fridays per month, effectively furloughing all state workers, including the staffs of his fellow executives. However, his mandate legally could not apply to his colleagues, who promptly ignored the order. Sharp disagreements also surfaced between the legislature and the state's controller, John Chiang, with regard to the issue of temporary pay cuts for lawmakers who submitted a budget that "simply did not add up" in 2011.[6] Based on his interpretation of the recently passed Prop 25, Chiang refused to pay legislators after the governor's veto rendered the budget late. Legislators sued to recover lost wages, and a state judge ruled that only the legislature has the authority to control the budget process—thus preventing the controller from withholding disputed legislative paychecks during a budget delay and thwarting the people's intent (the controller has appealed the ruling, and the appeal is pending at this writing). One lesson to be gleaned from this example is that an organizational structure that allows Democrats and Republicans to share executive power virtually guarantees that differences in governing philosophies and approaches will exist, but it usually takes a looming crisis to make those differences visible and put them to the test.

Administrators and Regulators

A great checkerboard of departments, administrative offices, boards, and agencies form the state's bureaucracy. Almost all are linked to the governor through cabinet secretaries whom he or she designates to head each department. All the departments and state agencies these secretaries lead are organized either by statute or by initiative and are designed to help the governor execute state law faithfully.

Bureaucratic reorganization occurs periodically, but the "superagency" scheme of Governor Pat Brown—not to be confused with his son, Governor Jerry Brown—has stuck since the 1970s. The superagencies act as umbrella organizations for the smaller departments, boards, and commissions nested within them. The seven superagencies are (1) Business, Consumer Services, and Housing; (2) Natural Resources; (3) Corrections and Rehabilitation; (4) Transportation; (5) Health and Human Services; (6) Environmental Protection (EPA), and (7) Labor and Workforce Development. For example, the Transportation Agency houses six entities, including Caltrans, the Department of Motor Vehicles (DMV), and the state highway patrol. The state EPA oversees the Air Resources Board and five other major offices that regulate or assess pesticides, toxic substances, water resources, and other health hazards. The secretaries of these seven superagencies plus those of remaining departments, including several "superdepartments" that employ many specialists—the Departments of Finance; Food and Agriculture; and Veterans Affairs (see Figure 5.2)—constitute the governor's cabinet. Working for them are 198,100 full- and part-time public employees who make up the state bureaucracy—a workforce that decreased almost 20 percent from 2009 to 2013.[7] Governor Brown eliminated several departments in 2011 to help close the budget gap and continues to identify and purge duplicative state organizations.

The governor's stamp is also seen in membership appointments to about three hundred commissions and boards that share some governing authority with him or her in advisory, regulatory, administrative, or marketing capacities. Among these are large entities such as the California Public Employees' Retirement System (CalPERS) and smaller ones such as the boards overseeing professional licensing for dentists, nurses, accountants, and so forth. Most boards consist of four or five members and some meet only twice a year. Full membership turnover of a board rarely occurs during a governor's term; thus, competing ideological viewpoints are often represented on boards depending on who appointed whom. In addition, many organizations operate autonomously, meaning that they don't need to consult the governor or other elected officials before taking independent action on an issue, although the latter are ultimately responsible for their actions. Together, these unelected authorities make rules affecting Californians in virtually every imaginable way, from making beaches accessible to determining trash dump locations.

Conclusion: Competition for Power

The Progressives' lack of faith in political parties and mistrust of elected officials have left a legacy of many individuals at the top both sharing and competing for power. Ironically, although no single person is in charge, most Californians believe the governor is and blame him or her when things go awry. Perhaps not surprisingly, then, citizens are also unwilling to vest more power in that office and have, for example, rejected proposals to allow the governor to cut the budget more easily.[8]

What are we to make, then, of California's plural executive? In the first place, the division of labor among high-profile officials can mean that each brings a different kind of energy and focus to his or her specialized role. The splintering of authority among many offices also provides checks against the concentration of authority, but, perversely, this arrangement also obscures accountability. Decentralized decision making means that voters cannot hold anyone but the governor accountable for decisions produced at the state level, even though he or she may not be the source of their discontent.

In the second place, no one is truly "in charge" of the state, and fragmented authority places limitations on the governor's ability to coordinate a political agenda. The governor may be vested with "supreme" administrative authority by the constitution, but he or she can no more tell the controller what to do than the secretary of state can. State executives are entitled to their own approaches, initiatives, and budgets, and they use them to defend their individual reputations and, indirectly, in pursuit of other offices. They have little incentive to set aside their ideological differences or to coordinate their activities. The executive branch lacks the tools needed to build consistent, integrated policies, and Republicans and Democrats continue their work in spite of each other. Shared partisanship helps smooth out their differences, which the 2010 elections facilitated when Democrats captured all eight top offices (excluding the Board of Equalization).

FIGURE 5.2 Organization Chart of California's Executive Branch

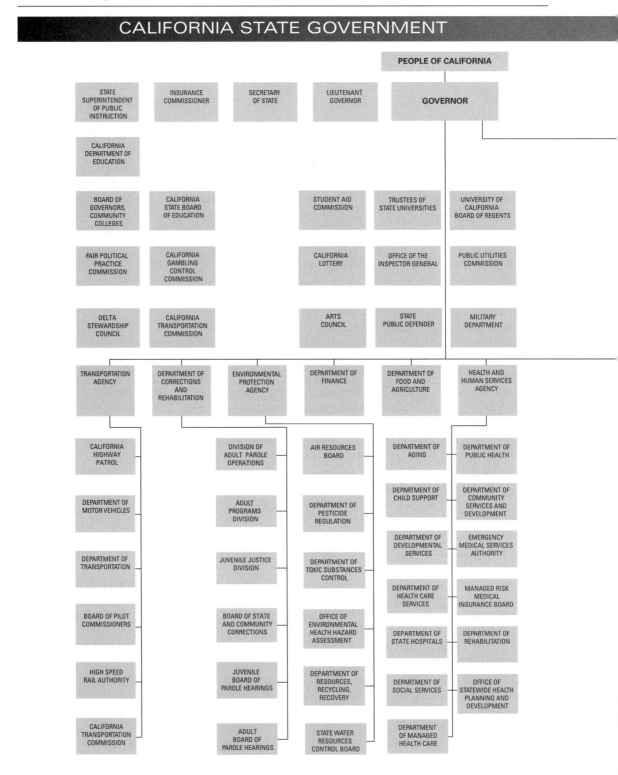

THE EXECUTIVE BRANCH

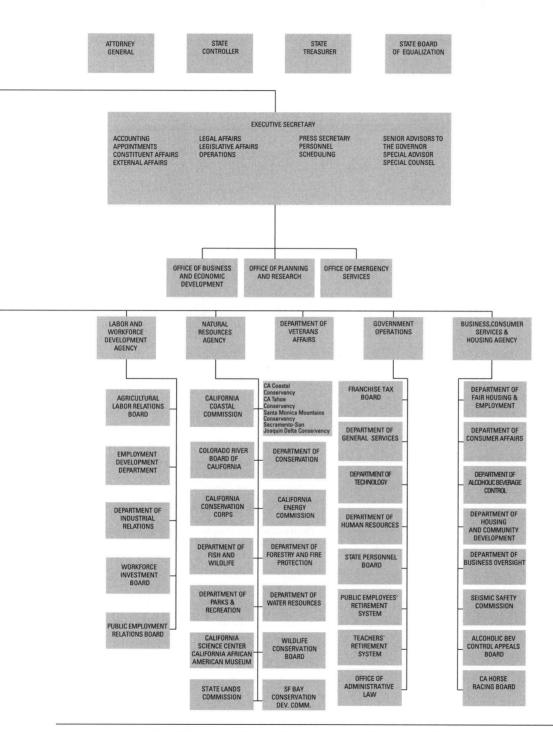

ATTORNEY GENERAL

STATE CONTROLLER

STATE TREASURER

STATE BOARD OF EQUALIZATION

EXECUTIVE SECRETARY

ACCOUNTING
APPOINTMENTS
CONSTITUENT AFFAIRS
EXTERNAL AFFAIRS

LEGAL AFFAIRS
LEGISLATIVE AFFAIRS
OPERATIONS

PRESS SECRETARY
PERSONNEL
SCHEDULING

SENIOR ADVISORS TO THE GOVERNOR
SPECIAL ADVISOR
SPECIAL COUNSEL

OFFICE OF BUSINESS AND ECONOMIC DEVELOPMENT

OFFICE OF PLANNING AND RESEARCH

OFFICE OF EMERGENCY SERVICES

LABOR AND WORKFORCE DEVELOPMENT AGENCY

NATURAL RESOURCES AGENCY

DEPARTMENT OF VETERANS AFFAIRS

GOVERNMENT OPERATIONS

BUSINESS,CONSUMER SERVICES & HOUSING AGENCY

AGRICULTURAL LABOR RELATIONS BOARD

CALIFORNIA COASTAL COMMISSION

CA Coastal Conservancy
CA Tahoe Conservancy
Santa Monica Mountains Conservancy
Sacramento-San Joaquin Delta Conservancy

FRANCHISE TAX BOARD

DEPARTMENT OF FAIR HOUSING & EMPLOYMENT

EMPLOYMENT DEVELOPMENT DEPARTMENT

COLORADO RIVER BOARD OF CALIFORNIA

DEPARTMENT OF CONSERVATION

DEPARTMENT OF GENERAL SERVICES

DEPARTMENT OF CONSUMER AFFAIRS

DEPARTMENT OF INDUSTRIAL RELATIONS

CALIFORNIA CONSERVATION CORPS

CALIFORNIA ENERGY COMMISSION

DEPARTMENT OF TECHNOLOGY

DEPARTMENT OF ALCOHOLIC BEVERAGE CONTROL

WORKFORCE INVESTMENT BOARD

DEPARTMENT OF FISH AND WILDLIFE

DEPARTMENT OF FORESTRY AND FIRE PROTECTION

DEPARTMENT OF HUMAN RESOURCES

DEPARTMENT OF HOUSING AND COMMUNITY DEVELOPMENT

PUBLIC EMPLOYMENT RELATIONS BOARD

DEPARTMENT OF PARKS & RECREATION

DEPARTMENT OF WATER RESOURCES

STATE PERSONNEL BOARD

DEPARTMENT OF BUSINESS OVERSIGHT

CALIFORNIA SCIENCE CENTER CALIFORNIA AFRICAN AMERICAN MUSEUM

WILDLIFE CONSERVATION BOARD

PUBLIC EMPLOYEES' RETIREMENT SYSTEM

SEISMIC SAFETY COMMISSION

STATE LANDS COMMISSION

SF BAY CONSERVATION DEV. COMM.

TEACHERS' RETIREMENT SYSTEM

ALCOHOLIC BEV CONTROL APPEALS BOARD

OFFICE OF ADMINISTRATIVE LAW

CA HORSE RACING BOARD

Source: Adapted from California Online Directory, "California State Government—the Executive Branch," http://www.cold.ca.gov/Ca_State_Gov_Orgchart.pdf. Updated July 1, 2013.

For the most part, however, California's executive officers coexist in pursuit of the same basic goal: to allow the state to prosper. Their collective inability to do so signals the intractability of California's problems and illustrates how the constitutional division of powers complicates the job of finding clear solutions. Nevertheless, a governor can exert strong pull over state policy and can influence state affairs to a much greater degree than any other state executive could. The extent to which he or she successfully uses instruments of power such as the signing of legislation, vetoes, appointments, and annual budgeting to coordinate "the big picture" is a measure of California's governability.

Notes

1. Most state workers are members of the powerful union known as the California State Employees Association.

2. According to the Assembly Clerk's Office (personal correspondence with author, June 2013), there were a series of veto overrides in 1979–1980, but the last occurred when the senate overrode a gubernatorial budget line-item veto on September 5, 1979 (Senate Journal, p. 7174). The assembly overrode this line-item veto on February 4, 1980 (by a vote of fifty-five to twelve), but a motion to reconsider was noticed. The motion to reconsider lapsed on February 5, 1980, so the override took effect on that day (Assembly Journal, p. 11086).

3. According to the Human Resources Department at the Department of Finance, the number of employees in May 2013 was 470. This represents a 10 percent increase from 2011. Although the number fluctuates, it is not expected to decrease.

4. See Paige St. John, "Jerry Brown Grants Clemency to 79 Individuals," *Los Angeles Times,* PolitiCal blog, December 24, 2012, http://latimesblogs.latimes.com/california-politics/2012/12/jerry-brown-clemency-list .html. St. John also notes that Brown made 403 acts of clemency during his first years in office (1975–1983). More recently, Brown granted 65 pardons on the eve of Easter 2013. State of California, "Governor Brown Grants Pardons," press release, March 30, 2013, http://gov.ca.gov/news.php?id=17981. For the reasons behind Brown's decisions, see *Executive Report on Pardons, Commutations of Sentence, and Reprieves,* issued annually by the governor's office under statutory order.

5. California State Board of Equalization, "The Agency and Its History," accessed August 30, 2013, http:// www.boe.ca.gov/info/agency_history.htm.

6. John Chiang is quoted in the Sacramento superior court judge's opinion in *Steinberg Perez v. Chiang* (2011), filed January 1, 2012, Introduction, Section 2, supra 12.

7. The total number was 198,090 as of May 2013, including part-time workers and excluding employees of the California State University system. In June 2009 the comparable state employee workforce numbered 244,061. California State Controller's Office, "State Employee Demographics," May 2013, http://www.sco .ca.gov/ppsd_empinfo_demo.html.

8. The most recent examples are Proposition 76 in January 2006 and Proposition 1A in May 2009, both of which were resoundingly defeated.

The Court System

The state courts' place in a separated system of powers is to verify that the actions of the executive and legislative branches—and also popular will as expressed in initiatives—are lawful and, more generally, to provide "fair and equal access to justice for all Californians." In one of the largest court systems in the world, more than two thousand judicial officers and nineteen thousand court employees handle 9.5 *million* cases annually.[1] Chances are good that every Californian at some point in his or her life will engage the justice system directly as a juror, to resolve family matters resulting from divorce or child custody disputes, or because of a traffic violation—the top reasons people connect to California's courts.

Impartiality forms the judicial system's core, but the branch is political nevertheless. Progressives realized this when they established nonpartisan elections for judges in 1911, but there is no avoiding the fact that many judges must run retention campaigns that can be expensive and further politicized when outspoken donors or independent spenders try to influence election outcomes. Judges are also appointees who make policy through their interpretation of laws, and they are often chosen by governors because of the imprints they make on civil society through their decisions. In addition, the yearly appropriations process politicizes the courts, especially in bleak budget years, because lower funding levels hurt residents' ability to get the help they need to navigate a judicial system that intimidates the average citizen. Year after year, budget reductions have forced those who run the courts to make unsatisfactory decisions that inevitably cause some citizens to suffer more than others.

California's constitution guarantees citizens the right to a jury trial for both criminal and civil cases, but chronic underfunding has led to overworked employees, shortages of judges, huge trial backlogs, and long delays for those involved in lawsuits—not to mention severe jail overcrowding. The judicial branch is withering from the largest reduction in funding in state history—$1 billion over five years.[2] What Chief Justice Tani Cantil-Sakauye has called "devastating and crippling" cuts have translated into seething frustrations for regular citizens.[3] Waits for regular trials and adjudications in family court can seem everlasting, and rural residents now must travel hours to a courthouse because of unprecedented court closures: 22 courthouses and 114 courtrooms had been closed as of mid-2013. Domestic violence victims find it hard to secure restraining orders quickly. Court reporters have been eliminated for civil and family matters. Fewer employees at every level means that what used to take a few minutes to resolve now takes hours, and what took days now takes weeks. Even after the state raided special accounts intended for infrastructure repairs to cover the courts' operating expenses, very little additional funding for courts was included in the 2013–2014 state budget—certainly not enough for the system to recover from a 65 percent reduction in state funding over the past half decade. For millions of people who rely on the courts to deliver justice, it will be many years before they find that the system is restored to full capacity.[4]

The Three-Tiered Court System

As in the federal judicial system, California courts are organized into three tiers, and the legislature controls the number of judgeships. At the lowest level are trial courts, which are also known as superior courts, located in each of California's fifty-eight counties. In a trial court, a judge or jury decides a case by applying the law to evidence and testimony presented. Working at this level are more than 1,600 judges and 360 subordinate judicial officers such as commissioners, and they deal with virtually all 9.5 million civil and criminal cases that begin here. Most citizens who use the courts are involved in resolving minor *infractions* for which a fine rather than jail time is imposed, including traffic violations such texting while driving. Infractions, which are heard by a judge only, make up about 60 percent of the superior courts' docket. The next-higher level is a category of crime called *misdemeanors,* for which the maximum punishment is a $1,000 fine and up to a year in a county jail. Examples include drunk driving, vandalism, and petty theft. Finally, an accused criminal may be charged with a *felony,* which is a serious and possibly violent offense, punishable by a state prison sentence or possibly death. Examples of felonies include murder, robbery, rape, and burglary of a residence. County district attorneys (DAs) bring cases against the accused, and anyone who cannot afford to pay for his or her own legal defense is entitled to help from a public defender. California's DAs have a conviction success rate of around 80 percent.[5] Sentencing outcomes depend on the severity of the crime, the offender's criminal history, and the court's discretion.

Civil suits, on the other hand, usually involve disputes between individuals or organizations seeking monetary compensation for damages, usually incurred through injuries, breaches of contract, or defective products. Limited civil cases involve damages valued at less than $25,000, whereas unlimited civil matters exceed that threshold. The huge number of civil lawsuits in the state, about 1.2 million annually,[6] reflects a general acceptance of litigation as a "normal" way to resolve problems. The state attorney general can also bring civil cases against companies that break environmental, employment, or other types of state laws. Civil suits typically result in monetary judgments. Unlike criminal defense, the state does not supply legal representation for citizens who are involved in civil cases.

From left to right, California Supreme Court justices Joyce Kennard, Tani Cantil-Sakauye (chief justice), Marvin Baxter, Ming Chin, and Goodwin Liu enter a courtroom during a California State Supreme Court hearing in San Francisco.

Finally, juvenile, family, and probate cases are specific types of civil cases that are also heard in superior court. Family matters typically involve divorces, marital separations, and child custody cases. Parties might also ask a judge to rule on a family member's mental competence, settle an inheritance dispute, or legally change a name. A single judge or a trial jury may decide a case at this level.

If the losing party in a case believes the law was not applied properly, he or she may ask the next-higher district **court of appeal** to hear the case. There are no trials in district appellate courts, although three-judge panels commonly hear lawyers argue cases. Spread across nine court locations are 105 appellate justices who review approximately twenty-five thousand cases for errors, improprieties, or technicalities that could lead to reversals of the lower courts' judgments; they dispose of more than half these cases without issuing written opinions. On the whole, appellate court decisions clarify and actually establish government policy, as the state supreme court allows the great majority of these decisions to stand.

The highest judicial authority is vested in a seven-member **supreme court**, whose decisions are binding on all California courts. Headquartered in San Francisco, the justices of the supreme court also hear oral arguments in Los Angeles and Sacramento about cases appealed from the intermediate-level district courts throughout the year, but they automatically review death row cases and exercise original jurisdiction over a few other types. Of roughly ten thousand cases appealed to it

FIGURE 6.1   California Court System

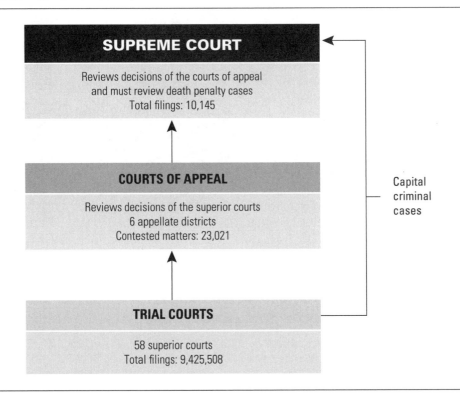

SUPREME COURT

Reviews decisions of the courts of appeal
and must review death penalty cases
Total filings: 10,145

COURTS OF APPEAL

Reviews decisions of the superior courts
6 appellate districts
Contested matters: 23,021

TRIAL COURTS

58 superior courts
Total filings: 9,425,508

Capital
criminal
cases

Sources: California Courts, "About California Courts," December 2012, http://www.courts.ca.gov/2113.htm; Judicial Council of California, Administrative Office of the Courts, *2012 Court Statistics Report: Statewide Caseload Trends, 2001–2002 through 2010–2011* (San Francisco: Judicial Council of California, 2012), http://www.courts.ca.gov/documents/2012-Court-Statistics-Report.pdf.

in 2010–2011, the court issued a mere ninety-eight written opinions, made available to the public on the court's website (http://www.courts.ca.gov) and through published official reports. The justices are not required to review all cases and therefore have wide discretion over case selection, concentrating mostly on those that either address important questions of law or promote uniform judgments across the system. They spend considerable time choosing cases, and each justice employs support staff and permanent staff attorneys to assist him or her. Their interpretations of the law define the boundaries of acceptable behavior for businesses, government, and citizens. As the principal supervisor of the lower courts, the chief justice shoulders more responsibility than the other justices. As spokesperson for the judicial branch, Chief Justice Cantil-Sakauye delivers the "state of the judiciary" address annually to the legislature and has become the system's "chief lobbyist" for restoring state funding to the court system. The court's reputation at any given time reflects its collective policy decisions, both in the questions the justices choose to address or ignore and in their interpretation of the wording and intent of specific laws.

Controversy often stems from the supreme court's review of initiatives, political measures that can only be ruled on after passage and are often overturned in whole or in part for violating the state constitution. Proposition 8, a constitutional amendment that eliminated same-sex marriage by defining marriage as between a man and a woman only, became a hot potato in 2009 for the justices, who were threatened with recall if they overturned it. (They didn't, although three supreme court justices in Iowa did legalize same-sex marriages and were ousted by that state's voters in 2010.)

On and Off the Court

An attorney who has practiced law in California for at least ten years may become a judge, but individuals usually enter the position through gubernatorial appointment rather than by first running for office. Those who are interested in becoming judges may apply through the governor's office. A governor has ample opportunity to shape the long-term ideological bent of the judiciary by selecting individuals whose partisanship and political principles are reflected in their judicial philosophies. When then attorney general George Deukmejian (1982–1991) was asked why he was running for governor, he replied, "Attorney generals don't appoint judges. Governors do."[7] Governor Arnold Schwarzenegger was far less partisan in his judicial appointments than his predecessors: just over half of his appointees were Republicans, about a third were Democrats, and the remainder were undeclared.[8] Governors also directly affect the demographic composition of the bench, which today remains disproportionately male, middle-class, and white—in contrast to the state's heavily ethnic prison population (see Table 6.1 and Box 6.1). Vacancies are unpredictable. In the seven years between November 2003 and December 2010, Governor Schwarzenegger made 627 appointments to the bench. Between January 2011 and June 2013, Governor Brown appointed 103. Whereas Schwarzenegger appointed two of the seven supreme court justices, shortly after taking office Jerry Brown had an opportunity to fill a vacancy on the state's highest court. Justice Goodwin Liu is currently the only supreme court jurist appointed by a Democratic governor.

Superior court justices serve for six years without term limitations, and if they were first appointed to office and not elected, they must become nonpartisan candidates for their offices when their terms expire. Longer terms are intended to increase the judiciary's independence and consistency over time by reducing the frequency of distracting campaigns that can create potential conflicts of interest with campaign contributors. Contested elections are rare, and unopposed judges usually win.

Appointees to the six appellate courts and the supreme court also require the governor's nomination, but they must first be screened by the State Bar's Commission on Judicial Nominees, a state agency whose members represent the legal profession, and then confirmed by the Commission on Judicial Appointments. Members of the latter include the attorney general, chief justice of the supreme court, presiding judge of the courts of appeal, and at-large members of the legal community; together, they evaluate appointees' fitness for office. Confirmation allows a justice to fulfill the remainder of his or her predecessor's twelve-year term, but the judge must participate in a nonpartisan "retention election" at the next gubernatorial election, at which time voters are asked to vote yes or no on whether he or she should remain in office. The judge may seek unlimited terms thereafter.

Voters rarely reject judges. Defeat requires public outrage fed by a well-publicized, media-driven campaign, as three supreme court justices found in 1986. Having earned reputations for being "soft on crime" at a time when rising crime rates were rattling the public, Chief Justice Rose Bird and

TABLE 6.1   Diversity of California's Justices and Judges (in percentages)

Court (persons reporting)	Female (N = 519)	Male (N = 1137)	Black or African American (N = 101)	Hispanic or Latino (N = 138)	Asian (N = 96)	White (N = 1183)	Native American (N = 5)/ Other/More than one (N = 59)	Information not provided (N = 49)
Supreme court (7)	57.1	42.9	0	0	28.6	42.9	28.6	0
Court of appeal (100)	31.0	69.0	5.0	5.0	3.0	79.0	6.0	1.0
Trial court (1,549)	31.2	68.8	6.2	8.6	5.9	71.1	3.8	3.1
Total	31.3	68.7	6.1	8.2	5.8	71.4	4.0	3.0

Source: California Courts, "Demographic Data Provided by Justices and Judges Relative to Gender, Race/Ethnicity, and Gender Identity/Sexual Orientation," December 31, 2012, http://www.courts.ca.gov/documents/2013-Demographic-Report.pdf.

two of her colleagues were targeted for their opposition to the death penalty. For the first time in California history, three justices lost their retention bids, and Governor George Deukmejian replaced them with conservative justices.

Although judges rarely lose elections, they are not immune to campaign or interest group pressures. In their primary role as defenders of law and order, judges are expected to be independent arbiters of justice, but elections can jeopardize their impartiality. In the thirty-three states that directly elect judges, the price of judicial campaigns—even for retention elections—is rising, a trend that alarms court observers. Nationwide, several judicial elections in 2010 were targeted by "super spenders" and ideologically based interest groups hoping to sway the courts, a trend also apparent in state supreme court elections (such as in Michigan in 2013) and smaller-scale contests.[9] In 2010, for example, an outspoken Christian conservative group tried to unseat four superior court judges in San Diego by promoting its own candidates, sparking a larger debate over the integrity of California's court system. (All four judges managed to keep their jobs, despite relatively low voter turnout.)

Judges can also be dismissed for improper conduct or incompetence arising from a range of activities, among them bias, inappropriate humor, and substance abuse. Hundreds of complaints are filed each year with the Commission on Judicial Performance, the independent state agency that investigates allegations of judicial misconduct. The commission does not review a justice's record but focuses instead on personal behavior that may warrant a warning letter, formal censure, removal, or forced retirement. Only a tiny fraction of judges face disciplinary action; the great majority have internalized the norms of judicial propriety that are imparted through law school and the legal community.

Court Administration

Like the U.S. federal court system, the state judicial branch is headed by a chief justice. However, a formal organization, the thirty-one-member **Judicial Council of California**, which the chief justice chairs, sets policy for the state's court system. This public agency is tasked with policymaking, establishing rules and procedures in accordance with ever-changing state law, making sure the court is accessible to citizens with diverse needs, and recommending improvements to the system. The council also controls the judiciary's annual budget and reports to the legislature and responds to its mandates. A subagency of the Judicial Council, the Administrative Office of the Court (AOC), is made up of staff who actively implement the council's policy decisions. Administrative officers throughout the state manage the court system by supervising a supporting cast of thousands who help run the court system day to day. They make information available to the public, keep records, hire interpreters, schedule hearings, and, when times are prosperous, create task forces to study issues such as foster care or domestic violence, among many other activities.

Juries

Barring a traffic violation, jury duty tends to be the average citizen's most direct link to the court system. Names of prospective jurors are randomly drawn from lists of registered voters and names provided by the Department of Motor Vehicles. Under the "one day–one trial" program, prospective jurors are excused from service at the end of a single day if they have not been assigned to a trial, and they only need to respond to a summons to serve once a year. If assigned to a trial, jurors consider questions of fact and weigh evidence to determine whether an accused person is guilty or not guilty. Convincing citizens to fulfill their duty to serve as jurors isn't easy, and juries tend to overrepresent those who have relatively more time on their hands, such as the elderly, the unemployed, and the wealthy. About 9 million people are summoned to serve on juries each year in California, although only about 3.5 million of them are eligible and able to sit on a trial.[10] All jurors are compensated $15 per day starting with the second day of service plus thirty-four cents for mileage one way. There are no plans to raise this rate, although it is well below the national average of approximately $19 for the first day and $25 for the second day of service.[11]

Grand juries are impaneled every year in every county to investigate the conduct of city and county government and their agencies. Each contains nineteen members, except for Los Angeles's grand jury, which has twenty-three members due to the city's large population. During their one-year terms, grand jurors research claims of improper or wasteful practices, issue reports, recommend improvements to local programs, and sometimes indict political figures for misconduct, meaning they uncover sufficient evidence to warrant a trial.

Criminal Justice and Its Costs

About 90 percent of cases never make it to trial. High costs and delays associated with discovery, investigations, filings, and courtroom defense encourage out-of-court settlements and mediation, and the chance to receive a lesser sentence for pleading guilty results in plea bargains that suppress prison crowding. Although California's crime rates have declined over the past two decades, the state's prisons have been bursting at the seams for years. With 163,000 inmates in facilities designed to hold about 85,000, by the Department of Corrections and Rehabilitation's own admission the state's prisons were 185 percent above capacity in early 2011.[12] "Bad beds" have been crammed into prison libraries, gymnasiums, day rooms, and other areas not intended for sleeping bunks. By June 2013 the inmate population had been reduced to 119,200—still 149.5 percent of capacity.

The "three strikes" initiative is largely to blame for the blistering growth of the prison population. In 1994 voters were horror-struck at the abduction and murder of twelve-year-old Polly Klaas, a crime perpetrated by a man with a long and violent record. Klaas's family and others lobbied vigorously for tougher sentencing of repeat offenders, and their efforts culminated in the "three strikes and you're out" law: anyone convicted of a third felony is sentenced to a mandatory prison term of twenty-five years to life without the possibility of parole, with enhanced penalties for second-strikers. Today, approximately forty-two thousand inmates are serving time for second and third strikes, most of which were nonviolent offenses.[13] Some of those convictions will be reconsidered due to the passage of Prop 36 in 2012, which revises the law to impose a life sentence only when a new, third felony conviction is serious or violent and authorizes resentencing for current inmates if they were imprisoned for nonviolent offenses. This will release some pressure from the system, but hardly enough to repair it.

Longer sentences translate into an aging prison population with expensive health care issues, and under the Eighth Amendment's prohibition against cruel and unusual punishment, inmates are the only population in the United States guaranteed the constitutional right to receive adequate health care—although the quality of that care is often in doubt. Prompted by a class-action lawsuit in 2001 alleging dire conditions and the state's slowness to reform, a federal court removed control of prison health care from the state and appointed a federal receiver to help raise standards to an acceptable level. Immediately the receiver demanded that at least $8 billion more be invested in upgrades to compensate for historically insufficient funding.

Underfunding of the correctional system has been the default option for state lawmakers because prisoners are esteemed by no one: spending cuts to prisons represent a rare convergence point for those on the left, who would prefer more spending on rehabilitation and crime prevention programs, and those on the right, who tend to equate spending with unfair comforts for criminals who deserve to pay for their crimes. In fact, cuts to prisons and corrections are the only ones that citizens consistently say they would make in order to balance the annual budget: 62 percent supported this choice in a May 2011 poll.[14] The receiver has remained in charge since 2005, and with lawmakers' authorization, major improvements to on-site medical facilities have been made, including a new $839 million inmate medical complex in Stockton.[15] Despite those investments, deliberate cuts over the years have led to deteriorating facilities, and the state has failed to build more penitentiaries; the result is a prison population that remains dangerously dense.

Skyrocketing costs are also connected to overcrowding. In 1980 the total prison population was 22,500, and in 1985 it cost less than $100 million to run the entire correctional system. Today the correctional system devours $11.2 billion (from the general fund, special funds, and bonds, 2013–2014). At a projected yearly cost of about $59,000 *per inmate,* California pays far more than other states, where the costs are closer to $30,000 per offender.[16] The higher costs are attributable mainly to expenses for security personnel and medical care. For each inmate approximately $17,500 is spent on pharmaceuticals and medical, mental, and dental care; about $31,000 goes to staff salaries, benefits, and administrative costs; and the remainder covers facilities, food, record keeping, rehabilitation, and educational and drug treatment programs. It costs less to send California prisoners to out-of-state facilities in states such as Arizona, Mississippi, and Oklahoma, where approximately 8,500 prisoners are incarcerated, although Governor Brown has begun to curtail the practice. In addition, about 18,300 felons who are not legal U.S. residents also cost the state more than $900 million per

Enacted budget 2013–2014:	$8.89 billion (general fund), $11.17 billion (total)
Cost per inmate, 2013–2014 (estimated):	$59,000*
Staff, 2013–2014:	59,856
Total number of inmates (estimated):	119,214** (June 2013)
Lifers:	25,927*
Prisoners on death row:	725 (including 19 women)
Parolees:	49,726** (June 2013)
Most common crime:	Property crime (86% of reported crimes)
Number of prisons:	34, minimum to maximum security, and including 1 new medical prison, plus 42 adult firefighting camps, 1 community prisoner mother facility, and 1 female rehabilitative correctional center
Mean age:	39 (male), 38 (female)
Gender of inmates:	95.5% male, 4.5% female

Racial composition of inmate population:

Category	Inmate population
White, non-Hispanic	23.1%
Hispanic/Latino	41.0%
Black	29.6%
Other	6.3%

Sources: California Department of Corrections and Rehabilitation, Offender Information Services Branch, Estimates and Statistical Analysis Section, Data Analysis Unit, "Prison Census Data," December 31, 2012, http://www.cdcr.ca.gov/reports_research/offender_information_services_branch/Annual/Census/CENSUSd1212.pdf. Budget statistics from California Department of Finance, "Governor's Budget 2013–14," http://www.ebudget.ca.gov.

*Figure calculated by the Legislative Analyst's Office (Mac Taylor, January 2013) based on 2013 data.

**Due to reductions mandated by the federal government, this number is expected to decline further. See California Department of Corrections and Rehabilitation, Offender Information Services Branch, Estimates and Statistical Analysis Section, Data Analysis Unit, "Weekly Report of Population," http://www.cdcr.ca.gov/Reports_Research/Offender_Information_Services_Branch/WeeklyWed.

year because the federal government only reimburses about 5 percent of the costs associated with their incarceration.

Indefensible overcrowding resulted in a federal court order for the state to cap the prison population at 137.5 percent of capacity, to which Governor Brown responded by signing AB 109 in 2011, the "Public Safety Realignment" law. Realignment policy shifts the responsibility for locking up about 34,000 low-level, nonviolent, non–sexual offender adult felons to county governments and aims to transfer 46,000 state parolees to county probation departments, representing a small step toward solving a much larger problem in the state penitentiaries but a bigger drain on county resources. Even as counties receive more state funding to defray the cost of expanded jail services, they will inherit demands that they cannot meet long-term, including the burdens of providing adequate health care

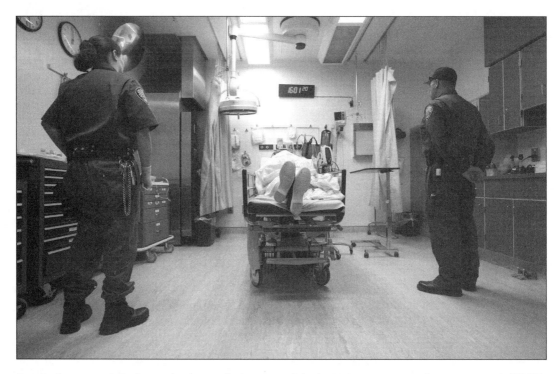

An aging inmate population has made prison medical care a costly business; the average annual cost per person is $17,000, with much higher price tags for specialized care—for example, it costs more than $800,000 a year to care for and guard a prisoner lying in a vegetative state not only because of necessary medical equipment and round-the-clock care, but also because of the high-security environment.

facilities, space and beds to house inmates, and personnel to supervise and help rehabilitate those on probation. County jail systems were not designed to hold convicts sentenced for longer than one year, and many have population caps that are being exceeded. In addition, the varying economic environments, local policies, and political will across fifty-eight counties will inevitably translate into differences in the ways that inmates are treated, raising further questions about fairness and equality.

In June 2013 federal judges lost their patience with the slow rate of attrition and threatened to release 9,500 "low-level" prisoners by the end of 2013 if the state did not meet mandated targets. As of this writing, the state continues to argue that options are limited and releasing prisoners will endanger citizen safety. There are no easy political solutions to prison overcrowding.

Crime rates have fallen in California since peaking in 1992, and many point to the three-strikes law as the reason. Crime rates and imprisonment trends in states that lack three-strikes penalties are similar to California's, however, and researchers have shown the cause-and-effect relationship to be complicated by other variables. Yet voters believe it works. Until 2012 they were unwilling to soften the law, but enough voters changed their minds as the costs of overcrowding became apparent. Because voters approved Prop 36 in 2012, three-strikes sentencing is now restricted to those who commit violent and serious offenses.

Conclusion: Access to Justice

How much access to justice can Californians count on? Chief Justice Cantil-Sakauye has stated that current funding levels for the judicial branch "absolutely won't be enough to provide the kind of access to justice the public deserves."[17] The cumulative impacts of five years of budget cuts have been spread broadly, and they fall especially hard on Californians who already have difficulty accessing the courts because they live far from an operating courthouse, or who have little daytime to spare outside their jobs, or who require interpreters, or who don't have the money to hire lawyers to defend themselves in civil suits. It will take years for the court system to dig out of the fiscal hole that the legislature has created for it, and years to achieve the "fair and equal access to justice" guaranteed by the state constitution.

Chronic underfunding has also beleaguered the correctional department, which remains under federal court order to reach and stay at (or below) 137.5 percent of population capacity, and has a recovering health care system under the treatment of a federal receiver. Although crime rates have declined steeply since the 1990s, an aging prison population with increasing medical needs and high personnel expenses has driven up costs that California taxpayers find difficult to stomach. Where the courts and prison populations are concerned, the lack of robust lobbying efforts—the kind perfected by most special interest groups—and the inability to generate public sympathy are problematic in a political system that is responsive to such pressures.

Judicial branch politics and flaws in the correctional system also shed light on the complexity of governing. Prison overcrowding, an inmate population that is about three-quarters ethnic minority, and crowded court dockets are outcomes of other political and social issues that require legislators' attention, namely, poverty, lack of education, racism, unemployment, access to mental health care, and homelessness. Such social problems are manifest in crimes ranging from minor to serious and are inherent indicators of Californians' quality of life. Only a governing approach that comprehensively addresses the relationships among these issues can bring about fair, equitable, and accessible justice for all Californians—a daunting responsibility indeed.

Notes

1. California Courts, "About California Courts," December 2012, http://www.courts.ca.gov/2113.htm.
2. Five years refers to the number of budget cycles from 2008 through 2012, as reported on the official website of the California courts. California Courts, "InFocus: Judicial Branch Budget Crisis," http://www.courts.ca.gov/partners/courtsbudget.htm#ad-image-0.
3. Shane Goldmacher, "Chief Justice: 'Crippling' California Court Cuts Would Be 'a Blow against Justice,'" *Los Angeles Times,* PolitiCal blog, June 14, 2011, http://latimesblogs.latimes.com/california-politics/2011/06/chief-justice-crippling-california-court-cuts-would-be-a-blow-against-justice-.html.
4. For those who can afford it, alternative dispute resolution (ADR), also known as mediation or legally binding arbitration, offers a quicker way to decide cases. ADR relieves some of the pressure on the state's overall caseload, but it creates further divisions between those who can pay for high-priced mediators and those who must depend on state services.
5. Mac Taylor, *California's Criminal Justice System: A Primer* (Sacramento: California Legislative Analyst's Office, January 2013), http://www.lao.ca.gov/reports/2013/crim/criminal-justice-primer/criminal-justice-primer-011713.pdf.

6. Judicial Council of California, Administrative Office of the Courts, *2012 Court Statistics Report: Statewide Caseload Trends, 2001–2002 through 2010–2011* (San Francisco: Judicial Council of California, 2012), http://www.courts.ca.gov/documents/2012-Court-Statistics-Report.pdf.

7. Governors' Gallery, "George Deukmejian," http://governors.library.ca.gov/35-deukmejian.html.

8. Julie Patel, "Forum Sheds Light on How Judges Are Screened, Chosen," *San Jose Mercury News,* June 4, 2006.

9. For more information about the politics and costs of judicial elections, see James Sample, Adam Skaggs, Jonathan Blitzer, and Linda Casey, *The New Politics of Judicial Elections 2000–2009: Decade of Change* (Washington, DC: Justice at Stake Campaign, Brennan Center for Justice at NYU School of Law, August 2010), http://www .justiceatstake.org/media/cms/JASNPJEDecadeONLINE_8E7FD3FEB83E3.pdf; and Lester Graham, "The Influence of Money and Politics in Michigan Supreme Court Elections," Michigan Radio, February 18, 2013, http://www.michiganradio.org/post/influence-money-and-politics-michigan-supreme-court-elections.

10. California Courts, "About California Courts." Approximately 9.4 million persons completed jury service in 2008; the number was 8.67 million in 2010–2011. "Completed service" means the individual appeared at the court on the appointed day, although he or she may not have been assigned to a trial and was dismissed at the end of the day.

11. According to data collected by the National Center for State Courts in 2007, the average compensation rate was $18.75 (plus mileage) for the first day of service and $25.30 for the second day (assuming the juror was sworn in by day two). Data for some states were incomplete. See Gregory E. Mize, Paula Hannaford-Agor, and Nicole L. Waters, *The State-of-the-States Survey of Jury Improvement Efforts: A Compendium Report* (Williamsburg, VA: National Center for State Courts, April 2007), http://cdm16501.contentdm.oclc.org/cdm/ref/collection/juries/id/112.

12. California Department of Corrections and Rehabilitation, Offender Information Services Branch, Estimates and Statistical Analysis Section, Data Analysis Unit, "Monthly Report of Population as of Midnight April 30, 2011," May 3, 2011, http://www.cdcr.ca.gov/Reports_Research/Offender_Information_Services_ Branch/Monthly/TPOP1A/TPOP1Ad1104.pdf.

13. See California Department of Corrections and Rehabilitation, Offender Information Services Branch, Estimates and Statistical Analysis Section, Data Analysis Unit, *Second and Third Striker Felons in the Adult Institution Population* (Sacramento: California Department of Corrections and Rehabilitation, September 30, 2012), http://www.cdcr.ca.gov/Reports_Research/Offender_Information_Services_Branch/Quarterly/Strike1/ STRIKE1d1209.pdf.

14. Mark Baldassare, Dean Bonner, Sonja Petek, and Jui Shrestha, *Californians and Their Government* (San Francisco: Public Policy Institute of California, May 2011), http://www.ppic.org/content/pubs/survey/ S_511MBS.pdf.

15. According to Taylor: "The federal court stipulated that the transition from the receivership back to state control will begin when the administration can demonstrate both (1) the ability to maintain an inmate medical care system that provides care as good as or better than that being delivered under the Receiver and (2) that any outstanding construction or information technology projects initiated by the Receiver would not be jeopardized. Likewise, the federal court overseeing inmate mental health care recently expressed satisfaction with progress made to date by the department towards a constitutional level of mental health care." Taylor, *California's Criminal Justice System,* 66.

16. Data provided by the Legislative Analyst's Office, June 2013. These numbers are based on actual per capita expenditures of $51,889 in 2011–2012, estimated costs of $56,421 per inmate in 2012–2013, and current policy and budget allocations in 2013–2014.

17. California Courts, "Chief Justice Issues Statement in Response to 2013–2014 Budget," press release, June 27, 2013, http://www.courts.ca.gov/22629.htm.

CHAPTER 7

Other Governments

Californians fall under the jurisdiction of many governments operating within the state's borders. Counties, cities, special districts, and regional governments share responsibility for delivering essential services that both protect and enhance residents' quality of life—from hiring police officers to making sure clean water flows beneath paved streets. Yet even in prosperous times these governments struggle to fund baseline operations with scarce taxpayer dollars. Demand for services generally outpaces voters' willingness to pay higher taxes for them, although voters tend to make exceptions for new taxes that have concrete, dedicated purposes and are temporary. In the worst of times, these governmental bodies may declare bankruptcy, and taxpayers end up paying the long-term costs of failed governance.

The state's patchwork of subgovernments reflects historical demands for services along with the desire of communities for self-rule. In cases where one entity cannot or will not deliver a service, new ones have been created without regard to centralized planning. Bottom-up solutions are joined to state and federal mandates in a functionally segmented system—one that works with surprising efficiency considering the enormous number and scope of issues encompassed and the limited budgets available to local governments today.

County Government

The revised state constitution of 1879 subdivided California into fifty-eight counties created to deliver services and carry out programs created by the state government, and their boundaries have remained untouched since then. If we picture the state as a tall cabinet with fifty-eight different-sized drawers, then the counties represent the drawers, which are filled with cities, some almost completely, some only partially, and three without any (Alpine, Mariposa, and Trinity Counties do not contain

MAP 7.1   California, 2010 Population by County

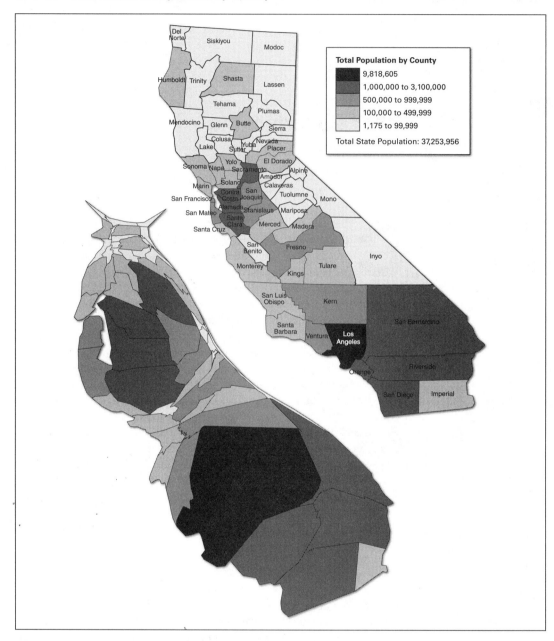

Total Population by County

■	9,818,605
■	1,000,000 to 3,100,000
■	500,000 to 999,999
■	100,000 to 499,999
□	1,175 to 99,999

Total State Population: 37,253,956

Source: U.S. Census Bureau, 2010 census, http://www.census.gov.

Notes: Geographic area and population are two variables used to measure the size of California's fifty-eight counties. Geographic boundaries are shown in the top map with shadings for population density, and the lower "cartogram" illustrates the relative distribution of population by county.

BOX 7.1 **FAST FACTS on California's Other Governments**

Number of counties:	58
Number of cities:	482
Number of federally recognized tribes:	110
Number of school districts:	1,043
Number of special districts:	4,770
Five largest cities by population:	Los Angeles, 3,863,839
	San Diego, 1,326,238
	San Jose, 984,299
	San Francisco, 825,111
	Fresno, 508,483
Largest county by area:	San Bernardino, 20,052 square miles
Smallest county by area:	San Francisco, 47 square miles
	(10,000 people per square mile)
Largest county by population:	Los Angeles, 9,958,091
Smallest county by population:	Alpine, 1,087
Largest city by population;	Los Angeles, 3,863,839
Number of chartered cities:	121 (25%)
Number of general law cities:	361 (75%)
Number of cities with directly elected mayors:	149 (30%)

Sources: California Department of Finance, "E-1 Population Estimates for Cities, Counties, and the State—January 1, 2012 and 2013," http://www.dof.ca.gov/research/demographic/reports/estimates/e-1/view.php; California League of Cities, "Learn about Cities," http://www.cacities.org/Resources/Learn-About-Cities; California Department of Education, "State Reports" (statistics for 2011–2012), http://www.ed-data.k12.ca.us.

cities). San Francisco is the only combination city/county, having consolidated the functions of both into one government. The areas that do not fall within city boundaries are considered "unincorporated," and all counties contain large swaths of unincorporated areas, where more than 20 percent of Californians live. County governments directly provide services and local political representation to those residents.

County lines drawn in 1879 bear no relation to population density or economic activity today, and all counties are expected to provide the same kinds of services to their constituents regardless of population size or geographic area. This means that the largest county by population, Los Angeles, about 10 million people, maintains the same baseline political departments, elected officials, and responsibilities as tiny Alpine, population 1,100. The legislature endows each county with the responsibility to provide for residents' health and welfare, and can either delegate state functions to the counties or revoke them.

The constitution permits general law and charter counties, with the main difference lying in how officers are selected and organized. All counties are governed by five-member *boards of supervisors*

(San Francisco's board has eleven members and a mayor). Supervisors face nonpartisan elections every four years, and most are reelected overwhelmingly unless they cannot run due to term limits, and that depends on whether voters in a specific county have enacted such limits via local initiative. Many termed-out state lawmakers are prolonging their political careers as county supervisors, putting their knowledge and "institutional memory" about state issues and systems to good use by helping run the state's largest subgovernments. Forty-four counties are the **general law** variety, organized according to state statute. Each county must elect a sheriff, district attorney, and assessor, and may appoint or elect a variety of other officers, such as a medical examiner and public defender. Fourteen counties are organized under **charters** that allow flexibility in governing structure: apart from elected supervisors and the above-named officials, they can determine the other types of offices, whether they will be combined (will they have an assessor/recorder/clerk or a recorder/clerk?), whether they will be appointed or elected, and if they will be elected at-large or by district.

County officials such as the sheriff and treasurer/taxcollector/assessor help the board of supervisors supply basic but vital social and political services in many areas:

- *Public safety:* courts, jails, probation, public defense, juvenile detention, sheriff, fire, emergency services
- *Public assistance:* housing, services for the homeless, food stamps, state welfare programs
- *Elections and voting:* voting processes, voter registration
- *Tax collection:* county, city, special districts, schools
- *Environment and recreation:* parks, facilities, open space, waste removal and recycling, air quality, land use policy, water
- *Public health:* hospitals, mental health clinics, drug rehabilitation programs
- *Education:* libraries, schools
- *Social services:* adoptions, children's foster care
- *Transit:* airports, bus and rail systems, bridges, road maintenance
- *Vital records:* birth, death, marriage certificates

Counties finance these operations by levying sales taxes and user fees and through state government funds, property taxes, and federal grants. They spend the most on public safety and public assistance (see Figures 7.1 and 7.2). State budget crises stem the flow of revenue, typically forcing counties to lay off employees, cut services, and raise fees to make ends meet. Even after economies are in recovery mode, it takes years before the state restores funding to previous levels, and counties continually struggle to fulfill their state-mandated obligations—from preventing disease to ensuring foster children's safety—with relatively meager funding.

Municipal Governments

Communities in unincorporated areas of a county may want more control over land use in their neighborhoods, better services, or a formal identity. They can petition their state-chartered local agency formation commission, or LAFCO, to incorporate as a city or municipality if the residents generate enough tax revenues to support a local government. The average size of a California city is 65,000, with a huge span between the smallest (Vernon, population 112) and the largest (Los Angeles, population 3.8 million).

Much like counties, cities provide essential public services in the areas of public safety and emergency services; sewage and sanitation; public health; public works, including street maintenance; parks and recreation; libraries and schools; and land-use planning. Sometimes these overlap or supplement county programs: for example, a city might maintain its own library and also contain two or three county library branches. If lacking their own facilities, cities can contract with counties for services, pool their resources in a joint-powers agreement, or contract with private firms. A new trend among cities, especially as public employee pension obligations have grown over the years and residents have refused to pay higher taxes, has been to cut personnel and public works costs through outsourcing. One such "contract city" is the town of Half Moon Bay, which since 2011 has outsourced recreation services, engineering, legal services, code enforcement, and police protection, mostly to private contractors, the neighboring city of San Carlos, and San Mateo County. Similarly, as cities in Orange County have multiplied, the OC Fire Authority has continued to provide critical fire services to them under contract, and contracted county sheriffs patrol municipalities that cannot afford their own police forces.

More than 75 percent of California's 482 cities have incorporated under **general law,** meaning they follow state law in form and function. The remaining **charter cities** are creatures of local habits, formed through city constitutions that grant local government supreme authority over municipal affairs. This **"home rule" principle** permits municipal law to trump similar state laws. The city of Bell in the Los Angeles area serves as an uncomfortable reminder of this fact: using home rule to evade salary limitations that are set by state law, Bell's city leaders voted themselves exorbitant pay raises that technically were legal. When finally exposed, the city manager was making almost $800,000 a year in salary and benefits—more than four times the governor's salary.

Virtually every city is governed by a five-member **city council** that concentrates on passing and implementing local laws, called **ordinances**. Thus, unlike how state and federal governments separate powers among different branches to ensure checks and balances, legislating *and* executing local law blends in city councils. City councils rely heavily on small boards and **commissions** filled by local volunteers or appointees to help recommend and set policy relating to the special needs of citizens and businesses. For example, the city of Gardena has seven commissions, including a Youth Commission and a Senior Citizens Commission, tasked with creating helpful and appealing programs for those city residents. To facilitate public participation in these and other public-planning bodies, as at the state level, all city and county governing institutions must abide by the **Ralph M. Brown Act**, which mandates advance notice of all meetings, "open" meetings that do not take place in secret, and full public disclosure of the proceedings.

City council members are reelected every four years in nonpartisan elections, usually by the entire city's electorate in an **at-large election** rather than from separate **districts**. Many city councils are now subject to local voter-imposed term limits, and the list of term-limited cities grows each year. If the **mayor** is not elected at-large (meaning that the whole city votes for mayor), council members designate one among them to act as a ceremonial mayor, typically on a rotating basis, for one or two years at a time. Each city makes its own rules regarding how long and how often city council members can act as mayor and whether the appointment will be automatic, by acclamation, or by election. Automatic rotation creates opportunities for many young council members to assume the role of mayor, and mayors in their twenties are not altogether uncommon. Ceremonial mayors lack veto power, and their vote on the council is equal to the votes of their colleagues. In place of an elected mayor, the council hires a manager to run city operations.

If the mayor's authority exceeds that of the city council members, such as the power to veto city council actions or hire and fire high-profile appointees to help run city operations, a **strong mayor** form of government is in place. Some 30 percent of California cities maintain this form of municipal government, partly because a sole individual can offer a clear agenda and be held accountable for its success or failure. The far more popular **council-manager system** exists in nearly 70 percent of

FIGURE 7.1   County Revenues and Expenses, 2010–2011

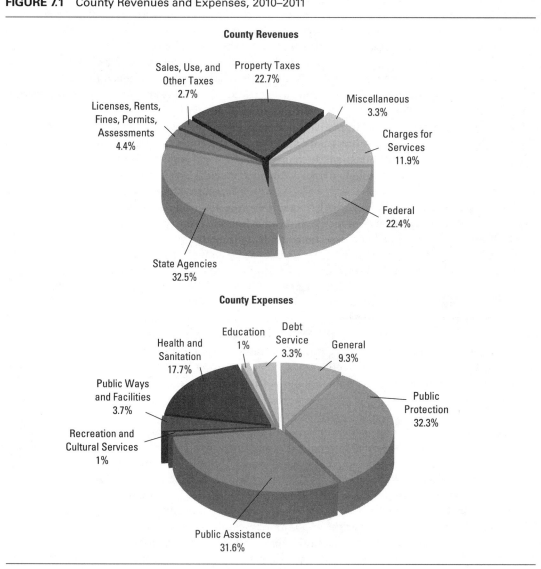

County Revenues

Sales, Use, and Other Taxes 2.7%
Property Taxes 22.7%
Licenses, Rents, Fines, Permits, Assessments 4.4%
Miscellaneous 3.3%
Charges for Services 11.9%
Federal 22.4%
State Agencies 32.5%

County Expenses

Education 1%
Debt Service 3.3%
Health and Sanitation 17.7%
General 9.3%
Public Ways and Facilities 3.7%
Public Protection 32.3%
Recreation and Cultural Services 1%
Public Assistance 31.6%

Source: California State Controller's Office, "Cities Annual Report," prepared September 11, 2011.

Notes: Excludes the city/county of San Francisco. Figures may not add to 100 percent due to rounding.

cities, an institutional legacy of Progressives who believed that efficient city management required technical expertise because "there is no partisan way to pave a street." In most cities, then, a council retains a ceremonial mayor but hires a professional **city manager** to budget for, manage, and oversee the day-to-day operations of a city. As a city's "chief executive officer," the city manager is authorized to make decisions independent of the council and thus wields great power behind the scenes. The office handles hiring and firing decisions, as well as the supervision of all city departments. Most city managers possess a master's degree in public administration and have experience managing local government departments. Typically, the highest-paid city employee is the professional city manager, who earns more than $175,000 per year on average—although again the numbers vary widely, with some city managers making little (less than $20,000) and others making a lot (more than $300,000). The average annual wage for all types of California city employees is $61,000, but the pay scales vary immensely, and so do the numbers of city employees, resident-to-employee ratios, and the types of professionals in any given municipality.[1]

Cities depend heavily on taxes and fees to finance operations. Prior to Proposition 13, property taxes constituted 57 percent of combined city and county revenues annually; in 2011–2012 property

City councils make laws (their legislative function includes passing ordinances) and also execute laws by implementing city plans or programs. The San Bernardino city council regularly meets twice weekly, compared to Los Angeles's city council, which meets three times a week, and the councils of smaller cities, which commonly meet twice a month. At a typical meeting council members might discuss pending litigation, decide land-use matters, pay tribute to community heroes, approve expenses and payments for city services, establish new fees, vote on contracts for city services, and/or listen to citizens' concerns.

taxes represented only 8 percent of the average aggregate city budget. The bulk of funding now comes from sales and use taxes; fines and developer fees; service charges for public utilities and transit; a variety of taxes on hotels, other businesses, and property; and state and federal agencies.

FIGURE 7.2 City Revenues and Expenses, 2010–2011

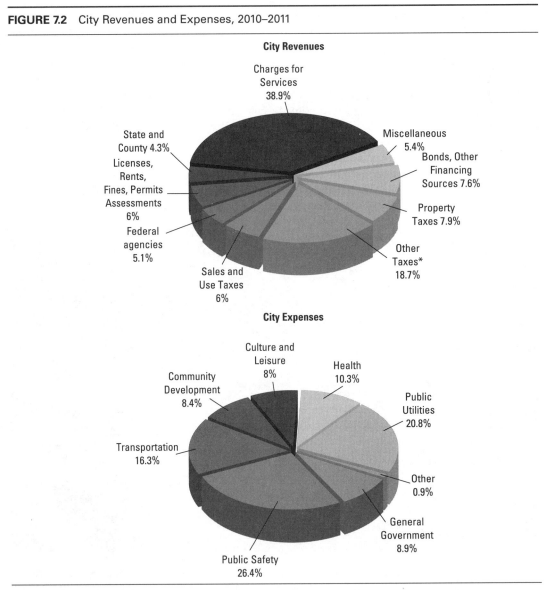

City Revenues

- Charges for Services 38.9%
- Miscellaneous 5.4%
- Bonds, Other Financing Sources 7.6%
- Property Taxes 7.9%
- Other Taxes* 18.7%
- Sales and Use Taxes 6%
- Federal agencies 5.1%
- Licenses, Rents, Fines, Permits Assessments 6%
- State and County 4.3%

City Expenses

- Culture and Leisure 8%
- Health 10.3%
- Public Utilities 20.8%
- Other 0.9%
- General Government 8.9%
- Public Safety 26.4%
- Transportation 16.3%
- Community Development 8.4%

Source: California State Controller's Office, "Cities Annual Report," prepared September 11, 2011.

Notes: Excludes the city/county of San Francisco. Figures may not add to 100 percent due to rounding.

*Includes transportation, transient lodging, franchise, business license, real property transfer, utility user, and other nonproperty taxes.

Assembly members and senators perform economic gymnastics to balance the state budget during hard times, and their routine includes yanking property taxes and other fees previously committed to cities to backfill the state's budget hole. In an effort to stop such state "raiding" of local funds, cities and counties sponsored a constitutional amendment (Proposition 1A in 2004) to prevent state legislators from transferring locally generated property taxes, vehicle license fees, and sales taxes into the state's general fund. The state, however, can override some of those restrictions during fiscal crises, effectively diverting millions of dollars away from the cities and counties in which they were generated.

Local governments scramble to find substitute revenue sources. One popular strategy at the city level is to charge developers heavy fees for new construction projects or saddle them with the costs of constructing new streets, schools, lighting, sewers, or any infrastructure improvements related to population growth. These fees are then imposed on home buyers. Mello-Roos fees, for example, can amount to thousands of dollars a year for home owners who live in houses constructed in previously undeveloped areas. Assessed as a special lien against each property that will be in effect for as long as forty years, the annual charges can vary dramatically from area to area, and even house to house. In counties such as San Diego, the average home owner in a Mello-Roos-related district pays an additional $1,826 per year on top of property taxes, with these fees totaling $195 million in San Diego County in 2012 alone.[2]

Another strategy is to base land-use decisions on a project's net fiscal impact, a phenomenon known as the **fiscalization of land use.** In practical terms this means that cities today have incentives to entice and keep retail businesses that can generate substantial sales taxes, as local governments receive 1 percent of state sales taxes collected in their jurisdictions. Auto dealerships, shopping malls, and big-box retailers like Wal-Mart are therefore favored over low-income housing and service-based industries that will further stress city resources—in other words, decisions are made without regard to the intrinsic value of, or need for, a project.

Borrowing large sums to upgrade city services with better technology, to cover payment obligations, or to rebuild schools, for example, has also become a favored tool for local governments of all types. Debt typically takes the form of a voter-approved **bond**, which can range from hundreds of thousands to hundreds of millions of dollars. Taxpayers "issue" (sell) bonds to lenders and commit to repay them, with interest, after twenty or thirty years, for example. Bonds are also used to cover financial obligations such as long-term leases. One source estimates that California city and county bond debt is over $90 billion, and when school districts and other special districts are included, the total is closer to $200 billion—numbers that underestimate current debt because of reporting delays.[3]

Debt can also take shape in long-term commitments to pay for hefty projects that may or may not generate income, such as a water treatment plant that local citizens pay for through higher sewage bills. So-called **unfunded liabilities** probably constitute the most hazardous type of debt; this catchphrase refers to whatever a city or county legally owes in future payments but does not yet have the financial reserves to cover. Historically California's cities and counties have negotiated retirement and health care benefits in contracts with public employees, such as firefighters and police, but those commitments have drained—and continue to threaten—public treasuries to the point of bankruptcy. Generous employee labor contracts have been based on optimistic projections of tax receipts and returns on investments, and governments have been banking on higher rates of return than an unanticipated economic downturn could deliver. Even if return rates improve, municipalities and counties owe no less than an estimated $20 billion in pension payments—*plus* health care benefits (which are likely to *triple* those outlays).[4]

How will local governments fulfill these colossal pension obligations without going broke? Residents in some cities, as in San Diego, have passed local initiatives eliminating pensions and switching to 401(k) plans for new city employees. Other cities simply can't avoid running out of money. Following Vallejo's lead, the cities of San Bernardino and Stockton filed for Chapter 9 **bankruptcy** protection in 2012 in hopes of erasing soaring debt loads that have been pushed into the stratosphere by employee compensation and pensions, bond repayments for ill-advised infrastructure projects, and general financial mismanagement by city officials. City payouts have shot up while tax receipts have plummeted. To recover, a bankrupt local government must raise taxes to pay its bills and curtail virtually every service it provides to citizens as it charges higher fees. Crime rises as the police force dwindles, the city's ability to borrow vanishes along with its good credit ratings, the roads become gutted with potholes, and tourism evaporates. Creditors are repaid pennies on the dollar, and the city's long-term debt is reduced through the renegotiation of current labor contracts—yet huge pension obligations remain.

To date, the courts have treated retirees' pensions (earned retirement benefits, with interest) as ironclad contractual obligations, and labor unions have fiercely defended them as vested rights. If judges decide that pension systems can be treated as all other creditors and these contracts can be broken, then cities will have a greater incentive to bargain for lesser payments or to declare bankruptcy, and retirees will see drastic changes in their long-anticipated retirement incomes. Municipalities now considered financially vulnerable by big credit-rating agencies, including Los Angeles and San Jose, which spend tens of millions of dollars (roughly 20 percent of their annual budgets) on these expenses, would find this option irresistible.

Special Districts

A **special district** is a geographic area governed by an autonomous board for a single purpose, such as running an airport or providing a community with street lighting or a cemetery. Arguably the most abundant power centers in California, but virtually invisible to the average citizen, special districts proliferate because they are created to meet critical needs that cities and counties lack the will or capacity to address. Like regular governments, they can sue and be sued, charge users for their services, and exercise the right to eminent domain (the taking of property for public use). Unlike most governments, however, they may cover only a portion of a city or stretch across several cities or counties.

Of 4,770 special districts in the state, two-thirds operate independently with their own boards of governors chosen by voters in low-profile elections; the remainder are controlled by counties or cities through appointments. About 2,700 special districts independently generate their own revenue as enterprises through fees or by providing services and charging their customers, while the remainder depend on counties and cities for their funding. The majority of special district services are paid for through property-related service charges or special assessments that initially require a two-thirds majority vote. In other words, the total fee per property owner is a percentage of a property's assessed value, so neighbors might pay different rates for the same services. Hospital, rat and mosquito control, trash disposal, fire protection, irrigation and water delivery, bus and rail transit, and utility districts proliferate. The Southern California Metropolitan Water District (MWD) epitomizes this type of fee-based service organization: created by the legislature in 1928, its mission is to provide adequate, reliable supplies of high-quality drinking water to current and future residents in Southern California. Today, twenty-six cities and water districts coordinate their activities through the MWD to provide drinking water to nineteen million residents in six counties,

Clothing, cars, furniture, electronics, and many other goods pass through this important special district, the Port of Los Angeles at San Pedro, before being transported to stores across the United States. Located twenty miles from downtown Los Angeles, the port occupies forty-three miles of waterfront and features twenty-four cargo and passenger terminals, making it the busiest cargo port in the nation. Ports are major economic engines, worth billions of dollars to the local and state economy, and they create employment for more than one million Californians. Together, the Port of Los Angeles and the neighboring port in Long Beach constitute the eighth-largest port in the world, following those in Asia.

delivering more than 1.7 billion gallons of water daily. In addition to paying their local water district for the water they use, Southern California residents see charges listed on their annual property tax bills for basic MWD services.

School districts constitute a separate but most familiar category of special district: more than 1,000 provide K–12 education for about 6.2 million students attending almost 10,000 different schools; an additional 72 districts encompass 112 community colleges.[5] Created by state law, nonpartisan five-member boards of education (Los Angeles's board has seven) govern their school districts by following the detailed operating instructions of the state's education code and heeding the State Board of Education's mandates. A superintendent manages the local system, which may be responsible for more than 662,000 students—as is the case in the gargantuan Los Angeles Unified School District—or fewer than 100 students. Governing boards handle issues relating to nearly every aspect of student life, from regulating students' cell phone use to defining nutritional needs to designing appropriate curricula, and they must weigh the concerns of vocal parents and special interest groups trying to influence their decisions against the concerns of those who do not speak up so forcefully.

State-funded, K–12 public **charter schools** operate outside the jurisdiction of the local school board; these are organized by parents, teachers, and/or community groups to provide specialized programs of instruction that may have a particular emphasis in the performing arts, sciences, languages, or college preparation, for example. Since a 1992 state law enabled charter schools to form, their number has increased annually, reaching 1,018 in 2012. Charter schools are free and open to all students, and if a school receives more requests to attend than it has spots available, it must hold a blind lottery to determine which students can attend.

Proposition 98 dedicates approximately 40 percent of the state's general fund budget to K–14 education, yet schools receive funding from a variety of sources. Using the 2012–2013 fiscal year as a point of reference, just over 70 percent of K–12 public school funding is sourced through Prop 98 with general fund money and local property tax revenue. The rest comes from a variety of sources: approximately 10 percent from federal dollars, and miscellaneous sources supply the remaining 20 percent, including bond payments, the state lottery (a mere 1.5 percent), special local parcel taxes, and donations funneled through private foundations that have been formed to supplement operations by buying equipment or hiring specialized teachers (music or arts instructors) that districts cannot afford.

Regional Governments

Unlike governments that make and enforce binding laws, **regional governments** provide permanent forums in which local elected officials can exchange ideas and information, plan, and coordinate their policies across county and city boundaries, usually for land-use and development-related activities arising from population growth and change. State law allows for the creation of a variety of regional governments with joint powers authority (JPA), and these **councils of government** (COGs) plan for future populations by addressing common issues that encompass a wide spectrum of infrastructure-related needs, including housing and transportation, water and food availability, toxic waste disposal, public safety, and environmental quality. COGs in California, therefore, are a collection of local officials and agencies that voluntarily agree to share responsibility for solving collective problems. There are at least thirty-five major COGs that have organized in California and have formed joint-powers agreements.[6]

COGs coordinate rather than dictate because they cannot force decisions on local governments. Their governing boards are composed of mayors, city council members, and county supervisors, making them *intergovernmental* entities. In these collaborative forums to promote regional planning, they receive input from research specialists and advisers from federal departments, special districts, state agencies, and even sovereign nations such as California Native American tribes and Mexico. Their planning activities include reviewing federal grants-in-aid and proposing legislation. They do not deliver public services.

COGs can take the form of *transportation planning agencies* or *commissions,* such as the Contra Costa County Transportation Authority, which coordinates freeway expansions and improvements, maintains emergency roadside call boxes, helps fund bus transit, oversees bicycle paths, and encourages ridesharing. Nineteen COGs are also federally designated *metropolitan planning organizations* (MPOs), legally responsible for researching, designing, and finding funding for regional transportation plans for areas with more than 50,000 people. MPOs include associations like the San Joaquin COG (SJCOG) and the Santa Barbara County Association of Governments

(SBCAG). Other COGs are *planning councils* with wider scope, like the Tahoe Regional Planning Agency, through which elected officials from surrounding areas create overarching plans that have vital impacts on construction, recreation, water quality, and the environment around Lake Tahoe. Their boundaries can be extensive, such as the Association of Bay Area Governments (ABAG), which unites local elected officials from nine counties and 101 cities to deal with housing, open space, employment, waste, transportation, recreation, and equity challenges posed by a population that is seven million and growing.

Regional government may also take the form of regulatory entities that set rules for environmentally sensitive activities. These bodies are authorized by state law to set rules and enforce them. For instance, California's thirty-five "air districts" are dedicated to controlling pollution from stationary sources (Air Pollution Control Districts, or APCDs) and promoting air quality (Air Quality Management Districts, or AQMDs) through comprehensive planning programs that include the setting of compulsory rules for residents and the enforcement of those rules, air quality monitoring, research, public education, and the issuing of special business permits.

Federalism

Whereas the state authorizes county governments, local jurisdictions, and special districts to perform necessary functions, the U.S. Constitution guarantees that states share governing power with the national government, although states' authority has diminished as both the federal purse and federal capacity have grown. The U.S. Congress discovered long ago that **funding** is a convenient instrument for enticing states to adopt federal goals by granting or withholding moneys in exchange for new state policy. In this way, highway funds have been exchanged for lower speed limits and a minimum drinking age of twenty-one—issues that only the states can legislate.

California is also subject to **unfunded mandates**. These are federal laws that require the states to provide services, but no federal funds are supplied to implement them. Such mandates amount to hundreds of millions of dollars in various areas, including social services, transportation, education, health care, and environmental cleanup. For example, holding an average of 15,000 to 18,000 undocumented immigrants in state correctional facilities daily costs the state upward of $1 billion per year. The federal government's State Criminal Alien Assistance Program (SCAAP) provided only $51 million in 2012–2013—about 5 percent of the average cost to house inmates[7]—and the U.S. Department of Justice zeroed out the SCAAP budget for fiscal year 2014, considering the funding levels "so low as to render the program ineffective."[8] Mandates also can take the form of **preemptive legislation,** which prohibits a state from passing certain laws; the federal government has used legislation of this kind to prevent some of California's progressive environmental rules and legislation from taking effect, such as a ban on ride-on lawn mowers—a move that would have negative impacts on the states where the mowers are manufactured.

California remains dependent on the federal government to balance its ledgers, receiving billions for major programs such as welfare and health coverage. Federal money flows to individuals in the form of Social Security checks, for example, and also through the state budget. The Legislative Analyst's Office estimates that in federal fiscal year 2009–2010, Californians received $330 billion from the U.S. government—roughly three times the amount of state spending, a figure that includes

BOX 7.2 California's Landmark Climate Change Law: AB 32

California set itself apart again when the state's majority-Democratic legislature joined Governor Arnold Schwarzenegger in crafting the Global Warming Solutions Act of 2006, otherwise known as Assembly Bill 32 (AB 32), the world's first law establishing a program of regulatory and market mechanisms to curb emissions of greenhouse gases. Although businesses and antiregulatory interests continue to oppose the law strongly, anticipating higher costs because of its mandates, voters beat back an initiative (Proposition 23) to rescind it in 2010. The law aims to promote a "green economy" by encouraging jobs that promote more efficient, renewable energy sources that improve air quality and authorizes the state's Air Resources Board (ARB) to set new fuel efficiency standards for new cars, trucks, and sport utility vehicles sold in California; establish a statewide emissions cap for 2020 based on 1990 emissions levels; adopt mandatory reporting rules for significant sources of greenhouse gases; create advisory boards to assist with planning; and write mandatory reporting rules for significant sources of greenhouse gases.

Most notably, ARB has enacted the nation's first **cap-and-trade program** for greenhouse gas (GHG) emissions. Modeled on other successful market-based pollution reduction programs, California's version is designed to reduce the overall amount of GHGs by setting an upper limit, or cap, on the aggregate amount of statewide emissions from 85 percent of GHG sources. About 360 "polluters" (businesses creating carbon and other gases linked to climate change, representing 600 facilities) were initially given trading credits, or allowances, for the normal amount of GHGs they produce. These large businesses, such as electricity generators, emit more than 25,000 metric tons of carbon dioxide annually. Chevron's Richmond refinery is the biggest source, producing 4.5 million metric tons of an overall estimated 447 million metric tons in the state yearly; the University of California is another large emitter. Every year the total cap on statewide emissions will decline by 2–3 percent (the total number of allowances will decline), providing incentives for polluters to invest in more efficient technologies or fuels that will reduce their own emissions, thereby creating for them a surplus of carbon trading credits that they can sell at a quarterly online auction. Companies in capped industries must register and report their emissions annually (also subject to independent verification), a requirement imposed in 2008, and the Air Resources Board has designed the process to protect against collusion, cheating, and price manipulation. Advocates of the cap-and-trade approach tout the facts that no new taxes are directly assessed and businesses have flexibility to alter their practices to be compliant. Opponents bemoan the new layer of regulations and paperwork and costs of compliance, and equate new costs with indirect taxes. California plans to link to cap-and-trade markets in Quebec, Canada, on January 1, 2014.

2010 Emissions by Sector

Source: California Environmental Protection Agency, Air Resources Board, "Greenhouse Gas Inventory Data—Graphs," http://www.arb.ca.gov/cc/inventory/data/graph/graph.htm.

Note: Total gross emissions for 2010: 451.6 million metric tons of carbon dioxide equivalent.

Initially the act was fiercely opposed by a tight coalition of automobile, manufacturing, and energy industries, which challenged the new law as going "too far" by setting stricter standards than the federal government—despite the fact that the federal Environmental Protection Agency (EPA) had never set a greenhouse gas emissions standard. Ruling that AB 32 superseded federal authority to maintain clean air standards, the EPA under the George W. Bush administration denied California a waiver from adhering to clean air standards lower than those set in the Federal Clean Air Act. On June 30, 2009, the EPA under the Barack Obama administration reversed the ruling, giving California and thirteen other states the green light to proceed with implementation and enforcement of laws like AB 32. Governor Schwarzenegger crowed: "After being asleep at the wheel for over two decades, the federal government has finally stepped up and granted California its nation-leading tailpipe emissions waiver. . . . A greener, cleaner future has finally arrived."* According to a U.S. Energy Information Administration report in 2013, however, California remains the second-highest producer of carbon dioxide, behind Texas and ahead of Pennsylvania.

Source: California Environmental Protection Agency, Air Resources Board, "About the ARB," last reviewed April 26, 2012, http://www.arb.ca.gov/html/aboutarb.htm.

*California Governor's Office, "Governor Applauds EPA Decision Granting California Authority to Reduce Greenhouse Gas Emissions," June 30, 2009, http://gov.ca.gov/issue/energy-environment.

Social Security and Medicare checks, defense and homeland security, state health care including Medi-Cal, education, transportation, and more. Money that went straight to the state amounted to $80 billion in the 2011–2012 fiscal year, or 38 percent of total state spending, which neared $209 billion. Given California's staggeringly high population, position as a military gateway to the Pacific, and importance to the nation as an agricultural hub and economic powerhouse, federal dollars will continue to backfill permanent and growing needs.

Tribal Governments

An often-overlooked class of government functions alongside state and local entities, and also under the thumb of the federal government: that of sovereign tribal nations. Tribal governments operated in relative obscurity until recently. Isolated on one hundred thousand acres of mostly remote and frequently inhospitable reservations throughout California, the state's 110 federally recognized tribes had minimal impact on neighboring cities or state government. Native groups were defined politically by their interaction with the U.S. Congress and federal agencies such as the Bureau of Indian Affairs, as well as by prior case law that treated them as wards of the federal government rather than as fully sovereign nations. In the main, California governments could ignore them.

Gaming changed all that. As bingo halls flourished in the 1970s and blossomed into full-scale gambling enterprises by the late 1980s, states began looking for ways to limit, eliminate, tax, influence, or otherwise control this new growth industry, one whose environmental and social effects on surrounding communities were proving significant.

After the U.S. Supreme Court ruled in 1987 that tribes do indeed have the right to run gambling enterprises on their lands, Congress exercised its supreme lawmaking authority (to which tribes

FIGURE 7.3 Tribes Are Recognized Sovereigns

The U.S. Constitution explicitly recognizes four sovereigns:

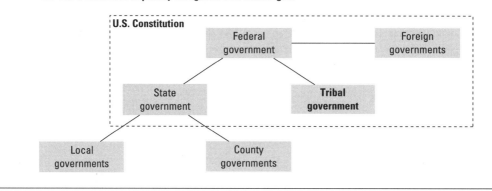

Source: Kate Spilde, Kenneth Grant, and Jonathan Taylor, "Commentary: Social and Economic Consequences of Indian Gaming in Oklahoma," *American Indian Culture and Research Journal* 28, no. 2 (Los Angeles: UCLA American Indian Studies Center, 2004). Reprinted with permission of the authors.

are subject) and wrote the **Indian Gaming Regulatory Act (IGRA)**, a law that restricts the scope of gaming and defers regulatory authority to the states. The IGRA also stipulates that tribes within a state and the state itself must enter into compacts to permit certain forms of gaming irrespective of tribal sovereignty. In California, casinos with 350 or more slot machines are considered Class III gaming operations and are subject to compacts. Class II gaming includes card rooms and bingo played for monetary prizes.

No state can tax a tribal nation, but California governor Gray Davis used this point as a bargaining chip with sixty-one tribes during their compact negotiations in the late 1990s. The final compact specified that in exchange for permitting Las Vegas–style gambling, tribes would participate in revenue sharing with nongaming tribes and also contribute to a fund for reimbursing casino-related costs to cities and counties, such as those stemming from traffic congestion, public safety concerns, and gambling addiction. California voters overwhelmingly approved this first compact as Proposition 5, which was superseded two years later by constitutional amendment Proposition 1A in 2000. Gaming compacts that are renegotiated over time eventually take the form of referenda submitted to voters for approval. This recently occurred when several Southern California tribes negotiated a deal to add thousands of slot machines in exchange for millions more paid annually into the state's general fund. Native American groups spent a combined $108.4 million to convince voters to approve four propositions in 2008, and each passed by at least 55.5 percent.[9]

Today, the state's casino industry is exceeded in size only by that of Nevada, and more than half of the state's slot machines are located in three Southern California counties: San Diego, Riverside, and San Bernardino. Eleven Native American casinos were expanded or renovated before 2010, and a few more have been authorized since then, bringing the total number of authorized gaming machines to more than 72,000. Sensing opportunity with an improving economy, a few smaller, more remotely located tribes have recently angled into the gaming business. As of 2013, California had ratified gaming compacts with seventy tribes, and a total of fifty-nine casinos were in operation, plus eighty-eight card rooms and a smattering of satellite slot arcades, which do not require compacts. The fact that casinos must be located on existing tribal lands limits their proliferation, but a few tribes have successfully taken additional land into trust with the consent of the federal government, enabling them to erect casinos in higher-trafficked areas. Seventy-three tribes without casino operations receive an annual payout from the Indian Gaming Revenue Sharing Trust Fund (to which large gaming tribes contribute) amounting to $1.1 million per tribe annually.

Clearly, "tribal sovereignty" has limits with regard to both federal and state law. Tribes retain control over political activities within their reservations' borders, and their governments usually take the form of all-powerful tribal councils vested with executive, legislative, and judicial powers. Councils have full control over tribal membership, which numbers more than fifty thousand registered individuals in California alone, and they implement federal assistance and grants covering health care, education, and other social needs, which amounted to about $278 million in direct payments and grants in 2009.[10]

The Morongo Casino Resort and Spa rises above the desert floor near the San Jacinto Mountains. The Morongo Band of Mission Indians in Cabazon, California, operates one of fifty-nine tribal gaming enterprises in the state; California has ratified compacts with seventy tribes. Gaming revenues have helped reduce the proportion of Native American families living in poverty, which hovered at 22 percent in 2011.

Gaming operations have laid the foundation for socioeconomic and political development in and around tribal territories. Relative prosperity has transformed tribal governments into fully staffed operations that have increasing institutional capacity to provide services that the state can't or won't provide; however, local governments are obligated to provide services such as law enforcement, road access and repairs, and emergency services. Tribes are now important participants in regional planning, and cities, counties, and local communities benefit from their charitable donations as well as from the jobs and tax revenues the casinos generate. Additionally, the state benefits from the tribes' ability to obtain federal dollars for improvement projects, such as widening roads and building bridges in cases where such upgrades are otherwise unaffordable. Fourteen California tribes also make annual payments to the state's general fund, amounting to approximately $364 million out of a total estimated $6.95 billion in casino revenues in 2009.[11]

Gaming enterprises have transformed tribal governments into major players at both the state and national levels, enabling them to lobby for or against policies of interest to them and to donate heavily to campaigns. Tribes nationwide contributed approximately $17.2 million to federal candidates and political campaigns in the 2011–2012 election cycle and spent another $47 million on lobbying activities. California tribes constituted five of the top ten donors at the national level, and among them were Southern California's San Manuel, Pechanga, and Morongo bands.[12] Among twenty tribes in California that lobbied either the governor's office or the legislature in 2011–2012, these three were also the heaviest spenders, forking over almost $3 million out of almost $6 million spent by all on lobbying activities.[13] Like many other special interests, Native American tribes have "found a voice" in the political system through the power of money.

Conclusion: The State's Interlocking Systems

California's state government is much more than a mega-institution with a few major components. The "big" institutions that include direct democracy, the legislature, state executive offices, and the courts may generally set overarching policies for the state, but they tend to obscure the importance of the thousands of local and regional directives that have immediate impacts on everyday life—laws and rules that are crafted by thousands of people working in elected and unelected capacities across county, city, special district, and regional governments, as well as in tribal nations. In ways both small and large, their decisions directly condition the health and livelihoods of communities throughout the state. These entities assure that clean drinking water is flowing from taps, safely dispose of millions of cubic feet of trash daily, kill mosquitoes that spread disease, hire more than 300,000 teachers across the state, and assume responsibility for solving these and other significant collective action problems that transcend boundaries but require local input and cooperation to solve.

The state's government should therefore be viewed as a complex organism, with approximately 6,500 identifiable working parts that have specialized and localized functions. Each part contributes to the welfare of the whole, either singly or in conjunction with others, but never in isolation. When dissected, the system appears as a bewildering mess of overlapping boundary lines, yet with remarkable success, these interlocking systems provide essential services that citizens need and will continue to demand.

Notes

1. California State Controller's Office, "Government Compensation in California, California Cities 2011," http://publicpay.ca.gov/Reports/Cities/Cities.aspx. The posting includes reported information for 462 cities.

2. Kevin Crowe and Joanne Faryon, "Do You Pay Extra Property Taxes? Mello-Roos: Who's Paying What," KPBS News, inewsource, May 29, 2013, http://www.kpbs.org/news/2013/may/29/mello-roos-taxes-vary-dramatically-whos-paying-wha.

3. California Public Policy Center, "Calculating California's Total State and Local Government Debt," Spring 2013, http://californiapublicpolicycenter.org/calculating-californias-total-state-and-local-government-debt. See also California State Treasurer's Office, "Debt Issuance Data Summary Tables," June 19, 2013, http://www.treasurer.ca.gov/cdiac/debtdata/debtdata.asp.

4. California Public Policy Center, "Calculating California's Total State and Local Government Debt." Health care costs are notoriously difficult to estimate.

5. These statistics are for the 2011–2012 school year, published on the California Department of Education's data website, http://www.ed-data.k12.ca.us (see the section on state reports). See also California Department of Education, "CalEdFacts," http://www.cde.ca.gov/re/pn/fb.

6. The exact number of COGs is difficult to calculate because a number of transportation planning commissions, planning councils, and other more localized (but intergovernmental) organizations qualify as COGs. The California Association of Councils of Government listed thirty-five member organizations in 2013. CALCOG, "Find Your COG," http://www.calcog.org/index.aspx?nid=45.

7. The cost coverage is closer to 15 percent if the costs are calculated as the total amount the state would save if those inmates were not in the system, or $51.2 million reimbursed out of $338.9 million spent. The average per capita costs (maximum estimates) are reported in the text. Data supplied by the California Legislative Analyst's Office, July 2013. See also a recent report by the U.S. Government Accountability Office, *Criminal Alien Statistics: Information on Incarcerations, Arrests, and Costs* (GAO-11-187) (Washington, DC: U.S. GAO, March 2011), 40, http://www.gao.gov/assets/320/316959.pdf.

8. The program and the Department of Justice's decision are summarized in National Conference of State Legislatures, "The State Criminal Alien Assistance Program (SCAAP)," April 13, 2013, http://www.ncsl.org/issues-research/immig/state-criminal-alien-assistance-program.aspx.

9. Vote results supplied by California Secretary of State. Data from ballot measure summaries for Propositions 94–97 are from Follow the Money, "Ballot Measures," accessed September 17, 2013, http://www.followthemoney.org/database/StateGlance/ballot.phtml?m=493.

10. Data from U.S. Census Bureau, *Consolidated Federal Funds Report for Fiscal Year 2009:State and County Areas* (Washington, DC: U.S. Census Bureau, August 2010), http://www.census.gov/prod/2010pubs/cffr-09.pdf.

11. See California Department of Finance, *2013–14 Governor's Budget Summary* (Sacramento: California Department of Finance, January 10, 2013), appendix 17, http://www.dof.ca.gov/documents/FullBudgetSummary_web2013.pdf. The National Indian Gaming Commission reported that total revenues for forty-nine gaming operations in California and northern Nevada tribes were $6,969,881 in FY 2008 and $7,363,493 for fifty-nine operations in FY 2008. National Indian Gaming Commission, "Tribal Gaming Revenues by Region, Fiscal Year 2009 and 2008," http://www.nigc.gov/linkclick.aspx?fileticket=goZCPYPDuT4%3d&tabid=67.

12. Kent Cooper, "Indian Tribes Gave Record Amount," *Roll Call,* Political MoneyLine blog, March 1, 2013, http://blogs.rollcall.com/moneyline/indian-tribes-gave-record-amount.

13. Author's calculations based on lobbying reports for 2011–2012, California Secretary of State's database "Lobbying Activity: Employers of Lobbyists," http://cal-access.ss.ca.gov/Lobbying/Employers.

The California Budget Process

*The best evidence of the fairness of any settlement is the
fact that it fully satisfies neither party.*

—Winston Churchill, 1926

Annual budgeting at the state level is a grueling process of translating social and political values into dollars, a set of interrelated decisions that creates winners and losers. A budget is a statement of priorities, the result of intense bargaining, and the product of a sophisticated guessing game about future income and economic trends that provides risk-averse politicians with incentives to respond to the most vocal and powerful interests participating in the political system. All the while, larger economic conditions provide a context for decision making that can set the stage for massive heart attacks (from ballooning deficits that require terrifying cuts, for instance) or just mild heartburn (from conflicts over how best to spend unexpected revenues).

California's annual budget, around $100 billion, represents a temporary answer to the state's infinite needs and wants and, despite its enormous scale, still makes many Californians wonder, "Why do we pay so much in taxes, but the state never has enough?" This chapter examines the budgeting process and explores the reasons for California's budgetary dilemmas—dilemmas that force representatives to make painful choices among alternatives.

California Budgeting 101

California's fiscal year begins July 1 and ends June 30. By law a new budget must be passed by June 15 or lawmakers forfeit their pay (a condition imposed by voters in 2010). The governor must then sign the budget by July 1 or the state cannot write checks for services or goods in the new cycle. In past years the budget was routinely completed late, triggering more uncertainty and panic for Californians dependent on state services, but the on-time budget three years in a row (2011, 2012, 2013) indicates the power of unified government: that is, when one party dominates both the legislative and executive branches. Excluding delays, it takes at least eighteen months to construct the state's spending plan.

Advance work begins in the governor's **Department of Finance (DOF)**, which is staffed by professional analysts who continuously collect data about state operations. Each branch of government and executive department itemizes its own programmatic budget needs, from personnel to project costs, including items such as habitat restoration (Department of Fish and Game), managed care for people with disabilities (Department of Health and Human Services), and trial court funding (judicial branch)—merely a sampling from among thousands of state government activities. The DOF's projections about how much money will be available through taxes and fees provide baselines for estimating how much *must* be spent on major existing programs and how much *can* be spent on new desired programs or services. **Mandatory spending** already committed through existing laws, such as Medi-Cal and debt payments, absorbs most of the approximately $85–$100 billion annual budget, leaving limited room for legislators to duke it out for the **discretionary funds** used to cover all other state services, from monitoring the safety of amusement park rides to sheltering victims of domestic violence.

Guided by the governor's initiatives, political values, and stated objectives, the DOF prepares a budget by assigning dollar amounts to state programs and services. The governor submits his or her budget to the legislature by January 10, whereupon it is routed to the legislature's own **legislative analyst** for scrutiny. Heeding recommendations from the Legislative Analyst's Office and anticipating the governor's updated version that accounts for actual tax receipts (the **May Revision or "May Revise"**), throughout the spring the legislative budget committees and subcommittees work on the legislature's own competing version of the budget. State analysts testify before the committees, as do officials, lobbyists, and citizens representing every sector of society and local government as they seek protection for existing benefits or beg for more.

Once the budget committees finalize their work and the legislature resolves its differences into a comprehensive budget bill (usually through the help of a conference committee made up of three members from each house), legislative leaders and their staffs begin negotiating with the governor and his or her staff to reach compromises. Will money be set aside for emergency spending? If so, will that money come from cuts to mental health programs or after-school care? How much of a "hit" will the college and university systems bear? Will domestic violence shelters be closed? Hundreds of decisions like these play into negotiations that routinely used to include the party leaders from both houses (along with the governor, they constitute the **"Big Five"**) until the primary responsibility for passing the budget was shifted to the majority party (according to Proposition 25 in 2010, only a simple majority is sufficient to pass it). As was the case following the 2010 elections, when the same party controls the governorship and both legislative chambers, minority-party leaders will ultimately be excluded from the top-level negotiations if they refuse to compromise on issues the majority party considers fundamental, and if the minority's votes are not ultimately necessary for passing the budget. Thus, the **"Big Three"** (the governor, the Speaker, and the president pro tem, all Democrats) have been the key negotiators since 2011.

Final agreements also hinge on the governor's line-item veto power (see chapter 5). Eventually, often after considerable debate and struggle, the budget is passed and signed into law, as are "**trailer bills**"—a package of omnibus or large bills that make the necessary policy changes to the state laws and codes outlined in the budget plan.

Mechanics of Budgeting: Revenue

A budget reflects the governor's and legislature's educated guesses about how much money the state will collect in taxes, fees, and federal grants during the coming year, as well as the state's commitments to spending or saving what it collects. All budgets are built on economic data, assumptions, and formulas designed to produce accurate forecasts about dollar amounts and the numbers of people who will demand the services and products these dollar amounts cover. Relatively small numerical shifts in these formulas can equal hundreds of millions of dollars. For instance, the state controller reported that in June 2013 the state's three largest sources of revenue were either above or below the amounts

Governor Jerry Brown signed the annual state budget into law a few days ahead of deadline on June 27, 2013, flanked by Assembly Speaker John Pérez, Senate President Pro Tem Darrell Steinberg, and Senate Budget Committee Chairman Mark Leno. Because Democrats maintained supermajority status in both houses, the "Big Three" enacted the FY 2013–14 budget without Republican leaders' cooperation or Republican votes.

predicted just one month earlier in the May Revision: personal income taxes rose $496 million, or 7.7 percent above projections; sales taxes were up 0.1 percent, or $1.3 million; and corporate taxes were 15.5 percent below projections, or $306 million short. Larger economic forces produce discrepancies like these that simply cannot be estimated precisely. Nevertheless, sophisticated assumptions about how much will be coming into the state's coffers serve as a foundation for balancing the budget—or at least making it temporarily *appear* balanced.

Revenue is another word for income. The largest revenue streams are provided by **taxes** and **fees** for services, and in 2013–2014 these helped raise the state's general fund revenues to $96 billion, or a total of $145.3 billion if special funds and bonds are taken into account. Taxes are deposited into the state's general fund or redistributed to county and local governments; special fuel taxes go into the transportation fund. It should be noted that property taxes are raised at the local level and mainly used to fund schools; they do not augment the general fund. **Bond** funds are borrowed funds that are designated for specific purposes. In 2013–2014 bonds contributed $7 billion to the total state budget.

A separate stream of revenue, **federal grant money**, is funneled through the federal fund, representing billions of dollars from the U.S. government that go to state and local governments to subsidize specific programs, such as job retraining, or to local entities for a variety of items, such as low-income housing or school lunches. The Department of Finance estimated federal transfers to be $87.6 billion for FY 2013–14. When these federal dollars are included, the entire state budget for FY 2013–14 is actually close to *$232.9 billion.*

The state relies on several major categories of taxes, all of which are highly sensitive to larger economic trends. In other words, taxes rise and fall with the economy, creating unpredictable swings in tax collection. **Personal income taxes** contribute the greatest portion of state revenues in California (as they do for virtually all states), totaling almost $63 billion in FY 2013–14, nearly *two-thirds* of the state's general fund revenue. (The figure is about 45 percent of the *entire* budget, which includes revenue from all state sources, meaning all taxes, special funds, and bonds, but excluding federal funds.) California's personal income taxes are progressive, meaning that tax rates increase along with income so that people at the higher end of the income scale are charged a greater percentage in taxes than those at the lower end. On top of base taxes, marginal tax rates (as of 2013) for single or married individuals range from 1 percent to 13.3 percent, reflecting a temporary increase of 1–3 percent for those making $250,000 or more, tax hikes approved by voters in 2012 (Proposition 30). For example, a person making $15,000 would pay a base tax of $75.82, plus 2 percent of the amount over $7,582. For someone making $300,000, the base tax is $21,207.75 plus 10.3 percent of the amount over $254,250. This policy of "soaking the rich" means that California relies disproportionately on higher-income taxpayers to fill its coffers, although taxpayers can receive various exemptions and credits to offset the total they owe.

Retail sales and use taxes are the second-largest source of California's income, accounting for almost a third of the state's general fund revenue (about 25 percent of the total budget). Sales are anticipated to bring in $34 billion in taxes in FY 2013–14, an amount based on the base state sales tax rate of 7.5 percent, a rate that voters temporarily raised 0.25 percent through Prop 30 to help fund education. Of the base tax, 6.5 percent goes to the state (some of which funds local activities) and 1 percent is reallocated to local governments (although consumers typically pay higher sales taxes due to extra rates imposed by counties and cities). Consumer spending on everything from fuel to clothing directly affects how much money is available to cover state expenses.

Corporate income taxes represent a much smaller piece of the revenue pie (estimated to be $11 billion in FY 2013–14, or 6.2 percent of the total budget), as do a variety of other sources, including (all in FY 2013–14): motor vehicle fees (4.3 percent), fuel taxes (4.5 percent), insurance taxes (2.2 percent), and taxes on tobacco and alcohol (1 percent). The remainder comes from fees and fines imposed on a wide range of activities (parking at state parks, fines for crimes, professional licensing, and so forth), rental income on state property, and surcharges on energy and other commerce (totaling approximately 12 percent).

Apart from taxation, state **borrowing** to plug budget holes and to finance megaprojects has become so commonplace that the average bond measure is in the $5 billion range, and the state now carries more than $95 billion in bonded debt, excluding billions more in bonds that have been authorized and will be issued in the coming years. Most of the debt comes from voter-approved general obligation bonds dedicated to school construction and remodeling, public

FIGURE 8.1   State Revenue, 2013–2014

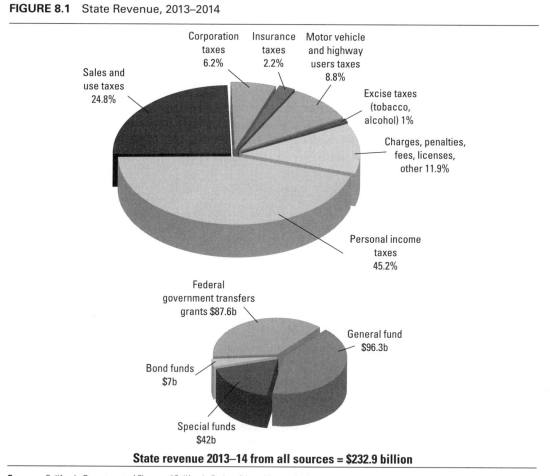

State revenue 2013–14 from all sources = $232.9 billion

Sources: California Department of Finance, "California Budget," http://www.ebudget.ca.gov.

Note: Percentages are based on general fund and special funds totaling 138.3 billion. Figures may not add to 100 percent due to rounding.

transportation projects (including a record-setting $19.9 billion omnibus transportation bill approved in 2006), and environmental and natural resource projects such as beach restoration and flood control. These measures veer sharply from the "pay-as-you-go" schemes typically used to finance large infrastructure projects in the past. Unfortunately, bonds will cost about twice their "face value" in the long run because of compounded interest. The state's dismal credit ratings (assigned by the nation's independent credit-rating agencies) have also driven up costs by forcing the state to borrow at higher interest rates, adding billions more to the state's bond repayment obligations.

Mechanics of Budgeting: Deficits and Expenditures

The state commits to a spending plan before it knows how much will actually arrive in the state coffers. Legislative and Department of Finance analysts do their best to predict how much unemployment benefits, welfare, housing assistance, health coverage, and a host of other services will be needed, but the costs of these services depend on how the economic winds blow. A struggling economy typically means more residents lose jobs and less is paid in income taxes; financially distressed consumers spend less, so the state collects less in sales taxes. Meanwhile, the state has already committed to a spending plan, but government expenses in the form of unemployment checks, health coverage, and other social services spike during economic hard times, and these imbalances translate into billions of dollars that policymakers cannot quickly replace. In one year alone (FY 2008–09), the state's collections for three major taxes—personal income, retail sales, and corporate—declined *$12.1 billion.*[1]

When expenses exceed revenues, **deficits** result. Legislators and the governor must return to the negotiating table to reconcile the differences, or "close the budget gap," which they can accomplish through reducing benefit checks, cutting state workers' salaries and/or benefits, eliminating or reducing services, changing tax policies, borrowing, or any combination of these. Elected officials have relied on all available options, including borrowing billions to cover portions of the deficit during the 2000s and "borrowing" from the state's other accounts, such as those dedicated to schools—about $35 billion that must be repaid, a large chunk of what Governor Brown calls the state's "wall of debt" (see Table 8.1). State officials also took advantage of temporary federal stimulus funds beginning in 2009 ($85 billion in total, parceled out over several years across state, local, and nonprofit agencies), sliced state programs by billions of dollars (more than $14 billion in cuts negotiated in spring 2011 alone), and resorted to "gimmicks" such as unrealistically assuming a much higher employment rate. Governor Brown rejected some of these tactics in June 2011 by vetoing the budget for the first time in state history, calling it "unbalanced" and citing "legally questionable maneuvers, costly borrowing and unrealistic savings."[2] In 2013 the state hit a milestone when Brown delivered a state budget without a deficit.

What does the state pay for? **Education** dominates the budget, and funding levels for this area are typically locked in through initiatives and statutes. For example, except in times of fiscal emergency, Proposition 98 mandates a minimum spending threshold that usually results in 40 percent of the budget being dedicated to K–12 schools and community colleges, systems that include 6.2 million schoolchildren and 2.4 million full- and part-time community college students. Annual K–12 per-pupil spending dropped precipitously from 2000 to 2012, to about $7,600 per student, although Prop 30 funds have stopped the downward slide.[3] According to the U.S. Census, California was

TABLE 8.1 California in Debt (as of end of FY 2011–12)

California carries several types of debt. **General obligation bonds** or lease-revenue bonds generally cover investments in infrastructure that shape the quality of life and commerce, such as better-networked roads and abundant water supplies. When times got tough in the late 2000s, to cover general fund expenses the state "raided" special accounts and also deferred payments that had been guaranteed to schools with promises to repay what it borrowed. That **budgetary borrowing** amounted to a $35 billion "wall of debt" in 2011. Then there are **unfunded liabilities**: promises made to future retirees in labor contracts, for example. The state's overall debt load looms large.

Category	Description	Main types	Amounts owed*
Bond debt	Long-term loans to cover infrastructure that shapes quality of life and commerce, authorized by voters or the legislature. Must be repaid in time (often 5, 20, or 30 years) with interest.	• General obligation bonds (GO) • Lease-revenue bonds (LR)** • Other; self-liquidating special funds (SF)	GO: $74 billion LR: $11.3 billion SF: $2.9 billion
		Approximate total bonded debt: $88.2 billion	
Budgetary borrowing	Long-term loans taken or payments deferred to cover shortfalls in the annual budget (most were incurred in late 2000s, forming what Governor Brown calls the **"wall of debt"**)	• Bonds ("economic recovery") • Internal loans • Unpaid costs to local governments and schools • Underfunding of mandated programs • Deferred costs and payments • Borrowing from special funds • Unemployment Insurance Fund loans (to U.S. government)	$26.9 billion $10.9 billion owed to U.S. government
		Approximate amount owed from budgetary borrowing: $37.8 billion	
Unfunded liabilities***	Promised benefits for current and future state retirees, negotiated and set in labor contracts but underfunded based on obligations	• Underfunded (future) pension payouts for state employees (CalPERS, CalSTRS) • Future health care liabilities	Pensions: $128.3 billion (2012 est.) Health care: >$50 billion(?)
		Approximate total unfunded liabilities: $180+ billion	

Sources: Bill Lockyer, "2012 Debt Affordability Report," California State Treasurer's Office, October 2012, http://www.treasurer.ca.gov/publications/index.asp; California Department of Finance, "California Budget 2013–14, Introduction," June 2013, http://www.ebudget.ca.gov; John Chiang, "Public Retirement Systems Annual Report, Fiscal Year 2010–11," California State Controller's Office, May 22, 2012, http://www.sco.ca.gov/ard_locrep_retirement.html.

*Amounts owed for bond debt come from the state treasurer's calculations at the end of FY 2012–13, minus economic recovery bonds. Amounts owed for budgetary borrowing were included in Governor Brown's budget (introduction), FY 2013–14. Unfunded liabilities were estimated by the state controller's office for FY 2010–11.

**"Lease-revenue" refers to debt incurred for facilities construction that will be paid through lease payments over time—hence "self-liquidating."

***Unfunded liabilities are generally difficult to estimate because fund levels depend on fluctuating rates of return over time, human longevity, and unknown future costs. CalPERS is the California Public Employees' Retirement System; CalSTRS is the California State Teachers' Retirement System. Health care costs will also be affected by the implementation of the Affordable Care Act.

FIGURE 8.2 State Expenses, 2013–2014

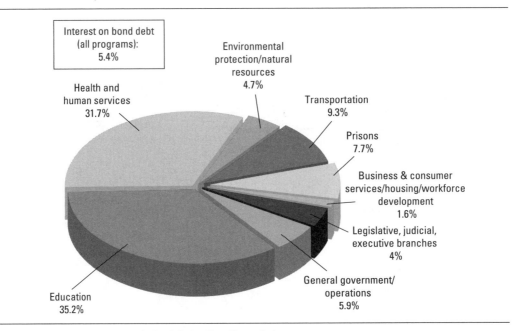

Interest on bond debt (all programs): 5.4%

Environmental protection/natural resources 4.7%

Health and human services 31.7%

Transportation 9.3%

Prisons 7.7%

Business & consumer services/housing/workforce development 1.6%

Legislative, judicial, executive branches 4%

General government/ operations 5.9%

Education 35.2%

Source: California Department of Finance, "California Budget," http://www.ebudget.ca.gov.

Note: Percentages are based on combined general, special, and bond fund expenditures of $145.3 billion. Total state expenditures were projected to be $232.9 billion, including $138.3 billion in general and special funds, $7 billion in bond funds, and $87.6 billion in federal transfers and grants.

ranked thirty-sixth in state spending in FY 2011, but the enacted budget for FY 2013–14 adds $1,045 per student, which improves its outlook.[4]

Spending on the two major public university systems, California State University and the University of California, is not included in Prop 98, and their funding has also sharply decreased during the past decade, despite total enrollment of about 660,000 students. After billions were slashed from *each* university system and tuition hikes became regular, Governor Brown banked on Prop 30 and stabilized funding for higher education, initiating a freeze on resident tuition increases for 2013–2014. All told, California spends about $50 billion on education annually.

Health and human services compete with education for the largest slice of the budget pie, representing almost 32 percent of the general fund in 2013–2014 and totaling $46 billion including special funds and bond funds. This category encompasses a range of essential services such as Medi-Cal, food stamps, residential care for the elderly, health care for children, and benefits for the disabled and unemployed—the last category having greatly increased during the economic downturn. Health care spending dominates, however: about one out of every five dollars spent by the state goes to Medi-Cal alone. To help meet the state's needs, the federal government transfers billions of dollars in welfare and other payments to California, which are both coordinated and redistributed through state agencies such as the Department of Health and Human Services.[5] In anticipation of the

FIGURE 8.3 Budgeting for Higher Education Programs in California, 2007–2014 (in millions)

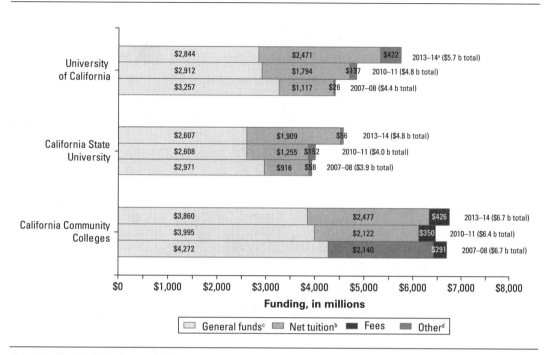

bReflects UC tuition after discounts provided through institutional financial aid programs.

cBeginning 2012-13, includes health benefit costs for CSU retired annuitants.

d"Other" category includes lottery funds, other UC core funds, American Recovery and Reinvestment Act of 2009 funds applied to all systems 2008-2011, and local property taxes for community colleges.

Source: California Legislative Analyst's Office, Higher Education Core Funding, www.lao.ca.gov/sections/education/ed-budget/Higher-Education-Core-Funding.pdf.

national Affordable Care Act's implementation, lawmakers have adopted simplified rules for Medi-Cal and expanded coverage to approximately one million more people, such as adults who earn up to 138 percent of the federal poverty level. The state will continue to expand coverage for health and mental health services and is counting on more federal dollars to follow.

The newly reorganized Transportation Agency manages about $20 billion for the state's **transportation** infrastructure, which encompasses Caltrans, the California Highway Patrol, and the Department of Motor Vehicles. Much of the agency's budget is derived from special funds (fuel taxes) and bond money, which is used to pay for the construction of state highways, rail routes, mass transit projects, and maintenance of 50,000 miles of road and highway lane miles, all overseen by Caltrans.

State government also incurs **general operational** costs: about $6 billion is spent to run the state's judicial, legislative, and executive branches, which contain eighteen thousand personnel positions (because some jobs are shared, there are actually more people employed).

At least another $11.2 billion goes to fund **prisons**, covering inmate medical care and rehabilitation programs as well as prison guard salaries and operating costs. As discussed in chapter 6, on average it costs California about $59,000 annually per adult inmate, a price tag that reflects the high costs of medical care and correctional officer compensation.

Finally, it should be noted that about 5.4 percent of the budget is dedicated to paying interest on general obligation or lease-revenue bonds, which represent the state's investments in infrastructure. This figure has risen as the state has assumed more debt over time, but it also varies with market conditions, such as the rates at which different bonds were sold.

Political Constraints on Budgeting

The budgeting process is far more than a series of steps. By nature it is political, involving many factors that condition and constrain policymakers' ability to make collective decisions. These factors help explain how budgets can be late and out of balance by billions of dollars within weeks of their passage, and why millions of Californians are both skeptical of elected officials' ability to solve problems and remain dissatisfied with the budget in any form.

Above all, the budget reflects the **larger economic climate**. State governments suffer the same economic challenges when the U.S. economy falters, and rise with the tide when the economy recovers. As unemployment climbs, recessions decimate revenue sources such as personal income and sales taxes, which happen to be the state's top-two largest sources of revenue—quite volatile sources on which California stakes its fortunes. Moreover, the state's tax policies have recently shifted some of the tax burden from corporations onto high-income individuals who largely rely on earnings from capital gains and businesses. The top 15.8 percent of taxpayers (those 2.4 million making more than $100,000 per year) paid 84.6 percent of all personal income taxes in the 2011 tax year. *The top 1.25 percent of taxpayers paid 44 percent of the state's income taxes,* including the contributions of about eighty billionaires who live in the state. Thus, the entire state budget critically depends on the financial fortunes of this small group (those making more than $400,000 a year).[6]

The **political climate** also influences what kinds of programs receive funding and how much. Public opinion shifts and public pressure cause some issues to gain political traction. In the 1990s crime dominated the political agenda; it could be education or health care in another year. Furthermore, to the extent that lawmakers know who the loyal voters are and respond to them, biases will result in their privileging some "special" issues—and interests—over others. Those who remain unsympathetic to those in charge will view these choices as wasteful, deleterious, or just plain ridiculous.

Anyone who has observed lawmaking will know that **special interests** and their **lobbyists** also unduly prevail throughout the process. Not only do they actively "educate" legislators about the effects of proposed budget changes, but they also threaten to use the initiative process to achieve what legislators may not deliver. Because they are usually "at the table" when the language of laws is being spelled out, their concerns are heard and can be accommodated. Business and union lobbyists vigorously promote their own companies, workers, industries, and causes, but among the most active advocates in California are those who work for subgovernments of the type described in chapter 7, "stakeholders" that include schools, counties, cities, and special districts. All send swarms of policy

FIGURE 8.4 The Annual Budget Process

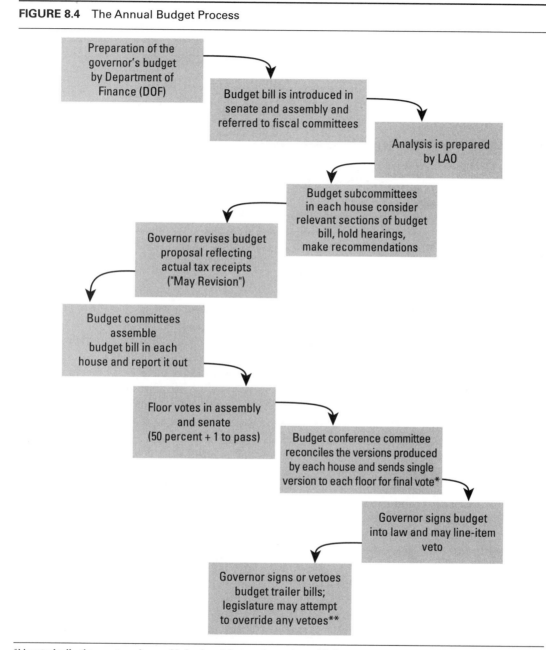

*More **typically, the senate and assembly leaders debate and negotiate with the governor** over final figures, with their staff members working overtime. If a conference committee meets, usually three people from each house participate. From this point, **permutations of the process occur with regularity.**

Leaders in each house help members construct many separate, omnibus **"budget trailer bills" that contain new policies or formalize legal changes reflected in the final budget figures. Trailer bills are processed through the houses, and the governor signs (or vetoes) each one. The legislature may attempt to override the governor's vetoes, but achieving the required two-thirds threshold is rare.

experts and lobbyists to press their cases to the state lawmakers, who help determine how much money they will receive and how it must be spent. Well-organized special interest groups are also behind some of the initiatives deliberately designed to limit legislators' budgeting flexibility. For example, a coalition of educators successfully endorsed Proposition 98, which guaranteed funding levels for public education.

Term limits have also contributed to the tangle by continually stocking and restocking the legislature with many novice lawmakers who lack big-picture understanding of how systems in the state interrelate and how cuts in one area will affect others. It takes more than one budget cycle for a legislator to gain a working understanding of how the process itself unfolds, and much longer to grasp how different constituencies are affected by changes. The ability to stay twelve years in one house may mitigate these dilemmas.

Use of the ballot box, or **ballot-box budgeting,** has fundamentally reshaped budgeting practices throughout the state as well. **Proposition 13** is a case in point. Prior to 1978, cities, counties, and schools relied on property taxes to finance their budgets. When Prop 13 capped property taxes at 1 percent of a home's or commercial building's purchase price and limited property assessment increases to no more than 2 percent per year, local governments were forced to look for other ways to pay for services (now mainly sales taxes and fees), and state government assumed responsibility for refilling local government accounts and funding schools. However, when times got tough, as they did in the early 1990s, the state substantially changed the way it allocated education funds, resulting in the redirection of yet more revenues away from local governments. Since then, state lawmakers have adopted the practice of occasionally "borrowing" property taxes from local jurisdictions to pay for schools or simply to plug large holes in the state budget. Thus, the burden of low property taxes has been shared by local governments, which have struggled to find alternative sources of revenue, and the state government, which cannot meet its obligations to fund local governments and schools when the general fund is empty and consequently still owes billions to local governments and schools. This constitutes a significant portion of the state's debt obligations. In addition, some ballot measures, such as mandatory sentencing laws for repeat offenders or sex offenders, unintentionally impose costly obligations on the state that drive up prison budgets.

In all of this, **rules matter**. Today the **two-thirds supermajority vote requirement to raise a tax or fee** hamstrings the majority party, which must seek a few votes from the minority party for it to pass—a nearly impossible task when the determined minority won't budge on principle. Unless fifty-four assembly members and twenty-seven senators are willing to hike sales taxes or vehicle license fees, or unless one party maintains supermajority status in both houses, the majority party will need several minority-party members' votes to implement such increases.[7]

Until 2010 one rule mattered most above all others: the two-thirds vote requirement for passing the budget. Because of their power to control the budget vote, minority-party members regarded the budget as their only opportunity to meaningfully influence public policy and force the majority to meet their demands. Over the past few years, long delays have resulted from the parties' inability to reconcile fundamental political differences (in 2010 the budget was one hundred days overdue), compelled by the minority Republicans' stand-pat refusal to compromise on tax increases and the majority Democrats' opposition to cutting certain services. In 2010 Californians lowered the threshold for passing the budget to a simple majority, meaning 50 percent plus one (forty-one assembly members and twenty-one senators), thus shifting the burden of constructing a balanced budget to the Democratic majority. In tough economic times this is easier said than done, however, as the majority party must make and take the blame for cuts to social services that people demand, or avoid cuts by raising taxes—a nonstarter for Republicans.

Generally speaking, representatives would rather give their constituents what they want than risk losing the next election because they "caused" their constituents to lose an important state service such as in-home elderly care for an aging mother, or receive a lower unemployment check, or lose health care coverage, or be unable to find day care for a child whose school year was cut short. Thus, **risk-averse politicians** who may be trying to promote the general welfare but shy away from making painful cuts help drive up deficits. This underlies the phenomenon of giant **structural budget deficits** after 2000 that were created by long-term commitments to programs that were initially paid for with increases in revenues that later disappeared. In other words, lawmakers used higher revenues from the "dot-com boom" to play catch-up with major programs that had been neglected or underfunded for years, but they found it difficult to reduce spending levels when revenue sources dried up. Imbalances have been carried over from previous years, further deepening the yearly budget shortfalls and underscoring the fact that every budget builds on the prior one. Cutbacks to state programs, along with higher revenues from an improving economy and a temporary sales tax hike (attributable to Prop 30), have finally brought spending in line with revenues; Governor Brown's hard-line approach has effectively eliminated the structural budget gap.

Tax Burden: Highest in the Nation?

It is a common complaint among Californians that they pay more in taxes than the average residents of other U.S. states. California's ranking in terms of overall state and local debt burden tends to justify that view: according to the state's nonpartisan Legislative Analyst's Office, the state placed tenth among the fifty states in 2010. However, if state and local revenues are considered as a share of economic wealth or income, the state's ranking is considerably lower.[8] The LAO calls the overall burden "somewhat above average" based on its calculation of state and local taxes: $11.30 per $100 of personal income, just above the national U.S. average of $10.59.[9]

The statewide base sales and use tax rate of 7.5 percent places California among the highest in the nation, and although variable local taxes can raise the total sales taxes paid, the Tax Foundation ranks California ninth for combined state and (average) local tax rates, which are 8.4 percent on average. Only New Yorkers pay more in state fuel taxes. Corporate taxes and personal income taxes also put the state near the top. As of January 2013, Californians who make less than $28,000 pay 6 percent, which is about average for all states. However, the rate jumps up for those making about $49,000 a year (9.3 percent, higher than almost all states), and voters imposed the highest rates among all states on those earning $300,000 or more. However, thanks to Proposition 13, individual property taxes remain relatively low and place the state near the bottom in rankings in that category, as do comparatively low "sin" taxes on alcohol and tobacco.[10] For example, as of 2013 California ranked thirty-second in cigarette taxes and twenty-ninth in beer taxes ($0.20 per gallon) and was almost the lowest-ranked state for table wine taxes ($0.20 per gallon). (By comparison, both Florida and Alaska impose taxes on table wine of more than $2.00 per gallon.)[11] It should be noted that this category represents less than 1 percent of the state's revenues; sales, income, and corporate taxes make up the lion's share of the state's general fund revenues.

These figures show that the amount of taxes paid varies greatly from individual to individual and among socioeconomic classes. It is critical to note that on an individual basis, whether a Californian

TABLE 8.2   State and Local Governments Rely on a Variety of Taxes

Type of tax	Current basic tax rate
Personal income	Marginal rates of 1 percent to 12.3 percent;* additional 1 percent surcharge for taxable income over $1 million
Sales and use	Average rate of 8.4 percent,* varies by locality
Property	1 percent of assessed value, plus rate needed to pay voter-approved debt (Assessed value typically grows by up to 2 percent per year.)
Corporation	8.84 percent of net income apportioned to California (10.84 percent for certain bank and financial companies)
Insurance	2.35 percent of insurers' gross premiums
Vehicle license	0.65 percent of depreciated vehicle value
Cigarette	87¢ per pack
Alcoholic beverage	Varies by beverage, from 20¢ per gallon of wine or beer to $6.60 per gallon of spirits (over 100 proof)
Vehicle fuel	36¢ per gallon
Diesel fuel	10¢ per gallon

Source: Mac Taylor, *Cal Facts* (Sacramento: Legislative Analyst's Office, January 2013), 12, http://www.lao.ca.gov/reports/2013/calfacts/calfacts_010213.pdf.

*Includes temporary tax increases imposed by Proposition 30 (2012).

pays more or less than taxpayers in other states depends greatly on which tax is being considered, how much the person earns, home owner status, regional location, and what goods and services that person consumes. These factors also influence individuals' perceptions of being overtaxed at least as much as their attitudes about public spending and the proper role of government do.

Yet when it comes to budgeting, not enough revenue has been collected to cover all that Californians appear to collectively want. Solid majorities oppose spending cuts to education and health and human services, but less than half support higher sales taxes or vehicle license fees, and the only category of cuts that most citizens support is in prisons and corrections—a category that the federal courts have determined is *under*funded.[12] However, it is worth noting that while Californians seem to have a penchant for keeping taxes low, time and again it has been shown that while they oppose general tax increases, they are much more willing to support specific taxes if they are assured the funds are designated for specific purposes—as they did in 2012 when they approved temporary tax hikes to pay for education.

Conclusion: Budgeting under Variable Conditions

As a U.S. state, California faces most of the same basic challenges as the other forty-nine, but as one of the world's largest "countries," its economy is intimately tied to global fortunes, and its fiscal dilemmas are comparable in scope and depth. The sheer volume of issues generated by its more than thirty-eight million residents is staggering, and the majority of those issues are reflected, though not always resolved, in the state's annual budgets. Above all, annual budgets provide a blueprint for the state's priorities, and the governor's perspective in particular. When one party controls both the legislature and the governor's office, as has been the case since Democrat Jerry Brown retook office in 2010, the budget reflects that party's outlook and it becomes easier for voters to hold that party to account for policy decisions and consequences.

Budgeting by nature is a rough-and-tumble business. Financial analysts in the executive (Department of Finance) and legislative (committee consultants and Legislative Analyst's Office) branches must perform the wizardry of forecasting without a magic crystal ball, relying on feedback, data, experience, statistical indicators, history, and tested formulas to predict the economic conditions for the coming year. Political representatives must then square their ideals with economic realities and reevaluate their preferences in the context of what is politically possible. Choices must be made; bargains must be struck; solutions must be fashioned through compromise. Legislators' behavior will be incentivized by majority rules such as supermajority votes that encourage hard bargains at the expense of simple majority rule, or exclusionary tactics that marginalize a minority party if its votes aren't needed. Budget meltdowns, delays, and austere spending cuts during the late 2000s and early 2010s illustrated that effective governing requires rules to facilitate rather than obstruct compromise.

After negotiations have ended, the legislature has passed the budget bill, and the governor has signed it into law, the $100 billion (or so) annual budget is then assaulted by forces largely beyond the government's control. National and international crises may trigger severe and unanticipated drop-offs in tax revenues, leaving the state in the lurch. In times like those, representatives have almost no fiscally sensible ways to deal with such short-term crises because they cannot legally cut services immediately without undermining the state's contractual commitments to people and companies. On the other hand, unanticipated surpluses, however rare, allow state officials opportunities to fulfill more promises. Although the budget is assembled for the coming year only, its very design conditions future choices by shrinking or expanding the state's commitments, paying down old or incurring new debt, spending cash or stashing away funds for emergencies, and/or making investments in infrastructure or ignoring other long-term projects. Whether or not California is both livable and governable is a reflection of the annual budgeting process and the set of compromises it ultimately yields.

Notes

1. California State Controller's Office, "Statement of General Fund Cash Receipts and Disbursements," press release, July 2009, http://www.sco.ca.gov/Press-Releases/2009/07-09summary.pdf.

2. Shane Goldmacher and Anthony York, "Governor Vetoes 'Unbalanced' State Budget," *Los Angeles Times,* June 17, 2011, http://articles.latimes.com/2011/jun/17/local/la-me-0617-state-budget-20110617.

3. The number is based on 2011–2012 inflation-adjusted figures provided by legislative analyst Mac Taylor in *Cal Facts* (Sacramento: Legislative Analyst's Office, January 2013), http://www.lao.ca.gov/reports/2013/calfacts/calfacts_010213.pdf.

4. Mark Dixon, *Public Education Finances: 2011* (Washington, DC: U.S. Census Bureau, May 2013), 11, http://www2.census.gov/govs/school/11f33pub.pdf.

5. Compare figures from both the California Department of Finance ("Chart B: Historical Data, Budget Expenditures," July 2011, http://www.dof.ca.gov/budgeting/budget_faqs/documents/CHART-B.pdf) and the U.S. Census Bureau, which pegs the dollar amount of transfers to California at $53.8 billion in 2008. See U.S. Census Bureau, "Federal Aid to State and Local Governments by State: 2000 to 2008," in *Statistical Abstract of the United States,* 269, Table 431, http://www.census.gov/compendia/statab/2011/tables/11s0431.pdf.

6. Figures are from the California Franchise Tax Board for the most recent tax year available, 2008. See Franchise Tax Board, "Table B-4A.1: Personal Income Tax Statistics for Resident Tax Returns," in *2009 Annual Report,* http://www.ftb.ca.gov/aboutFTB/Tax_Statistics/Reports/Personal_Income_Tax/2009_B-4A.pdf.

7. The only exception involves the risky move of including one or more fee hikes in the budget itself, which requires just a simple majority vote for approval, such as when the majority Democrats raised vehicle license fees an additional $12 through the 2011–2012 budget without the approval of Republicans.

8. Tracy Gordon, "California Budget," Public Policy Institute of California, July 2009.

9. Based on the most recent figures available, 2009–2010, in Taylor, *Cal Facts,* 11.

10. Tax Foundation, "State Tax and Spending Policy," accessed September 3, 2013, http://www.taxfoundation .org/taxdata/topic/9.html.

11. Federation of Tax Administrators, "State Excise Taxes," January 1, 2011, http://www.taxadmin.org/Fta/ rate/tax_stru.html#Excise.

12. According to a 2011 survey by the Public Policy Institute of California: "When asked about cutting spending to help reduce the state budget deficit, solid majorities of adults and likely voters oppose cuts in three of the four largest budget categories: K–12 public education (76% adults, 73% likely voters), higher education (68% adults, 64% likely voters) or health and human services (66% adults, 61% likely voters). But they support cuts in the fourth category: prisons and corrections (62% adults, 70% likely voters)." These statistics are roughly mirrored in past state surveys that asked similar or the same questions. See Mark Baldassare, Dean Bonner, Sonja Petek, and Jui Shrestha, *Californians and Their Government* (San Francisco: Public Policy Institute of California, May 2011), http://www.ppic.org/content/pubs/survey/S_511MBS.pdf.

CHAPTER 9

Political Parties, Elections, and Campaigns

Political scientist E. E. Schattschneider wrote in 1942 that "modern democracies are unthinkable save in terms of political parties,"[1] and the same can be said of elections. Without parties, the scale and scope of conflict produced by countless disorganized groups would be unmanageable. Without elections, citizens would lack the means to hold their representatives accountable. Through both parties and elections, diverse interests are voiced, aggregated, and translated into policy.

Many Californians remain unconvinced. Fully three-quarters of voters believe that state government is run by a few big interests, and strong majorities across parties think they make better public policy decisions than elected officials do.[2] Most voters have faith in an initiative process that allows them to bypass a state government they generally despise— although less than half have confidence in their fellow voters when it comes to making public policy at the ballot box. The "no party preference" or independent voter category is the only one to have climbed upward since 1980, surpassing the 20 percent mark in 2009. Increasing percentages of college-educated and younger people (ages eighteen to thirty-four) refuse to affiliate with either of the two major parties. Voter turnout consistently remains low among Latinos, the state's largest ethnic group.

Political communities define themselves by how they use parties and elections, and these facts shed light on California's independent streak, its complex electorate, and its antigovernment political culture. Two other defining features of California's political landscape are also worth noting up front, both of which have important implications for governing. The first is an **east-west divide** that has opened along liberal-conservative lines, whereby the coastal regions are heavily liberal to moderate and trend Democratic, and inland counties are much more conservative and strongly

Republican. The second is that **citizens, residents, and voters are not the same groups of people**. Reasons for these trends and their impacts are discussed in this chapter, along with the style of California parties, the character of elections, and the conduct of campaigns.

Democratic Stronghold, but Weakly Partisan

Historically speaking, political parties in California have struggled for survival, not prospered. Much of their troubles date to Progressive reforms in the early twentieth century deliberately designed to strip them of their power. Idealizing politics without partisanship, Progressives overhauled election law by establishing new mechanisms for voters to sidestep parties altogether—the initiative, referendum, and recall being foremost among these. Other innovations included nonpartisan elections for local officials and judges and cross-filing at the state level for statewide elected officials (discussed in chapter 2). Through secret ballots, direct primaries, and a ban on parties' preprimary endorsement of candidates, party members were able to choose their nominees without the blessings of party bosses.

A good deal of the Progressives' antiparty program flourishes today. Cross-filing was eliminated long ago,[3] but the long-term consequences of the Progressives' attack on parties are still visible: there is no absolute majority political party in California, state party organizations remain relatively weak, and candidates tend to self-select and draw on their own resources rather than those of their parties. One of every five registered California voters is in the "no party preference" category, having chosen no party at all.

Parties are far from ineffective in the state, however, and they thrive within government. The goals, values, and agendas of the two major parties remain far apart. Democrats dominate. Yet, on balance, the evidence supports the judgment that California is not a strong party state. This can also be seen through a more systematic examination of four interconnected parts of the party system: party *in the electorate* (PIE), party *in government* (PIG), party *as an organization* (PO), and party in *informal networks* (PIN).

Party in the California Electorate

In one respect, a political party is made up of members who share similar beliefs about the role that government should play in their lives, but "party in the electorate" also refers to the generalized sentiment a party's members share about what it means to be a Republican, Democrat, or member of any other party. It is this sentiment that leads them to vote for certain officials and reinforces their attachment to the party's "brand name."

Almost three-quarters of registered California voters belong to one of the two major parties, Republican and Democratic, but that number is somewhat deceiving. According to a 2012 statewide survey, a majority of Californians think the state needs a third political party.[4] Because neither party has absolute majority status, independent voters provide the swing votes necessary to win in general elections. While California is commonly labeled a "blue state" based on registration statistics and statewide elections that have overwhelmingly favored Democrats, the reluctance of more people to join a party and the defection of many from the major parties has turned the state's political complexion slightly purple.

MAP 9.1 California's East-West Partisan Divide

Predominant* party registration
as of February 10, 2013:

Democrat

Republican

Evenly divided
(less than 1% difference)

*based on highest percentage registered

0   100 Mi
0   100 Km

In terms of party registration, California was a majority-Democratic state between 1934 and 1989; since then Democrats have made up the state's plurality party, topping Republicans by 15 percent in February 2013. Democrats today are first in registration at 44 percent, Republicans take second at 29 percent, and other parties collectively hold third place with a combined membership of just over 6 percent. Individuals who affiliate with no party constitute 21 percent of the state's electorate.[5]

A plurality of "no party preference" voters actually consider themselves politically independent (42 percent); the rest lean toward one party or another. Independents lean closer to the Democratic (41 percent) than to the Republican Party (29 percent) and confirm political scientists' findings that "leaners" usually vote for the parties they prefer. Historically they have cast more votes for Democrats than for Republicans in California elections. For example, exit polls showed that 56 percent of independents chose Democrat Jerry Brown over Republican Meg Whitman in the November 2010 governor's race, and 64 percent of them voted for Obama in 2008, compared to 92 percent of Democrats and 14 percent of Republicans.[6] Recent surveys of likely voters reveal that slightly more men have registered independent; independents also tend to be young and college educated and are

FIGURE 9.1   Party Registration in Presidential Election Years, 1924–2012

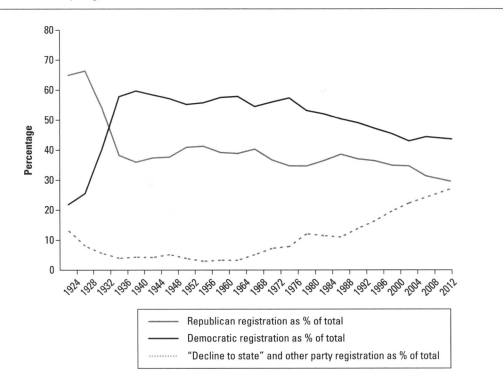

Source: California Secretary of State, "Report of Registration," November 2012.

Note: The percentages reflect the statistics from the closing date for registration in the general election.

To qualify as a new political party in California, a group must first hold a caucus or convention at which officers are elected and a name is chosen. Qualification may then proceed either by petition or by registration. Petitioners need to gather 1,030,040 signatures, a number equal to 10 percent of the total number of people who cast votes in the most recent gubernatorial (governor's) election, and they must file those petitions in several counties at least 135 days before the next election. The registration option requires that 103,004 persons (1 percent) complete an affidavit of registration at least 154 days prior to the next election—a difficult task to coordinate statewide, but a hurdle just cleared by a new party, Americans Elect, which qualified for the June 2012 primary election.

Registered Parties in California

- American Independent: http://www.aipca.org
- Americans Elect: http://www.americanselect.org
- Democratic: http://www.cadem.org
- Green: http://www.cagreens.org
- Libertarian: http://www.ca.lp.org
- Peace and Freedom: http://www.peaceandfreedom.org
- Republican: http://www.cagop.org

Parties That Have Failed to Qualify

- California Pirate Party
- California Moderate
- God, Truth, and Love
- The Good Party
- No Corporate Money
- Pot
- Reform Party
- Superhappy Party
- United Conscious Builders of the Dream

Source: California Secretary of State, "Political Parties," http://www.sos.ca.gov/elections/political-parties.

as diverse as the Democratic Party. San Francisco has the highest percentage of no party preference registrants in the state (31 percent in that city/county).

Current members of the Democratic Party in California tend to be ethnically diverse, in the low-to-middle income bracket, and younger than in the past. About one out of two Democrats is Latino, African American, or Asian, and 54 percent are white.[7] About a third of likely Democratic voters have household incomes of $40,000 or less per year, and a quarter of them are renters rather than home owners. Approximately 16 percent more women than men are registered as Democrats.

Republicans, meanwhile, tend to be white and middle- to upper-class, and they count more evangelical Christians among their ranks. In contrast to Democrats, 82 percent of likely Republican voters are white, and men outnumber women by about 5 percentage points. Majorities in both parties are college graduates, but almost half of Republicans who are likely to vote make $80,000 or more annually (47 percent), compared to 38 percent of both Democrats and independents.[8] More Republicans than Democrats are age fifty-five or older. Overall, these trends mirror those across the states.

About three out of four California Republicans describe themselves as **conservative:** they generally want a government strictly limited in size, are more responsive to business than to labor, do not believe in raising taxes, oppose homosexual marriage, favor strong laws restricting illegal immigration, and believe that "individual destiny should be in the individual's hands." About 75 percent of likely Republican voters prefer lower taxes and fewer services.[9]

California Democrats, on the other hand, tend to hold **liberal** views: 71 percent of likely Democratic voters would pay higher taxes in exchange for more government services; they want the government to promote equal opportunity in education and the workplace, they want wider access to health care, they favor pro-choice laws, and they are more responsive to labor than to business. There is nearly universal belief among Democrats that immediate steps should be taken to curb the effects of global warming or climate change, compared to about half (54 percent) of Republicans who hold that view. Half of Democrats say they are liberal, and about a third consider themselves moderates. In contrast, independents are distributed widely across the ideological spectrum: about a third of likely independent voters describe themselves as **middle-of-the-road**, and equal proportions (one-thirds) consider themselves liberal or conservative. They are about evenly split on raising taxes for more services or lowering them for fewer services (48/48 percent).[10]

Party in Government

Those most responsible for advancing a party's brand name through policymaking are current elected officials: the party in government. Approximately 20,000 officials in California hold elective office; of them, 132 hold statewide office and 55 represent Californians in the U.S. Congress. Governors, assembly members, senators, federal representatives, and others pursue agenda items that become associated with a party's name through fulfilling their chief purpose: *to organize government in order to achieve their policy aims.* Through their decisions and also by what they choose not to do, those in positions of power communicate what it means to be a member of a particular party.

Democrats have held the title of majority party for more than forty years in both legislative houses. The assembly and senate have been majority Democratic almost continuously since 1971, interrupted only by Republican rule in the assembly in 1995–1996. A high degree of ideological polarization pervades the capitol, especially with regard to taxation and spending: Democrats are more willing to raise certain taxes (income taxes paid by millionaires, for example), and Republicans are unwilling to raise them, period, instead insisting on shrinking government through cutting services.

Although neither Democratic legislators nor Republican legislators are all exactly alike, the basic ideological divide between Democrats and Republicans has been expressed in strong party solidarity and ideological rigidity, which voters hoped to alleviate through redistricting and the top-two primary. In the past, districts were engineered to guarantee the election of Democrats or Republicans, which led to the election of the most ideologically extreme candidates. The "real" competition took

FIGURE 9.2 Registration by Political Party in California, 2013

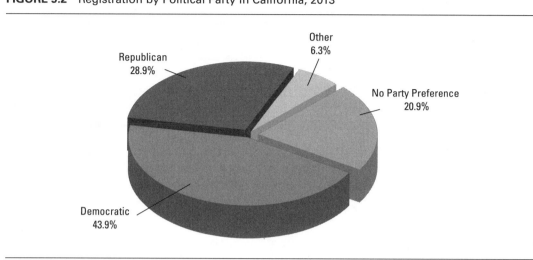

Other
6.3%

No Party Preference
20.9%

Republican
28.9%

Democratic
43.9%

Source: California Secretary of State, "Odd-Numbered Year Report of Registration, February 10, 2013," https://www.sos.ca.gov/elections/ror/ror-pages/ror-odd-year-2013/hist-reg-stats.pdf.

place during primary elections, as candidates of the same party vied for the votes of strong partisans in those low-turnout elections. Despite Prop 11's intentions, however, nonpartisan redistricting did not eliminate the tendency for districts to favor one party or the other (more often the Democrats). Likewise, the top-two primary has fallen short: so far there is little evidence that elections conducted under the new rules have markedly moderated legislative politics.

Democrats now dominate state government, having captured every executive office and a supermajority in the legislature in 2012. What accounts for their domination? Historically, competitive districts have not materialized because of attempts at *gerrymandering* and *natural sorting*. **Gerrymandering** refers to the act of manipulating district boundaries to include or exclude certain groups in order to benefit a party or an incumbent. Until 2010 state lawmakers—in actuality, the majority Democrats, in concert with the governor—were in charge of redistricting and tended to draw maps that guaranteed a Democratic majority and few competitive seats. "Bipartisan gerrymanders" were created when both sides agreed to maintain the status quo. In 2010, Californians joined a category of twelve states that entrust redistricting authority to citizen-controlled independent commissions. Under Prop 11, party leaders and legislators are barred from playing an active role in forming their own districts, although they are allowed to make the case to fourteen citizen mapmakers that respecting existing boundaries might help preserve consistency in representation, a point given due consideration—along with all the others voiced by citizens from across the state. After the commission concluded its process of redistricting for the first time, Republicans charged that the commission had gerrymandered districts to Democrats' advantage, although no evidence of that has been uncovered.

Other factors help determine the level of competitiveness in districts: higher Democratic registration, the Republican Party's unpopularity in the state, and natural **sorting**—that is, like-minded people with similar values tend to live near each other, and settlement patterns have produced a densely populated coastline that is more "blue" (Democratic) and an inland that is more "red" (Republican). Competitive districts are difficult to construct because the mapmakers are still bound to draw districts containing numerically equal populations that are as compact as possible, respect city and county lines, and do not split communities of interest. These conditions pit practicality against ideals, and, in the end, electoral interparty competition suffers. Regardless, citizens have been swayed by the argument that lawmakers in principle should not be in charge of drawing their own districts, whether or not more competitive districts are created.

The governor's office remains one place where Democrats' hold has been historically weak. Republicans have held the seat for almost fifty of seventy years since World War II. They have also managed to secure other statewide executive offices over the decades, preventing Democrats from monopolizing state administrative power.

Party Organizations

The concept of party also encompasses organizational bodies and their rules. It should be noted that when citizens register to vote they actually become members of their *state* parties, organized according to election codes in the fifty different states and the District of Columbia. This is why voter registration forms are addressed to a country registrar of voters rather than a national party association, and voters are given the option to register when they visit the Department of Motor Vehicles, a state agency. The national organizations known as the Democratic National Committee and Republican National Committee have little to no control over the state parties.

TABLE 9.1   Modern-Era California Governors by Party Affiliation

Term (years)	Governor	Party affiliation
1943–1954 (12)	Earl Warren	Republican*
1955–1958 (4)	Goodwin Knight	Republican
1959–1966 (8)	Edmund "Pat" Brown	Democrat
1967–1974 (8)	Ronald Reagan	Republican
1975–1982 (8)	Edmund "Jerry" Brown Jr.	Democrat
1983–1990 (8)	George Deukmejian	Republican
1991–1998 (8)	Pete Wilson	Republican
1999–2003 (5)	Gray Davis	Democrat
2003–2010 (8)	Arnold Schwarzenegger	Republican
2011–present	Edmund "Jerry" Brown Jr.	Democrat

*Warren also received the nomination of the Democratic Party.

Party organizations are well suited to fulfill another key party role: that of *nominating candidates for election and getting them elected.* At the top is the party **state central committee**, responsible for coordinating the local bodies that exist below it, for strategizing to win seats, and for assisting candidates with funding and other resources. These committees run the respective state conventions every year.

A state party chair acts as "CEO" of the party, and members of the state central committees include current statewide elected officials, nominees for statewide office, county-level party officials, and appointed and elected members from across the state. Democratic members of their state central committee number about 3,000, evenly divided between men and women and roughly balanced among age groups and races/ethnicities. The Republican state central committee has approximately 1,650 members (there are no gender, age, or race/ethnicity quotas). Beneath the major state party organs are fifty-eight **county central committees** for each party, also organized by the state election codes. Further down are low-membership local and regional clubs, which are home to impassioned party volunteers.

Party in Informal Networks

In California as elsewhere, informal political party groups formed through alliances among local powerbrokers also hold important keys to elections, thereby shaping the nature of the parties and their spheres of influence.[11] These informal groups include partisan business leaders, campaign donors and spenders, local officials, luminaries, and retired officeholders who may also participate in formal party committees. Located up and down the state, in and across cities and counties, they network in order to elect the candidates they prefer. Working "behind the scenes," often unofficially with the formal party apparatus but outside it, they seek and recruit candidates for all offices who embody their political values. They identify potentially viable candidates from their communities, invite them into their circles of influence, provide needed endorsements to cue voters, and work to get their picks elected. For instance, they may set up independent expenditure campaigns on behalf of a candidate, or pressure competitors to drop out of a race to clear the field for a preferred front-runner. These well-networked, ideologically driven groups of elites and party activists have a high degree of success in influencing elections, although their members and power remain largely invisible.

Elections: Continuity and Change

Like political parties, elections are a keystone of democracy, and voters continue to find ways to improve them, usually in order to address what they perceive as unfair advantages held by groups or individuals. Elected officials also occasionally initiate electoral changes, which might take the form of readjusted rules targeting the conduct of parties or candidates. Sometimes those reforms perform as intended, but often there are unanticipated or unintended consequences.

Propositions 11 and 14, already discussed elsewhere in this text, illustrate such outcomes. For example, newly redistricted maps in 2012 forced many incumbents into the same districts, which caused an unprecedented number to decline to run for reelection (six Democrats, nine Republicans, one independent). New challengers entered the fray, and in the end thirty-nine first-time legislators were elected, two seats switched parties, and only two assembly incumbents were defeated (compared to *zero* incumbent defeats in 2010).

Proposition 14 triggered a different set of outcomes. For years reformers tried to unlock primary elections so that a larger electorate (independents) could participate. Through regular **primary elections** for various offices, party members nominate candidates who will later compete head to head with the other party's nominees in the general election. For instance, six Republicans may jump into an assembly primary race, but only one will receive enough votes to become the Republican nominee for that seat (an incumbent invariably receives his or her party's renomination). That person will face the Democratic nominee in the **general election**.

Until 1996 the state had a **closed primary** system, meaning that only voters who declared their party affiliation prior to the election could participate in their own party's election. At the voting station a person would receive a Republican or a Democratic ballot listing party candidates for each office. Independent voters could not vote for partisan nominees, although they could vote on statewide initiatives, local measures, and nonpartisan offices. Proposition 198 (1996) changed the rules, but only temporarily. Californians approved the **blanket primary**, in which all registered voters could vote for any candidate. In 1998 primary election voters were given a single ballot listing each office and every possible candidate for it, just as in a general election. Two years later the U.S. Supreme Court ruled the scheme an unconstitutional violation of political parties' First Amendment right to free association. A **modified closed primary** took its place, and independents' votes counted if a party allowed it.

In June 2010 California voters decided again to switch to an **open primary**. In exchange for his vote to pass the budget in 2009, Republican senator Abel Maldonado demanded the legislature place a constitutional amendment on the ballot creating a **"top-two candidate"** open primary system, in which any registered voter may select a top choice from among all candidates for office. Even if one candidate receives a majority of all votes cast for that office, the top two winners advance to the general election for a runoff, be they two Republicans, two Democrats, one from each party, or otherwise. Reformers hoped to shake up the status quo by encouraging the election of moderate candidates who would need to appeal to a wider electorate and discouraging the election of ideologically polarizing lawmakers; they also sought to allow greater ballot access. Preliminary analyses of 2012 have found mixed results: although incumbents were challenged more and won with lower margins, newly elected legislators have not been markedly more moderate, though in a few districts the more moderate candidates, particularly Democrats, were favored over those perceived to be more ideologically extreme. Ironically, legislative parties in Sacramento work hard to keep their members in line, discouraging all forms of moderation that undermine party unity.[12]

Another extremely significant reform has been term limits for elected state officials, which have generated a slew of electoral consequences since their adoption in 1990. For one, the game of political office "musical chairs" now extends to all levels of government: competition for "down-ticket" elections such as seats on county boards of supervisors and big-city mayoralties has increased, and pitched contests over congressional seats have also multiplied as the pool of experienced candidates looking for jobs continues to swell. About two-thirds of all statewide officials attempt to run for another office within two years of being termed out. In the crusade to stay in office, it is also fairly common now for incumbents to be challenged by members of their own party—rivalries that used to be adroitly managed by party leaders or preempted by the advantages of incumbency that scared off good challengers (those with experience and money). Ironically, term limits have not affected incumbents' chances for reelection, however; officeholders continue to be reelected at near-perfect rates. Modifications to term limits that take effect for officeholders elected after 2010 will likely suppress the rate of turnover (they can now stay up to twelve years total in one or either house), although the goal of staying in public office will continue to motivate individuals to run when opportunities arise.

Special elections to fill vacant seats are also on the rise due to term limits, as politicians leave one office for another when it becomes available. The "domino effect" occurs when a state senator runs for an open U.S. Congress seat and a member of the assembly then runs for the subsequently vacated state senate seat; this then creates a third election needed to fill the empty assembly seat, and so on down the line. Between January 2011 and November 2013, twenty-one special primary and general elections were held to fill congressional or state legislative seats, most of which were vacated by ambitious elected officials. Unfortunately for cash-strapped counties, the average price tag for special elections can approach $1 million, and voter turnout for these elections is usually dismally low, averaging 19 percent turnout from 2011 to 2013. Turnout rates for special statewide elections called by the governor (or the legislature) are not usually much higher and cost upward of $100 million.

A few other noteworthy reforms continue to reshape California elections. First, the failings of punch-card systems laid bare by the 2000 presidential election between U.S. vice president Al Gore and Texas governor George W. Bush prompted the U.S. Congress to pass the Help America Vote Act of 2002. Every state received millions of dollars to replace older voting equipment with more accurate touch-screen and optical-scan machines. California's secretary of state, who has overseen the transition away from punch-card devices, monitors the new equipment for software glitches and intentional mischief. All counties are now outfitted with advanced voting technology—the need for which is increasingly offset by the numbers of registered California voters who "**vote by mail**" or are "permanent absentee" voters. More than half of voters now regularly cast mail-in ballots for general elections, and almost two-thirds of the 2012 primary election ballots were cast by mail. Voters are briskly opting for "permanent absentee voter" status (meaning they receive and submit their ballots only through the mail); more than 43 percent were permanent absentee voters in the general election of 2012, compared to 8 percent just ten years earlier.

One of the biggest technological developments affecting elections is **online voter registration**. As of 2012 Californians can register to vote via the Internet, a service already offered (or pending authorization) in sixteen other states, including Kansas and Arizona. To register, applicants can go to http://registertovote.ca.gov. If an individual does not have a signature that can be accessed from his or her California driver's license record, then a hard copy of the form that the applicant fills out online will be mailed for a signature. The secretary of state announced that online voter registration rates had increased noticeably just prior to the 2012 elections, when the system was activated (just a month before the election). It appears that young voters prefer this method of registering to mail-in forms, so this change has the potential to improve this voting group's historically dismal registration rates.

One other important change could take effect for the 2016 presidential elections: how California allocates its Electoral College votes for U.S. president. Under the U.S. Constitution, each state determines how it will cast its electoral votes. In order to avoid the dilemma that arises when a candidate receives the U.S. popular vote but loses the election, as was the case with Al Gore in 2000, California will direct its electors to cast their votes for the presidential candidate who wins the most popular votes in the United States. This proposed change will take effect only when enough states enact this "national popular vote" law (collectively they must possess 270 Electoral College votes, a simple majority). California was the ninth state to commit to implementing this plan.

California Campaigns

Given parties' relatively weak hold over Californians, the frequency of elections, a mobile population, and the immense size and density of districts, campaigns serve the important role of connecting citizens with candidates and incumbents. Across the state, virtually all campaigners face the same basic challenges: raising huge sums of cash to buy access to potential voters and convincing enough of those voters to reject their opponents.

Former assembly Speaker Jesse Unruh once proclaimed, "Money is the mother's milk of politics."[13] Indeed, incumbents cannot afford to stop raising money, waging what is known as the nonstop "permanent campaign." On average, a successful assembly campaign costs about $750,000, and a senate campaign can easily run more than $1 million.[14] But those costs depend critically on how strong the competition is: incumbents running in a general election usually face

Congresswoman (and former state legislator) Judy Chu, Assemblyman Mike Eng, and State Senator Ted Lieu marched with the Asian Pacific AIDS Intervention Team during the L.A. Pride Parade on June 10, 2012.

FIGURE 9.3 Vote by Mail Statistics, 1966–2013

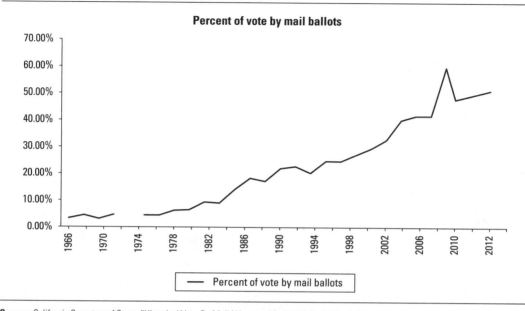

Percent of vote by mail ballots

Source: California Secretary of State, "Historical Vote-By-Mail (Absentee) Ballot Use in California," http://www.sos.ca.gov/elections/hist_absentee.htm.

Note: Data were not collected for 1974.

"sacrificial lambs" who spend almost nothing in their defense, whereas some incumbents without serious challengers still spend in excess of $1.5 million "defending" their seats. These sums do not include the many millions more that might be spent by outside groups independently to influence electoral races.

Open-seat elections, created regularly now by term limits, require far higher sums. Candidates for open assembly seats spend an average of $950,000; the most exorbitant races can cost candidates more than $3 million. Costs are also higher when there is a good possibility that the other party could win the seat: two senate candidates in 2008 spent a combined sum of more than $8.5 million, and the winner squeaked by with 857 votes. In July 2013, a Republican victory that denied senate Democrats supermajority status was the most expensive in Fresno history, costing the candidates and other spenders more than $5 million.

Among the most generous contributors to campaigns are trade and public employee unions, energy companies, general business interests (manufacturing, chemicals, food and beverage, tobacco), bankers and securities and investment companies, the state parties, agricultural interests, real estate institutions, and ideological or single-issue groups. Tribal governments, ranked among the top donors in 2008, dramatically curtailed their spending in 2010 and 2012 (to $6 million, down from $163 million). Oil and gas companies were also in the top five in 2010, but they reduced their spending from $69 billion to less than $6 billion in 2012. Out-of-state contributors also directly donate and independently spend multiple millions, although all donors are subject to limits on how

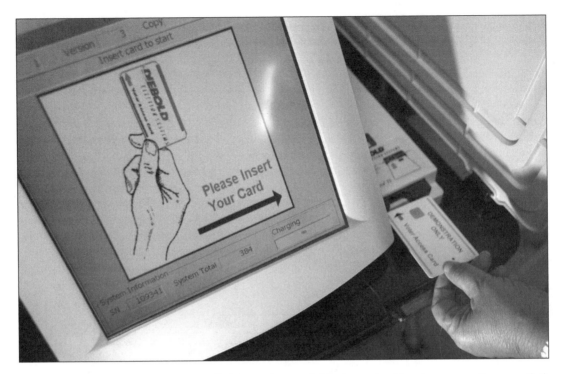

Touch-screen voting systems have been certified for use in every California county, although some counties use optical-scan machines that require voters to fill in bubbles on paper ballots that are then electronically scanned.

much money they may give directly to candidates. The only exception is that candidates enjoy the constitutional right to donate to themselves as much of their own money as they wish.

All campaign contributions and expenditures must be reported to the California secretary of state's office, which makes fund-raising activity publicly available pursuant to Proposition 9 (see http://cal-access.ss.ca.gov). The state's disclosure rules (dictating that information about donors must be made available to the public) survived a legal challenge after the U.S. Supreme Court ruling in *Citizens United v. Federal Election Commission* (2010) lifted a seventy-year-old ban on independent federal campaign expenditures by corporations and unions in the name of free speech. Large sums are now being spent in independently run *federal* campaigns without strict reporting and disclosure requirements, principally in the form of mass mailings and television and radio ads designed to defeat or endorse candidates. However, in California, large sums could already be spent independently on state elections, so these were minimally affected by *Citizens United*.

Why do candidates require colossal amounts of campaign cash? In districts as large as those found in California, paid media are the only realistic way to reach large numbers of potential voters. Advertising is especially pricey in urban media markets already crowded with commercial ads. Most candidates in the state invest heavily in this type of **wholesale campaigning**, or indirectly contacting voters through the airwaves and direct mail.

TABLE 9.2 Largest Campaign Contributors to State Campaigns by Industry, 2012

Industry	Contributions
Public-sector unions	$93,882,766
General business (food, hotel, alcohol, manufacturing, tobacco, recreation, tourism, business associations, gambling, entertainment, and so on)	$81,311,242
Finance, insurance, and real estate	$78,113,832
Ideological or single-issue groups	$58,177,627
Law firms and attorneys	$49,732,561
Agriculture	$48,835,188
General trade unions	$33,830,507
Party committees	$33,707,413

Source: Follow the Money, "California 2012, Independent Spending," accessed September 16, 2013, http://www.followthemoney.org/database/StateGlance/state_ie_spenders.phtml?s=CA&y=2012.

This is not to say that knocking on doors, attending community events, and "pressing the flesh"—types of **retail campaigning** that require a comfortable pair of shoes rather than large amounts of campaign cash—are unimportant in modern campaigns. Personal contact is particularly beneficial in local contests in which friends and neighbors help turn out the vote.

Professional campaign managers and consultants help candidates build efficient money-raising machines by coordinating other critical aspects of successful campaigns: access to donors, polling data, media buys, Web-based tools or social media outreach, targeted messages, and volunteers. Still, money isn't everything, even in statewide elections: in her losing gubernatorial contest with Jerry Brown, Republican candidate Meg Whitman spent a total of $178.5 million, or $43.25 per vote, compared to Brown's $36.7 million, or $6.75 per vote.

Conclusion: A Complex Electorate

Parties, elections, and campaigns have been the instruments of change and the targets of reform. Historical disdain for parties lingers in California's state election codes and permeates the conduct of elections, surfacing in initiatives that seek to empower individuals over organizations, such as Proposition 14, the "Top-Two Primary," which reformed primary elections by opening them to all voters, regardless of political party affiliation. It is also manifested in relatively weak formal party organizations, active informal party organizations, and ever-increasing numbers of independents.

Parties are far from dormant, however, and the strident partisanship displayed in the legislature accentuates their viability. They are relevant at every level of government, from running elections to organizing government, and they still provide the most important voting cues for the average citizen. The ideological divisions they represent are real, and the fact that Democrats hold a distinct party registration advantage and swept statewide elections in 2010 and 2012 signals their advantage over Republicans in the state, as well as Republicans' need

Mailers like these are designed to persuade voters and often are produced independently by outside spenders. This mailer, produced by Andy Vidak's 2013 state senate campaign, was distributed in a special election race in which more than $5 million was spent. Vidak's victory cost the Democrats their supermajority status in the senate.

to regroup in order to regain lost ground. Democratic supermajority status in both legislative chambers and executive office enables greater accountability, quite possibly rendering the state more governable—although that status is hardly permanent, as special election results have demonstrated. However, Democrats' consistent electoral successes tend to mask citizens' growing detachment from parties. It still remains to be seen whether the pairing of the open primary with a new redistricting process will result in campaigns, candidates, and winners who will exemplify the political moderation that characterizes most Californians and represents the politics that most of them desire.

Notes

1. E. E. Schattschneider, *Party Government: American Government in Action* (New York: Holt, Rinehart & Winston, 1942), 1.

2. The Public Policy Institute of California (PPIC) reports that 61 percent of all adults and 70 percent of voters feel this way. See Public Policy Institute of California, "Key Stats: Voter Attitudes," May 2013, http://www.ppic.org/main/keystat.asp?i=1281. A 2010 PPIC survey found that 44 percent have little trust in their fellow initiative voters. See Mark Baldassare, Dean Bonner, Sonja Petek, and Nicole Willcoxon, *Californians and Their Government* (San Francisco: Public Policy Institute of California, December 2010), http://www.ppic.org/content/pubs/survey/S_1210MBS.pdf.

3. Cross-filing—the practice of allowing candidates to file nomination papers with any party, appear on multiple ballots, and gain the nomination of more than one party—was finally eliminated through legislative action in 1959, and a ban on preprimary endorsements was found to be unconstitutional in 1989.

4. Mark Baldassare, Dean Bonner, Sonja Petek, and Jui Shrestha, "California's Independent Voters," Public Policy Institute of California, August 2012, http://www.ppic.org/main/publication_show.asp?i=784.

5. Data from California Secretary of State, "Odd-Numbered Year Report of Registration, February 10, 2013," https://www.sos.ca.gov/elections/ror/ror-pages/ror-odd-year-2013/hist-reg-stats.pdf.

6. Baldassare et al., "California's Independent Voters." See also Baldassare et al., *Californians and Their Government*; and national election data compiled from National Election Pool poll results reported on CNN Election Center 2008, http://www.cnn.com/ELECTION/2008/results/polls/#val=CAP00p1.

7. Baldassare et al., "California's Independent Voters."

8. Public Policy Institute of California, "Statewide Survey Interactive Tools," accessed September 3, 2013, http://www.ppic.org/main/survAdvancedSearch.asp.

9. Mark Baldassare, Dean Bonner, Sonja Petek, and Jui Shrestha, "California Voter and Party Profiles," Public Policy Institute of California, August 2013, http://www.ppic.org/main/publication_show.asp?i=526; and Mark Baldassare, *California's Post-partisan Future* (San Francisco: Public Policy Institute of California, January 2008), 5, http://www.ppic.org/content/pubs/atissue/AI_108MBAI.pdf.

10. Baldassare et al., "California's Independent Voters." See also PPIC, "Statewide Survey Interactive Tools."

11. See Seth E. Masket, *No Middle Ground: How Informal Party Organizations Control Nominations and Polarize Legislatures* (Ann Arbor: University of Michigan Press, 2009). See also Seth Masket, "Polarization Interrupted? California's Experiment with the Top-Two Primary," in *Governing California: Politics, Government, and Public Policy in the Golden State,* 3rd ed., ed. Ethan Rarick (Berkeley, CA: Berkeley Public Policy Press, 2013).

12. See Masket, *No Middle Ground.*

13. Quoted in Lou Cannon, *Ronnie and Jesse: A Political Odyssey* (New York: Doubleday, 1969), 99.

14. Based on 2008 and 2010 data; see Follow the Money, "California 2008," accessed September 3, 2013, http://www.followthemoney.org/database/state_overview.phtml?s=CA&y=2008, and "California 2010, Candidates," accessed September 3, 2013, http://www.followthemoney.org/database/StateGlance/state_candidates.phtml?s=CA&y=2010&f=0&so=a&p=6#sorttable. Averages reflect sums spent by winners. For the midterm 2010 election, the average was slightly lower for winning senate candidates, at approximately $885,000.

CHAPTER **10**

Political Engagement

Citizens and Politics

The Greek words *demos* and *kratos,* or democracy, translate literally as "the people rule." Democracy is therefore rightly associated with voting, but self-governance requires more than filling in bubbles on a ballot. Being informed, discussing public affairs, and contacting elected officials are essential elements of self-governance that allow a citizenry's will, demands, and needs to be expressed, and these are but a few ways a person might engage politically. Subgroups of citizens with similar interests try to influence the political system through political parties (the subject of chapter 9) or organized interest groups, of which there are thousands in the state of California alone. In addition, the mass media play a critical role in linking residents, interest groups, and government by distributing and analyzing information that influences how Californians behave politically.

News Sources and Media Habits

Californians know extremely little about state politics unless the subject is a crisis or an election, and their attitudes, opinions, and beliefs about government are molded by the way public affairs are reported and analyzed in the press. **Local television** news broadcasts remain the most popular sources of political news overall, but political coverage tends to be scant, sporadic, celebrity-centered, scandal-oriented, and big-event-driven. More than half of all voters watch daily news on television, but most of them (70 percent) are over age forty-nine.[1] Several large **newspaper** operations provide investigative journalism and in-depth treatment of political issues (*Los Angeles Times, Sacramento Bee, San Francisco Chronicle,* and several other major city papers), and information seekers can also look to **minority**

newspapers and publications such as the Spanish-language *La Opinión* for coverage of politics. Newspapers continue to struggle to retain and attract customers, although almost 40 percent of all voters read their local newspaper daily, whether online (35 percent) or in print (14 percent).[2] National Public Radio is popular with about one out of five voters, and voters have other **radio** program options (such as the conservative "John and Ken" talk show that airs in Southern California and New York). Other sources such as Cal-SPAN, the state's version of C-SPAN, which provides cable feeds of committee hearings and floor debates, attract tiny audiences. Today more and more young voters (20 percent of those ages 18–29) are using mobile devices such as smartphones or tablets to tap into the news on **Internet sites**, and more than half turn to **Facebook** for daily news and information.[3]

National trends affect state and local news coverage and consumption, with **media consolidation** topping the list. "One-newspaper cities" abound following the disappearance of local papers during the past few decades, and most of the state's big newspapers are owned by out-of-state corporations. Much of what is reported is delivered in bullet points and based on government reports and press releases, as well as on stories from the Associated Press (AP) wire service. Reporting news in entertaining ways, or "**infotainment**," has also entered the mix. At least 8 percent of registered California voters admit to getting their information about California politics regularly from *The Daily Show* on Comedy Central.[4]

The trend of getting news through mobile devices also bodes ill for investigative journalism but well for headline writers who can condense news into "byte-sized" pieces. Tweeted or texted information tends to be shallow and lacking context, misinformation can spread like wildfire without the ability to retract it fully, and public authorities tend to "script" their appearances because they know their gaffes could be broadcast on YouTube. It remains to be seen whether political participation based on social networking will yield the same kinds of benefits associated with traditional forms of participation, such as higher levels of political interest, feeling that one can make a difference, and closer ties and trust among community members.

Despite the proliferation of social networking and expanded forms of instant communication, like other Americans, most Californians do not follow state politics closely. Fewer than half of registered voters (41 percent) say they follow what's going on in government and politics most of the time, and about a quarter do not follow politics at all.[5] Certain groups in California, however, are more closely attuned to politics than others. Interestingly, Republicans seem to pay more attention to politics than Democrats (see Table 10.1), Northern Californians appear to be more politically attentive than Southern Californians, and those who identify with the Tea Party movement pay close attention to politics. Other news consumption patterns reflect behavior that has been well documented: younger people of all ethnicities, education levels, and income levels are far less attentive to government affairs than are older, white, more educated, and wealthier citizens. These trends demonstrate that **political interest** makes a huge difference in helping people connect to politics, and those who feel the impact of policies, recognize the immediate relevance of state government, and feel as if they can make a difference tend to seek more information that can lead to becoming involved politically.

Political Engagement and Disengagement

Feeling informed contributes to the sense that one can personally make a difference by participating in public affairs, and this sense of "efficacy" provides a stepping-stone to active participation in civic

TABLE 10.1 How Much California Voters Pay Attention to Government/Public Offices

	Percentage paying attention		
	Most of the time	Some of the time	Hardly at all
All registered voters	41	33	25
Party registration			
Democrat	41	34	24
Republican	50	29	20
Nonpartisan/other	30	37	32
Tea Party identification			
Identify a lot*	77	18	5
Identify some	46	37	17
Don't identify	35	34	30
Area			
Southern California	35	37	27
Northern California	50	28	32
Gender			
Male	47	30	22
Female	36	36	27
Age			
18–29	15	39	45
30–39	30	41	28
40–49	41	31	27
50–64	49	33	17
65 or older	63	25	11
Race/ethnicity			
White, non-Hispanic	47	30	22
Latino	25	40	33
Education			
High school graduate or less	31	31	36
Some college/college graduate	41	36	23
Postgraduate work	50	30	20
Household income (annual)			
Less than $20,000	26	37	36
$20,000–$39,999	34	36	29
$40,000–59,999	40	36	24
$60,000 or more	48	32	21

Source: The Field Poll, completed June 3–13, 2011, using a random sample of 950 registered California voters; sampling error ±3.3 percentage points.

Note: Figures have been rounded, and respondents with no opinion are not displayed in the table; percentages do not add to 100 percent.

*Small sample base.

or political settings. In addition to voting, which will be discussed below, Californians partake in a wide range of civic and political activities, though they rank lower than most U.S. citizens on most measures of civic engagement.[6] Studies consistently find that people are not more likely to engage in political activities online than offline.

At the lowest level of political involvement, individuals might indicate their political **likes and dislikes** on their Facebook pages, **follow** a political candidate or figure on Twitter, or join a **social networking group** dedicated to politics or a social issue (12 percent of adult Californians have joined online political groups).[7] They might also **discuss politics** with their friends and family, and just over a third of Californians report doing so weekly, while 25 percent of Californians report that they never discuss politics.[8] Like most Americans, more Californians of all ages still discuss politics *offline* than online, preferring to do so in person, on the phone, or in letters.[9] With some effort they might post a campaign **yard sign**, sport a campaign **sticker or T-shirt**, **encourage others to vote**, or try to **influence how others vote.** Higher up the scale, Californians **sign petitions** and may do so easily when electronic versions show up in their e-mail in-boxes; still, easy access has not translated into higher rates of petition signing (nation-wide, 22 percent of adults signed paper petitions during the past year, whereas 20 percent signed Internet petitions).[10]

It takes progressively larger investments to **call** or write **e-mails** or letters to elected officials in response to their solicitations for feedback or voluntarily to complain about a problem or ask for help with an issue, or to **boycott** a product for a political or social reason. About 14 percent of Californians have done at least one of these during the past year.[11] They also **attend local meetings** (9 percent), **attend rallies** or demonstrations, **work with informal groups** to address local problems, **work for campaigns**, or even **donate** to campaigns or incumbents. A tiny fraction become **active party members or officers**.

The same kinds of class biases and socioeconomic factors associated with use of news media are found in general patterns of political participation that political scientists have long observed at the national level. In addition to the variables already mentioned (age, ethnicity, income, nativity, and education), home ownership and length of residence are positively associated with civic behavior and activism; retirees and older residents who have lived in their homes for more than two decades are among the most reliable political participants. On the other hand, while disengaging from politics can certainly be a conscious choice, *not participating* is associated with these same factors, which are often beyond an individual's control. Poverty and lack of education limit an individual's skill set, leading to language deficits, a smaller knowledge base, a lower sense of efficacy, fewer chances to be contacted or mobilized, and/or less disposable time to participate in activities. Those who feel as if they will never be taken seriously will hardly waste their time trying to voice their opinions, and continuing disengagement leads to even greater disparities in skills and high levels of frustration and political apathy.

Of all these variables, **race/ethnicity** and **nativity** (whether one was born in the United States) best explain why participation rates in California generally lag behind the rest of the nation. California contains disproportionately large Latino and Asian populations with high percentages born elsewhere, and they are less inclined to discuss politics and to participate politically than are others. They are also less likely to register to vote, the topic of the next section.[12]

FIGURE 10.1 Party Registration by Race and Ethnicity, 2013

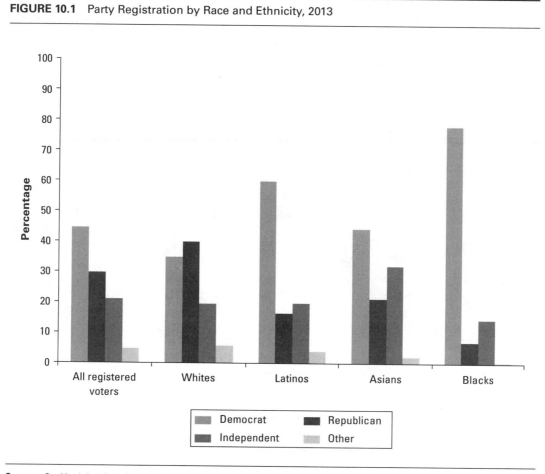

Sources: Combined data from Public Policy Institute of California Statewide Surveys: June 2013 (1,936 registered voters), July 2013 (1,691 registered voters), and September 2013 (1,429 registered voters).

Major Voting Trends

In a representative democracy the act of voting provides a critical check on officeholders, as it not only offers a means to reject undesirable representatives but also supplies cues about what policies a constituency prefers. In a direct democracy the voters represent themselves and "check" each other through the act of voting, but the majority of whoever turns out to vote wins. For these reasons, who votes in a hybrid democracy such as California's has profound implications for electoral outcomes, policymaking in the public interest, and, ultimately, the quality of representation and government.

Students at the Butte Community College campus are shown organizing in support of education as the state's shrinking budget threatened to bring higher fees and fewer classes.

The California electorate does not represent all Californians, nor does it reflect the size, growth, or diversity of the state's population. First, among those who cannot vote are approximately 3.4 million legal permanent residents, another estimated 2.6 million undocumented immigrants who reside and work in the state, and approximately 170,000 in prison or on parole.[13] Second, about 23 percent of those who are eligible to vote don't register; this equates to more than 5.6 million people who are not among what the Public Policy Institute of California calls the state's "exclusive electorate." Those who are not registered to vote differ from the pool of registered voters in several significant ways: more are renters (63 percent of all unregistered citizens), have only a high school diploma or less (68 percent of all unregistered), and are racial or ethnic minorities (77 percent of all unregistered).[14] Not registering to vote largely accounts for the low Latino vote share in comparison to that of whites.

Third, not all eligible voters vote in every election. Presidential elections, supercharged ballot issues such as gay marriage, and high-profile events such as the 2003 gubernatorial recall lure many more voters than "off-year" midterm elections, special elections, or primaries, which draw far fewer voters but more loyal partisans. Turnout over the past four presidential elections averaged 75 percent of all registered voters, and a much lower percentage—56 percent—of all *eligible* voters (2000–2012). Turnout sinks in the off-year elections, averaging 55 percent of all registered voters for the past three midterm elections (2002–2010), and just *40 percent* of all those eligible to vote. Stand-alone municipal elections obtain distinctly low turnout rates, usually ranging between 20 percent and 35 percent of registered voters.

FIGURE 10.2   Ethnic Makeup of California's Likely Voters

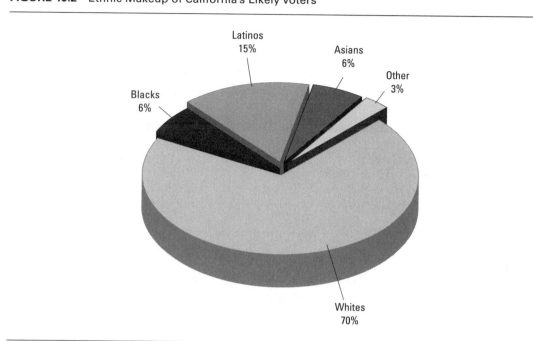

Source: Mark Baldassare, Dean Bonner, Sonja Petek, and Jui Shrestha, "California Voter and Party Profiles," Public Policy Institute of California, August 2013, http://www.ppic.org/content/pubs/jtf/JTF_VoterProfilesJTF.pdf.

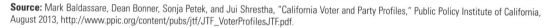

Fourth, among those who actually vote, different combinations of voters produce different electoral outcomes. For instance, voters "grouped" into assembly districts choose candidates who tend to reflect their characteristics and preferences, and, as a result, elected legislators resemble those localized voters. Initiative voters, on the other hand, hail from the entire state, and their votes reflect a different set of characteristics and preferences. The same is true for governors and statewide executives, whose constituency is the entire state. Fifth, the phenomenon of "roll-off" means that many voters cast their ballots only for the "big-ticket" offices such as president, skipping lower offices and ballot measures located further down the ballot, often because they do not feel informed enough to vote on them or because they view "down-ticket" items or offices as unimportant.

Who are California's likely voters? Non-Hispanic whites total just over 40 percent of California's resident population, but they constitute approximately *two-thirds* of all voters, who also tend to be slightly older, U.S.-born, and more conservative than nonvoters. Other important vote predictors are **age** (younger residents are more likely to be Latino, and both of these groups vote at the lowest rates), **nativity** (native-born residents are more likely to vote than foreign-born citizens), **education** (more highly educated individuals vote more), **home ownership**, and **income** (the higher the income, the more likely one is to vote). Clearly, the "haves" outshout the "have-nots" in elections.

As with other forms of political participation, differences in turnout are also related to variables such as **disposable time** (most people who don't vote work more than forty hours per week, and it takes time to become educated about the issues and candidates and to vote) and structural factors such as **registration requirements**, **timing of elections**, and the **perceived importance** of a given election. **Political interest** and **beliefs about government** are significant predictors of voting: two out of three nonvoters and infrequent voters believe that politics is controlled by special interests, and many of them (20 percent) find no candidates to believe in.[15] Having friends and family who value voting, or **living in a "pro-voting" culture**, also matters: two-thirds of those who speak Spanish and rarely vote also say that their friends hardly ever talk about politics.

Almost all of these characteristics are at least indirectly related to race/ethnicity and go a long way in explaining the large voting-related disparities that exist among ethnic groups. Nearly 40 percent of Californians are Latino, but they represent less than 20 percent of voters.[16] Stated differently, 60 percent of eligible Latinos did not turn out to vote in the 2012 midterm election, compared to 42 percent of non-Hispanic whites who didn't cast ballots.[17] The bottom line is that Latinos participate at much lower rates than their population numbers would predict, and the same is true for Asian Americans. High percentages of eligible African American voters tend to cast ballots in California.

Finally, different groups of voters represent different sets of values and priorities, determine who gets elected and who loses, and control which initiatives pass or not. Those who cast ballots generally hold very different views about the proper role of government than those who do not. For instance, when asked whether it was preferable to pay higher taxes and have a state government that provides more services or pay lower taxes and have a state government that provides fewer services, a majority of voters preferred the smaller-government option. However, a majority of infrequent voters preferred more services and higher taxes, as did a clear majority (60 percent) of those who were not registered to vote (see Figure 10.3). The results of low-turnout elections magnify the biases of narrow electorates.

Special Interest Groups: Indirectly Connecting Citizens to Government

Interest groups representing practically every aspect of the human experience advocate for government policies that will advance or protect their causes, and the benefits or changes they seek often extend to anyone who shares a key characteristic—which could be a medical condition, a position on gas fracking, or ownership of a certain kind of business. An organized group that makes its case to the government about its pet issue, or "special interest," is known as a **special interest group**. Such a group might therefore be a single entity such as the Catholic Church, a pro–gun rights organization, or a set of interrelated businesses such as the film industry. The term *special interest* can also be a vague reference to any group whose members share the same concerns and are willing to fight for them, such as beachfront property owners who want to protect their homes from beach erosion. In all cases, special interest groups are directly affected by public policy, and often they want something from government.

Though special interest groups are often regarded as self-interested, greedy political creatures, most citizens are unaware that they are indirectly linked to government through the interests and goals they share with many of them. A typical California college student is "represented" in the

FIGURE 10.3   Differing Perceptions about the Role of Government

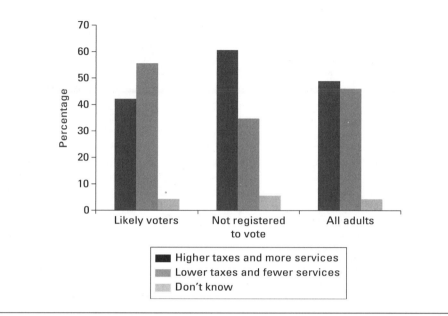

Source: Mark Baldassare, Dean Bonner, Sonja Petek, and Nicole Willcoxon, *Californians and Their Government* (San Francisco: Public Policy Institute of California, January 2011), http://www.ppic.org/content/pubs/survey/S_111MBS.pdf.

public sphere by a plethora of unobserved but well-organized interests, among them the university or college itself; the city, county, and region in which the student resides; hobby-, sports-, or activity-related groups such as the National Collegiate Athletic Association (NCAA); groups based on demographic characteristics such as economic status, ethnicity, religion, and more; health-related groups concerned with conditions such as allergies or disease; values-based associations focusing on rights, the environment, moral issues; and too many more to name. If employed, that student might also be linked to politics through membership in a labor union for working adults, such as the mighty California Correctional Peace Officers Association (CCPOA), which represents 30,000 prison guards and parole officers, or a trade association for professionals such as the 160,000-member California Association of Realtors, which facilitates state licensing requirements and advocates for laws and tax policies that will affect real estate agents or their clients. If that student comes from a family that owns a business, then there may be a natural political connection to an association such as the California Chamber of Commerce, which represents almost 13,000 California businesses both large and small (see Box 10.1).

Special interests are not all equal, however, and some in California carry disproportionate political weight because of advantages stemming from their resources, size, and/or perceived importance. In other words, legislators pay more attention to some interests than others. Among the most prolific, active, and influential special interests in Sacramento are actually **local governments** and **public**

BOX 10.1 **The Power of Organized Interests**

The California Teachers Association: Major Player in Education

If education was in the news this morning, chances are the powerful California Teachers Association (CTA) had something to do with publicizing it. As the state's largest professional employee organization, representing more than 325,000 teachers, school counselors, and librarians, the union helps bargain for higher salaries and benefits in local districts and provides assistance in contract disputes. As an advocacy group the CTA is committed to "enhance the quality of education for students" and "advance the cause of free, universal, and quality public education" through influencing state education policy.

Closely aligned with Democratic interests, the CTA participates at all stages of the bill-passage process by writing bills, testifying before committees, shaping legislation through suggesting amendments, donating to initiative campaigns, mobilizing citizens to support measures, and encouraging legislators either to support or to oppose bills. Most of this work is done through lobbyists, but members also are highly active, holding public demonstrations in local districts and loud rallies at the state capitol, organizing massive postcard campaigns, calling legislators to voice their views, and contributing through the union to state legislators' and initiative campaigns. When Governor Schwarzenegger proposed altering Proposition 98 to balance the budget in summer 2009, the CTA roared to life with a statewide ad campaign attacking his plan to "rob millions of dollars from public schools." During the busy election year of 2012, the CTA ran independent expenditure campaigns in support of Democratic candidates, donated directly to campaigns, and contributed large sums to pass Prop 30 and

When teachers speak, Democratic legislators—and sometimes the governor—listen. When education funding was cut in 2009, the group spent millions airing television ads in dissent; they organized statewide rallies in protest of cuts in 2011; they were instrumental in mobilizing support for Prop 30 in 2012.

defeat Prop 32—a whopping $43 million in all. The CTA also retained seven lobbyists and spent $8.392 million on lobbying activities in 2011–2012.

Sources: California Teachers Association, http://www.cta.org; California Secretary of State, http://cal-access.sos.ca.gov.

California Chamber of Commerce: Major Player in Business

Ever heard of a "job killer" bill? The California Chamber of Commerce (or CalChamber) has, and it aims to identify and destroy such bills before they impose new "expensive and unnecessary" regulations on California businesses. What is the chamber, and why is it so powerful?

Unlike professional associations that represent individuals (such as the CTA), the chamber's members are almost thirteen thousand California-based companies, from local shops to Microsoft, enterprises that employ a quarter of the state's private-sector workforce. The motto of the state's largest and arguably most important business organization is "Helping California business do business." Aided by seven in-house lobbyists, the chamber tries to help shape laws or administrative rules by educating policymakers about how proposed laws will critically affect California companies. It also donates to sympathetic candidates and officeholders, supports and opposes ballot campaigns through independent expenditures and direct donations, and helps incumbents through sponsoring events, among other activities. The member companies often team up to advocate for or against important bills. The chamber reported lobbying expenditures during 2011–2012 totaling $6.565 million and campaign-related expenditures and donations of about $3.4 million. These figures represent a fraction of what businesses spend to protect their interests in California. For example, the Walt Disney Company pays close to $750,000 a year for ongoing lobbying activities, and local chambers throughout California are also politically active.

Sources: California Chamber of Commerce, http://www.calchamber.com; California Secretary of State, http://cal-access.sos.ca.gov.

Calling attention to business-related issues is part of CalChamber's strategy to influence lawmaking and the regulatory environment. Chamber president and CEO Allan Zaremberg advances this objective through press interviews.

TABLE 10.2 Top Fifteen Spenders on Lobbying in California, 2011–2012

Name	Industry	Total amount spent
Western States Petroleum Association	Oil and gas	$9,972,580
California Teachers Association	Public-sector unions	$8,392,913
California State Council of Service Employees	Public-sector unions	$8,673,835
California Chamber of Commerce	Business	$6,656,838
City of Los Angeles + County of Los Angeles	Government	$6,118,937
Kaiser Health	Health services	$5,969,645
California Hospital Association	Health services	$5,042,077
California Manufacturers and Technology Association	Manufacturing	$4,572,317
AT&T	Business/utilities	$4,367,381
City of Vernon	Government	$4,319,069
Howard Jarvis Taxpayers Association	Taxpayer advocacy	$3,980,961
California School Employees Association	Public-sector unions	$3,654,399
League of California Cities	Government	$3,563,819
California Building Industry Association	Construction	$3,402,596
Sempra Energy	Electric utilities	$3,305,741

Sources: California Secretary of State, http://cal-access.sos.ca.gov; *Sacramento Bee* Lobbying Database, http://www.sacbee.com/2011/02/14/1728274/database-see-who-is-lobbying-state.html.

entities that carry out state programs for thousands or millions of Californians: public officials and experts working for cities, counties, and special districts often are in the best positions to judge the impacts of programs or predict how proposals will affect the public. Other groups are valued for their important roles in communities, such as **large employers** that provide jobs and subsidize local economies through the taxes they collect and pay, and **labor groups** that defend workers' rights. Representatives have incentives to please politically active constituencies, so any group or business that has the **ability to mobilize voters and influence, voters, public opinion** possesses significant advantages over those that cannot do so. Lawmakers also pay attention to organizations that share their issue positions or values, and they respond to individuals and groups that provide **support for their campaigns** through financial or in-kind donations.

The political power of special interests, therefore, is largely derived from what they can provide to decision makers, principally in the form of either **information, voters,** or **money**. In lawmaking environments good information is always in demand, and legislators and their staffs crave answers to questions about the potential impacts of their bills. To provide persuasive information, groups hire **professional lobbyists** who can be "educators" about the negative or positive effects pending legislation may have—framing a case that is sympathetic to their own interests, of course. So powerful are special interest lobbyists in Sacramento that they are collectively known as the "**third house**," a reference to the fact that they are crucial players in the lawmaking process. Lobbyists can make their clients' cases in face-to-face meetings with legislators or staff, but more often they do so by testifying in committee hearings where bills are vetted. They also perform research for bills and draft client-friendly legislation for lawmakers to sponsor.

Lobbyists also gain access to legislators by buying tickets to expensive fund-raising events (happening daily around Sacramento and elsewhere) and funneling **campaign donations** to state representatives, making sure that the interest groups they represent donate the maximum allowed. Although state law caps the amounts of direct donations that individuals, unions, and corporations can give to candidates, special interest groups may spend as much as they want independently to influence elections, and lobbyists help them decide how best to spend that money. A record $564 million was collectively spent on lobbying activities during the 2011–2012 term, and more than $138 million was contributed to the 2012 state legislative campaigns.[18] In state politics, organization, information, money, and status amplify voices and provide critical linkages to decision makers. The well-heeled few tip the playing field in their favor with the access their resources can buy. By extension, the unorganized and the poor are the biggest losers in politics.

Conclusion: An Evolving Political Community

Political parties, mass media, e-mail, social media, and even interest groups create the means for citizens to connect to government affairs, officials, and each other. Californians still rely most heavily on traditional media such as television, newspapers, and radio for their news, but very few people pay rapt attention to state politics, many pay no attention at all, and those in between are scarcely listening or do so only when crises, scandals, or elections occur. Being informed helps empower citizens to be politically active, and there is plenty of room for more citizen participation at all levels of government, because even though political scientists disagree about the minimum levels of knowledge, trust, and engagement needed to sustain a governing system for the long term, they generally recognize that "inputs" taking the form of civic involvement and political participation generally lead to more positive government "outputs." As it stands, rich corporations, well-heeled unions, and large, well-organized, resource-rich groups are perpetual, outsized contributors to California's political system and, consequently, benefit from their investments in politics. As the saying goes, the squeaky wheel gets the grease.

The most recognizable form of political participation—voting—carries intrinsic value as a democratic exercise and plays a vital role in linking citizens to their representatives. Uneven levels of participation, however, and higher rates of nonvoting among Latinos contribute to the governing dilemmas of policymakers as they weigh their responsibilities to serve the greater public interest but also respond to those who actually cast their ballots and are politically active. Those who are white, established, educated, and affluent tend to speak louder than the rest. Until the electorate more accurately reflects the entirety of the state's population, elected officials' decisions will continue to reflect the political, cultural, geographic, and demographic biases of those who vote. In the search for greater governability, expanding the electorate and raising levels of political participation would be surefire ways to make California's government more accountable and representative.

Notes

1. USC Annenberg–Los Angeles Times Poll on Politics and the Press, August 2012. Respondents were 1,009 registered voters nationwide, surveyed August 13–19; margin of error ±3.1 percentage points.

2. Ibid.

3. Ibid.

4. Mark DiCamillo and Mervin Field, "Release #2382," The Field Poll, June 27, 2011. Survey was conducted on 950 registered voters in California by telephone in English and Spanish, June 3–13, 2011, sampling error ±3.3 percent.

5. Ibid.

6. This deficit was recently verified by James Prieger and Kelly Faltis, who analyzed data from the Civic Engagement Supplement to the Current Population Survey, U.S. Census Bureau, collected November 2009. See James E. Prieger and Kelly M. Faltis, "Non-electoral Civic Engagement in California: Why Does the State Lag the Nation?," Social Science Research Network, Working Paper Series, January 2, 2013, http://papers.ssrn .com/sol3/papers.cfm?abstract_id=2195770. See also National Conference on Citizenship, California Forward, Center for Civic Education, and Davenport Institute for Public Engagement and Civic Leadership, *California Civic Health Index 2010: Financial Crisis, Civic Engagement and the "New Normal"* (Washington, DC: National Conference on Citizenship, November 10, 2010), http://www.ncoc.net/Political_Civic_Engagement.

7. Aaron Smith, *Civic Engagement in the Digital Age: Main Report, Part 1* (Washington, DC: Pew Internet & American Life Project, April 25, 2013), http://pewinternet.org/Reports/2013/Civic-Engagement/Main-Report/ Part-1.aspx.

8. See National Conference on Citizenship et al., *California Civic Health Index 2010,* 5; Prieger and Faltis, "Non-electoral Civic Engagement," 8, 18.

9. Smith, *Civic Engagement in the Digital Age.*

10. Ibid.; and Aaron Smith, Kay Lehman Schlozman, Sidney Verba, and Henry Brady, *The Internet and Civic Engagement* (Washington, DC: Pew Internet & American Life Project, September 2009), http://www .pewinternet.org/Reports/2009/15--The-Internet-and-Civic-Engagement.aspx.

11. Prieger and Faltis, "Non-electoral Civic Engagement." (Note that the data were collected in 2009.)

12. Ibid., 27.

13. Nancy Rytina, "Estimates of the Legal Permanent Resident Population in 2011," U.S. Department of Homeland Security, July 2012, http://www.dhs.gov/xlibrary/assets/statistics/publications/ois_lpr_pe_2011 .pdf; and Laura E. Hill and Hans P. Johnson, *Unauthorized Immigrants in California: Estimates for Counties* (San Francisco: Public Policy Institute of California, July 2011), http://www.ppic.org/content/pubs/report/ R_711LHR.pdf.

14. Mark Baldassare, *Improving California's Democracy* (San Francisco: Public Policy Institute of California, October 2012), http://www.ppic.org/content/pubs/atissue/AI_1012MBAI.pdf.

15. Reported statistics on nonvoters and infrequent voters in this paragraph come from the California Voter Foundation, "California Voter Participation Survey," 2005, http://www.calvoter.org/issues/votereng/votpart/ index.html.

16. See Mark Baldassare, Dean Bonner, Sonja Petek, and Jui Shrestha, "Latino Likely Voters in California," Public Policy Institute of California, August 2012, http://www.ppic.org/main/publication_show.asp?i=264.

17. Mindy Romero, "Changing Political Tides: Demographics and the Impact of the Rising California Latino Vote," California Civic Engagement Project, Policy Brief Issue 6, May 2013, http://regionalchange.ucdavis .edu/ourwork/publications/ccep/ucdavis-ccep-brief-6-impact-of-ca-latino-vote.

18. Follow the Money, "California 2012, Overview," accessed September 4, 2013, http://www.followthemoney .org/database/state_overview.phtml?y=2012&s=CA.

CHAPTER 11

Concluding Thoughts: Political Paradoxes and Governability

Governability suggests a good fit between the demands of a state's people and what its institutions deliver, that representatives understand their constituents' needs, and that decision makers grasp the dimensions of pressing problems and devise fair, responsible, timely solutions. Governability is enabled by rules that encourage participation, deliberation, and compromise, or by some combination of strong leadership and cooperation. How does California measure up?

Predictions of the state's demise rose to a fever pitch as high unemployment and a mortgage crisis drove the budget deficit to $27 billion in 2010, and flashing signals of government's failings were everywhere. Extremely low trust in government, partisan standoffs, yearly multibillion-dollar structural budget deficits that dwarfed the economies of small countries, a gross backlog of unfulfilled infrastructure needs, and growing debt created the perception that California's government was on the verge of economic ruin.

Although unemployment has remained higher than the national average and the state's long-term debt in the form of unfunded liabilities looms large, the improving economy has restored the state to solvency, at least in the short term (budget surpluses are projected!), and political reforms have altered the balance of power. The top-two primary and citizen-driven redistricting processes created new maps that enabled Democrats to dominate state offices, and the political majority has enacted on-time budgets without the encumbrance of supermajority rules since 2011. Under new term limits rules, incoming legislators will accumulate more policy expertise as the game of musical chairs slows from a frenzied scramble to a more measured pace. Governor Jerry Brown's approval ratings have risen, and Californians' overall ratings of the legislature have marginally improved.

These reforms scratch the surface of California's deeply rooted problems, some of which stem from the very design of its government. California's self-styled hybrid democracy splices the power of direct democracy with political representation, and the two coexist in a state of uneasy tension. This can be seen most clearly in voter-imposed laws intended to restrict political choices, such as in funding guarantees for big-ticket items like schools and practically unattainable thresholds for raising tax revenues (two-thirds voter approval for initiative tax measures and two-thirds of the legislature for revenue-raising bills). Incremental ballot-box reforms also forestall comprehensive approaches to problem solving, complicating the job of governing. Ironically, Californians demand strong and efficient leadership from all elected officeholders, yet ballot initiatives often limit authorities' power and therefore the ability of these officials to perform efficiently and effectively.

Furthermore, what was supposed to be a stopgap measure for keeping legislators in check is now an overworked policymaking machine, the gears of which are oiled by large campaign donors and shifted into overdrive by an electorate bombarded by distorted, oversimplified messages. Special interests parade as public interests, trying to drown out other voices in the political marketplace. The process is ripe for reform.

California politics is riddled with other ironies and paradoxes that go a long way toward explaining the current state of affairs. For example, Californians generally distrust politicians and are averse to political conflict, so they continue to reach for ways to take politicians—and politics, for that matter—"out" of politics; they resort to passing initiatives like term limits and open primaries that will automatically remove people from office at prescribed intervals and lessen political party control. Disappointment and resentment in the body politic continue to grow, however, because political systems are by nature designed to expose conflicting interests in the struggle to reach consensus, and the people not only need politicians to govern what is effectively one of the largest countries in the world, they need to organize in order to win, and political parties provide that reliable structure. Nevertheless, many Californians are unconvinced that parties matter, and increasingly they are registering as "no party preference" voters.

Paradoxically, Californians also expect that the public good will automatically be served when their personal needs are met. This may be possible with a government service like public education, a "good" that yields private gains with long-term public benefits, but this approach does not produce sustainable economic policies for large and diverse communities. To wit, Californians generally choose to pay lower sales, income, and property taxes if it helps their own bottom line, creating chronic underfunding of local and state governments that are burdened with meeting basic sanitation, education, health, transportation, and safety needs for all. This tendency has resulted in a heavy reliance on upper-income taxpayers, as well as a shift away from paying up-front costs and a pivot to long-term bond debt that costs twice as much in the long run, generating interest payments that place stress on the state's general fund by siphoning off money that could be used for other necessary budget items.

Quite apart from the institutional aspects of governing are socioeconomic and political issues that determine the state's political state of affairs—issues that involve more than thirty-eight million people who place myriad conflicting and ever-changing demands on the state. The multiethnic mix of children signals momentous change in the near future: nonwhites have accounted for all the growth in the youth population in the past decade, and Latinos are the largest ethnic group as of 2014. It is estimated that California will be an absolute majority-Latino state by 2040, and the population will reach fifty million by 2050.[1] How will decision makers nurture the educated workforce that will be needed to drive the state's service-based economy? Will voters be willing to extend helping hands to those on the bottom end of the socioeconomic scale? At least one in seven Californians will be sixty-five years of age or older by that time: How will the state provide for a large elderly population that places immense demands on health and residential care systems, with or without the Affordable Care Act? Already the state administration has estimated that to accommodate such growth, approximately $500 billion will be required to rebuild and expand aging transportation, school, water, and other systems in the next twenty years.[2] How will Californians be able to raise that kind of cash?

In many ways, political reforms brought California to this point, and political reforms will help transform its future. Yet institutional reforms can go only so far. Rules set boundaries for decision making but do not determine the choices people make, and choices must be based on realistic understanding about government's capabilities if the state's policies and laws are to work. For instance, many Californians presume that rooting out existing government waste would uncover enough revenues to pay for large government programs, as if saving millions of dollars could compensate for not raising billions through higher taxes. Voters' expectations and attitudes about government underscore California's ungovernability, but competent leaders who can convince citizens to reshape their expectations can counteract this drift.

Overall, California's government faces the same challenges as the governments of other states. What makes it distinct are the scope and scale of the state's issues, a hybrid governing structure in which voters can change the rules of the game for representatives, and constraints placed on authorities' power that range from term limits to supermajority thresholds that sacrifice majority will to the rival demands of a minority (usually the minority party). The issues are mostly the same across the nation, however, and they pose enormous challenges for state government now and for the foreseeable future. The extent to which these policy questions overwhelm capable elected officials is another measure of California's ungovernability:

- *Education:* Only an educated workforce can sustain a sophisticated, diverse, service-oriented modern economy. California continues to spend less on its K–12 students than almost all other states, meaning fewer days of instruction, lower pay for teachers, lack of instructional or supplementary materials, and shortages of reliable after-school care and programs. How will California schools prepare future citizens to meet state, national, and global communities' changing economic needs if the state lags behind the others? The fastest-growing segment of the population is Latino, but as a group these students trail behind in graduation rates and test scores. How will achievement gaps be closed? How will graduation rates be improved? Deep budget cuts also threaten to destabilize the state's premier college and university systems by carving away essential funding, much of which is used to hire and support the "best and brightest" who do research, teach, and prepare students for the workforce. State education is still a bargain compared to that available in other states, but California's master plan for providing tuition-free higher education has been abandoned. How will education funding deficits affect students' future job prospects and the higher education system's competitiveness?

- *Immigration:* California's immigrant population is the largest in the nation at about 2.6 million, equaling one in four current residents having been born outside the United States. Will voters be willing to extend to immigrant groups the same public benefits that they have enjoyed? If not, how might a service economy accommodate massive numbers of low-skilled, unemployed, low-educated residents who require state services to fulfill basic needs, from food to housing to employment?

- *Environment:* Climate change threatens California's basic lifelines. Erratic weather patterns are difficult to plan for. Rising temperatures bring less rain and lighter snowpack, as well as limited water supplies for thirsty farms, manufacturing plants, and homes. Alternatively, unpredictable rains can produce severe (and costly) flooding. Volatile weather patterns place stress on traditional recreation and tourism-related industries. Lower rainfall increases the risk of wildfires in bone-dry areas and increases airborne fine-particle pollution; wildlife unaccustomed to higher-than-average temperatures cannot quickly adjust, so biodiversity suffers. Rising sea levels threaten a densely populated coastline and imperil the Delta agricultural region (the source of drinking water for two-thirds of Californians and irrigation for 750,000 acres of croplands) with rising levels of salinity. California's AB 32, the nation's first greenhouse gas emissions law, remains under siege by those who object to the high costs of implementing its requirements. Can California make the investments necessary to bring about a "green" economy without creating a more hostile business environment? Can the government adequately respond and the economy readjust when environmental crises like earthquakes, heat waves, extensive wildfires, extended droughts, and torrential rains and resulting mudslides hit in quick succession?

- *Business and labor:* A large majority of California's 850,000 small and large business employers routinely complain about the regulatory difficulties they face, and *Forbes* ranks California near the bottom of U.S. states (forty-first in 2013) in business climate. Unemployment has remained higher than the national average. Meanwhile, multibillion-dollar unfunded liabilities, existing mostly as health care insurance and pension obligations for teachers and other public employees, menace the state's long-term financial outlook. How will the state balance its books, protect 12.7 million private-industry workers, and promote a clean environment while also making itself more attractive to companies that provide California jobs?

- *Water:* The northern part of the state receives about 75 percent of rainfall, but about 75 percent of residents live in Southern California. Between droughts and floods, policymakers have a hard time managing storage and distribution systems that move water to the south, dealing with water scarcity that pits urban against agricultural users, and addressing contamination from chemicals in farmland runoff and urban activity. Neighboring states and Mexico have prolonged disputes with California over equitable distribution of water from the Colorado River and estuaries. Degraded wetlands are the norm, as are declining native fish populations and inexplicable fish die-offs that are increasing in number. In many parts of the Delta region, where millions of people and animals reside and fertile lands are farmed, catastrophic levee failure due to earthquakes or flooding is a palpable risk. How will extremely costly solutions be implemented? Will California's leaders at state and local levels be able to craft strategic plans that comprehensively address the entire state's long-term needs?

- *Transportation:* The nation's highest number of cars on roads and freeways travel California's roadways, which are the most congested in the United States. The Legislative Analyst's Office notes that many of California's 50,500 miles of roads have either reached or will soon reach the end of their useful life, and while Caltrans estimates the costs of needed repairs at $7.4 billion annually, a paltry $1.8 billion is allocated for repairs each year. On top of hundreds of billions of dollars of deferred state highway and road repairs, local government officials estimate a price tag of $82 billion to fix the local streets that form more than 80 percent of the state's roadway mileage. Combined with trucks, buses, and farm and construction equipment, California's motorized vehicles also create dirty air that contributes to serious respiratory illnesses. Despite substantial investments in public transit since the 1990s, there has been virtually no reduction in the number of miles traveled by residents, and only 5 percent of Californians use public transit. California's airports, seaports, and railway systems contribute to pollution levels as well, an inevitable consequence of having the nation's busiest port (Long Beach), a gateway to Asia and South America. Can lawmakers improve California's air and travel systems by making them cleaner, safer, more navigable, and more efficient, and can they do so in cost-effective ways? Can they ensure the safety of residents as those systems take on larger proportions? How long will it take to reduce the state's extreme backlog of needs, and at what cost?

Less than a generation ago, California government was held up as a distinguished model of efficiency and planning. The state's fairly quick reversal of fortune is a testament to the power of rapidly changing social, economic, and political circumstances; the cumulative force of historical decisions; the power of culture; the consequences of rules; and the importance of collective choices. These conditions will continue to be at the heart of the policymaking that will define California's future and how well it will be governed.

Notes

1. California Department of Finance, Demographic Research Unit, "Report P-1 (County): State and County Population Projections, July 1, 2010–2060 (5-year increments)," January 31, 2013, http://www.dof.ca.gov/research/demographic/reports/projections/P-1.

2. Ellen Hanak, *Paying for Infrastructure: California's Choices* (San Francisco: Public Policy Institute of California, January 2009), 1, http://www.ppic.org/content/pubs/atissue/AI_109EHAI.pdf.

Image Credits

Chapter 1

Page 3, cartoon: ©Brian Fairrington/Cagle Cartoons.
Page 6, photo: Getty Images.

Chapter 2

Page 11, photo: © Everett Collection Historical / Alamy.
Page 12, figure: © Wikipedia Commons
Page 18, photo: © AP Photo/Lennox McLendon.
Page 20, photo: © Getty Images.

Chapter 3

Page 31, photo: © Getty Images.
Page 34, cartoon: ©WILLIS/San Jose Mercury News.

Chapter 4

Page 47, photo: © AP Photo/Susan Ragan.
Page 51, photo: © AP Images.
Page 56, photo: © Richard Cummins/Corbis.
Page 57, photo: © ASSOCIATED PRESS.
Page 58, photo: © Randall Benton/Sacramento Bee/ZUMA Press

Chapter 5

Page 63, photos: © Jerry Brown, Steve Granitz/WireImage; Kamala Harris, AP Photo/Rich Pedroncelli; Jerry Brown, Steve Granitz/WireImage; Bill Leonard, AP Images; Bill Lockyer, AP Photo/Lockyer for Treasurer; John Chiang, AP Photo/John Chiang For State Controller; Debra Bowen, AP Photo/Rich Pedroncelli; Gavin Newsom, AP Photo/Paul Sakuma; Dave Jones, Photo by Tia Gemmell, Riverview Media Photography; Tom Torlakson, The California Department of Education; Jerome Horton, Courtesy of the California Board of Equalization; George Runner, Courtesy of Senator George Runner (Ret.), Member of the California State Board of Equalization.
Page 65, photo: © Rich Pedroncelli/Associated Press.
Page 69, photo: © Photo by Michael Kovac/Getty Images for One Voice.

Chapter 6

Page 77, photo: © AP Photo/Paul Sakuma.
Page 84, photo: © AP Images.

Chapter 7

Page 93, photo: © AP Images.
Page 97, photo: © Courtesy of Renée B. Van Vechten.
Page 103, photo: © Kate Spilde, Kenneth Grant, and Jonathan Taylor.

Chapter 8

Page 109, photo: © Lezlie Sterling/Sacramento Bee/ZUMAPRESS. com/Alamy Live News.

Chapter 9

Page 125, Map 9.1: © Elizabeth Wu/Splash News/Corbis.
Page 134, photo: © Elizabeth Wu/Splash News/Corbis
Page 136, photo: © Getty Images.
Page 138, mailer: © Courtesy of Andy Vidak.

Chapter 10

Page 146, photo: © AP Photo/Rich Pedroncell.
Page 150, photo: © Kevork Djansezian/Getty Images.
Page 151, photo: © Aaron Lambert, CalChamber.

Chapter 11

Page 157, cartoon: © Kara Yasui and the Daily Bruin.

Index

Budgeting
  by assembly members, 95
  ballot-box, 118
  deficits, 112, 114–116, 154n6, 155
  Department of Finance involvement in, 108
  description of, 53–54
  for education, 112
  expenditures, 112, 114–116
  governor's power in, 66
  legislature involvement in, 53–54, 108
  mechanics of, 109–116
  overview of, 107–110
  political constraints on, 116–119
  revenue, 109–112
  schematic diagram of, 117
  signing of budget, 121
  structural budget deficits, 119
  variable conditions, 120–121
Bush, George W., 133
Business, 159

Cabrillo, Juan, 9
Cal Grants, 20
California Association of Realtors, 149
California Chamber of Commerce, 151
California Citizens Redistricting Commission, 33
California Coastal Commission, 55
California Correctional Peace Officers Association, 149
California Public Employees' Retirement System, 71
California State University, 114
California Teachers Association, 150–151
CalPERS. *See* California Public Employees'
    Retirement System
Cal-SPAN, 142
CalTrans, 159
Campaigns
  contributors to, 135–137, 153
  description of, 134
Cantil-Sakauye, Tani, 76–78, 85
Cap-and-trade system, 21, 100
Casinos, 102–103
Catholic missions, 9–10
Charter cities, 91
Charters, 90
Charter schools, 98
Chiang, John, 40n4, 70
Chief of security, 66–67
Chin, Ming, 77
Chinese immigrants, 11, 15

Choices
  importance of, 4
  rules and, 4
Chu, Judy, 134
Cities
  charter, 91
  employee salary ranges, 93
  initiatives of, 37
  municipal governments, 90–96
  property taxes for financing of operations in,
      93–94
  public services offered by, 91
  revenues and expenses of, 94
Citizens, 141
Citizens United v. Federal Election Commission, 136
City council, 91, 93
City manager, 93
Civil lawsuits, 76
Civil service exams, 14
Climate change, 100–101
Closed primary system, 132
Collective action, 4
Colorado, 26
Commander in chief, 66
Commission on Judicial Nominees, 79
Commissions, 91
Committees
  legislator participation on, 49
  standing, 49
Constituency service, 55
Constitutional amendment, 26
Controller, 68
Corporate income taxes, 110–111
Council-manager system, 92–93
Councils of government, 98–99
Counties
  description of, 87–90
  initiatives of, 37–38
  revenues and expenses of, 92
County central committees, 131
County government, 87–90
Court(s)
  administration of, 80–81
  caseload for, 75
  impartiality of, 75
  superior, 77
  three-tiered system, 76–79
  trial, 76

Median annual household income, 5
Mediation, 85n4
Mello-Roos fees, 95
Metropolitan Water District, 96
Mexican-American War of 1848, 9
Mexico, 9
Minimum wage, 50
Misdemeanors, 76
Missions, 9–10
Modified closed primary system, 132
Monetary flow, executive offices that regulate, 68–69
Monopolies, 13
Munger, Molly, 31
Municipal governments, 90–96

National Guard, 66
Nativity, 144
Natural sorting, 129–130
Newspapers, 141–142
News sources, 141–142
Nonpartisan offices, 13
Nuñez, Fabian, 66

Obamacare, 51
Office of Insurance Commissioner, 69
Online registration, of voters, 133
Open primary system, 132
Open-seat elections, 135
Ordinances, 91
Oregon, 26
Organized interests, 15–16
Overcrowding of prisons, 82–83

Pardoning, 66
Party as an organization, 124
Party in government, 124
Party in informal networks, 124
Party in the electorate, 124
"Pay suspension" rule, 40n4
Pension payments, 95–96
Pérez, John, 58
"Permanent absentee" voters, 133
Personal income taxes, 110, 119
Petition
    for city or county initiatives, 37
    signing of, 144
Petition referenda, 33
Plural executive, 61–64, 67, 71

Political campaigns, 134–137
Political culture, 4
Political disengagement, 142–144
Political districts
    drawing of, 44–45
    gerrymandering of, 129
    natural sorting of, 129–130
Political earthquakes, 23
Political engagement, 142–144
Political parties. *See also* Democrats; Republicans
    cross-filing effects on, 14
    Democrats, 44, 124, 126
    east-west divide, 123, 125
    in government, 128–130
    in informal networks, 131
    organization of, 130–131
    qualification as, 127
    registration for, 126
    Republicans, 44, 124, 126
    summary of, 153
Political reforms, 18, 157
Politics
    budgeting affected by, 116–119
    citizens and, 141
    description of, 1
    principles for understanding, 3–6
Population
    by county, 88
    diversity of, 19–21
    growth of, 14, 19
    post-World War II, 19
    statistics regarding, 5
    youth, 156–157
Portantino, Anthony, 55
Port of Los Angeles, 97
Poverty, 5, 144
Preemptive legislation, 99
President pro tem, 55, 57
Primary elections, 132
Prisons, 3, 81–82, 116
Progressives, 124
Progressivism, 13–15, 71, 75
Property taxes, 2, 23n5, 93–94
Proposition 1A, 17, 24n9, 27, 95
Proposition 5, 27, 102
Proposition 8, 27, 31–32, 79
Proposition 9, 27
Proposition 11, 27, 44, 129, 131

About the Author

Renée B. Van Vechten is associate professor of political science at the University of Redlands, where she teaches courses primarily in American Government and California Politics. She received her PhD in political science from the University of California, Irvine. In 2002–03, she was a Kevin Starr Fellow in California Studies, and in 2008, was honored with the Rowman and Littlefield Award for Innovative Teaching in Political Science, the American Political Science Association's national teaching award at that time. She is also engaged in the scholarship of teaching and learning. A lifelong resident of Southern California, she has spent the better part of her professional life studying, writing, and lecturing about California institutions.

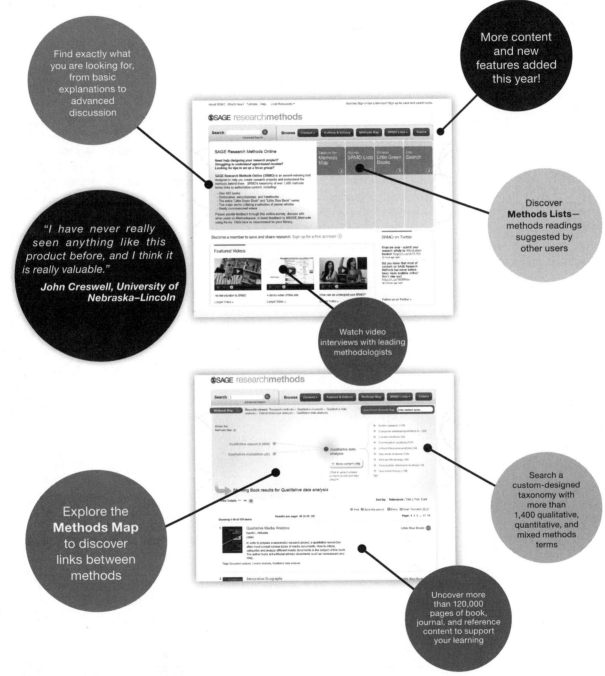

⊘SAGE researchmethods

The essential online tool for researchers from the world's leading methods publisher

Find exactly what you are looking for, from basic explanations to advanced discussion

More content and new features added this year!

"I have never really seen anything like this product before, and I think it is really valuable."

John Creswell, University of Nebraska–Lincoln

Discover **Methods Lists**—methods readings suggested by other users

Watch video interviews with leading methodologists

Explore the **Methods Map** to discover links between methods

Search a custom-designed taxonomy with more than 1,400 qualitative, quantitative, and mixed methods terms

Uncover more than 120,000 pages of book, journal, and reference content to support your learning

Find out more at
www.sageresearchmethods.com